Geoff Hamilton became universally recognised through BBC TV's hugely popular *Gardeners' World*, which he presented until his death in 1996. He was also wrote several bestselling books, such as *Geoff Hamilton's Paradise Gardens*, as well as regular columns for gardening magazines and the *Daily Express*. Geoff's books and programmes regularly featured his own garden Barnsdale, in Rutland, where he created many imaginative specialist gardens over the years.

Andi Clevely, who created this compilation, has been a professional gardener for thirty years. He is also the author of a number of books including a series of titles on particular types of plants. He recently wrote a series for Granada Television entitled *The Cook's Garden*.

Lynda Hamilton was a teacher before leaving to help Geoff full time at Barnsdale. She shared Geoff's concerns for the environment and has taken his place as vice president of Plantlife, the charity that protects British wildflowers.

GEOFF HAMILTON'S

YEAR IN YOUR GARDEN

A month-by-month
celebration of
a gardening genius
introduced by
Lynda Hamilton

Compiled by
ANDI CLEVELY
from articles written by
Geoff Hamilton
in the *Daily Express*
from 1991 to 1996

HEADLINE

First published in 1998 by HEADLINE
BOOK PUBLISHING

First published in paperback in 1999
by HEADLINE BOOK PUBLISHING

10 9 8 7 6 5 4 3 2 1

ISBN 0 7472 7502 5

Designed by Prue Bucknall
Picture research by Helen Fickling
Illustrations by Ann Winterbotham
Jacket by Head Design

Printed and bound in Great Britain by
Butler & Tanner Ltd, Frome and London

PREVIOUS PAGES A densely packed
kitchen-garden bed promises a varied
harvest of fresh home-grown produce.

THIS PAGE Swags of roses and clematis
over a clipped archway frame the view into
an inviting garden beyond.

contents

geoff in his garden

Lynda Hamilton

Geoff was passionate about gardening. He revelled in the physical work that it involved – being outside in all weathers, digging, sowing, hoeing, pruning and so on. But more than that, it was plants themselves that held him in thrall. Green shoots were the very basis of life, he said. They made his blood tingle.

In the years we shared together at Barnsdale, his enthusiasm for the garden never wavered. He was, at one and the same time, an idealist and a realist. He strove for the best – always. 'Spot on' he would say, or 'that's just right', but never 'that'll do'. But he would face setbacks with equanimity, openly admitting failure, but never defeat. Perhaps it was his willingness to share both his successes and his failures that made ordinary gardeners trust him. He certainly wanted to share the immeasurable joy that gardening gave him. Not only did it give him intense satisfaction and aesthetic pleasure, he also realised that it had a healing psychological role: gentle exercise and plenty of fresh air, fruit and vegetables are ingredients of any doctor's remedy for relieving stress. More importantly, the garden, Geoff felt, was the only place where most of our urbanised population can experience nature.

His absolute respect for nature was the bedrock of his deeply held belief in organic gardening. Long before organic gardening or 'green' issues became fashionable, Geoff had gardened in what he called 'the natural way'. As he saw it, organic gardening was 'very simply, a case of growing plants exactly as nature intended, only more so. Because we take much more out of our soil than nature does, we have to put more back.' Perhaps his chief concern – it was almost a mission – was to get people to stop using chemical pesticides and fertilisers. 'Just imagine,' he said, 'a garden filled with fabulous flowers, glorious greenery and perfect produce, and also buzzing with the activity of birds, bees, butterflies, hedgehogs, frogs, toads and all the rest of the gardener's friends.' Yes, of course

RIGHT Vegetables blend happily with flowers, as in this bed at Barnsdale where onions and beetroot mingle with fuchsias, petunias and marigolds.

LEFT Sweet peas and nasturtiums jostle for space on a fence at Barnsdale. Pots of summer bedding in the background echo the brilliant colours of the poppies and lupins in the borders.

it sounds almost too good to be true, yet Geoff proved that it was possible. Barnsdale has never been sprayed with a man-made chemical. And it thrives.

Although it is hard to believe now, Geoff was originally sceptical about the merits of organic gardening. He was trained as a commercial grower where rule number one was: 'If it moves – spray it.' So he started out with a trial aimed at proving that organic gardening didn't work. He set up four identical plots all growing the same vegetables and flowers. One was gardened organically, one with only chemicals, another with a mixture of the two, and finally there was a 'control' plot which had neither chemicals nor organic matter. In the first year the chemical plot produced very much better results. In the second there were signs that the organic plot was catching up. By the fifth year the organic plot was vastly outyielding the other three. And it was buzzing with insects while the chemical plot was sterile. So, although Geoff admitted that he couldn't honestly say whether the fruit tasted better or the flowers were brighter, he was absolutely convinced that they were healthier: the wildlife, he said, knew which plants were good for them.

But, again, he was a realist, and warned people what they might be in for if they tried this approach. 'If you decide to do away with chemicals entirely, you will be troubled with attacks from greenfly and caterpillars to begin with, and, in the first couple of years your crops might not be quite so good. But,' he said, 'nature's pest control methods are complicated. Every pest you consider your enemy has enemies of its own. Birds will eat caterpillars, slugs, snails, woodlice, greenfly and many other pests. Hoverfly larvae eat hundreds of greenfly, as do lacewings and ladybirds. Ground beetles go for slugs and caterpillars – if they get there before the frogs, the toads and the hedgehogs.'

To enlist the help of this green army, he suggested growing particular plants to attract specific insects and birds, but the first step, he said, was to grow a wide diversity of plants and pack them in together. 'Grow your flowers, fruit and vegetables, your roses, shrubs and herbaceous plants all in the same borders, just as the old cottage gardeners did. That provides cover for the shy species, and some food too. Provide trees for birds, and nesting boxes too if you

9

LEFT Geoff and Lynda in a corner of the courtyard garden at Barnsdale.

ABOVE Some of the loveliest violas have first appeared in private gardens. This is 'Barnsdale', an intriguing dark-coloured form which blooms profusely, especially in the cool shade that all violas prefer.

can, and think about making a pond somewhere for all the wildlife to drink.' Geoff also used physical barriers, netting fruit against birds, covering carrots with fine-spun polypropylene to protect against carrot fly and caterpillars, sticking bits of carpet underlay round the stems of cabbages to prevent cabbage root fly, and so on. 'Eventually you'll build up a balance of wildlife, but the process takes nerves of steel. You mustn't weaken once. If you do you'll be killing friends as well as enemies.'

Chemical fertilisers were also anathema to Geoff. 'They act fast and are like junk food to plants,' he said. 'They make them fat, soft, and attractive to diseases. Organic fertilisers, on the other hand, which feed the soil rather than the plant, are slow acting. They make for tough, strong plants which are much less prone to attack and better equipped to fight disease.' He explained that organic and chemical fertilisers work in different ways. 'Chemical growers don't rely on a fertile soil, often doing without manure or compost completely. Soil is used as an anchorage for the plants and as a store for water and plant food in solution. The growers add fertiliser that is immediately needed by the plant, which takes it up straight away and, it must be said, puts on a lot of growth. Organic growers rely on fertile soil that contains billions of micro-organisms. These slowly release plant food derived from organic matter, such as manure or compost, and any other organic fertiliser you may put on.' Geoff stopped using any of the suspect fertilisers from the time of the first BSE scare. Instead he used pelleted chicken manure and seaweed.

Geoff's concern with the environment went beyond the confines of his own garden: he was adamant that gardeners should stop using peat-based composts, or water-worn limestone for rockeries. He was horrified at the destruction of so much of our unique bogland and our limestone pavements, and spent a long time experimenting to find good substitutes. He found coir or coconut fibre worked well instead of peat, and also made his own soil-based mix using soil, garden compost, grit and chicken manure. And, after a spate of weekend trials, he found the perfect mix of hypertufa to give him artificial rock.

Serious as Geoff was about these issues, he had a huge sense of humour and could see the funny side of everything, including himself. Pinned up on a large notice-board in our downstairs loo – used by everyone who came to visit the garden, including the camera crews – were all the cartoons that poked fun at him, the photos that made him look ridiculous, and the rude letters that he'd received. He was always easy to tease and good-humoured about it – even when he was dunked in a water butt by three female production assistants who had been on the receiving end of one of his practical jokes. Geoff always had a fund of jokes and stories up his sleeve, which he would tell in the appropriate accent. And one of his favourite sayings, delivered at times of stress in the lilting Hertfordshire accent of an old and fondly remembered nursery colleague was, 'Thur's a whole noo day termorra, never bin star'ed.' He revelled in all aspects of the English language, especially puns, limericks and cryptic crossword clues.

He was a man without pretensions. Like the advice he gave, he was straightforward and honest. When he spoke or wrote, it was from the heart, about things that directly concerned him. That is why the articles on which this book is based, though compiled and edited, have been left largely untouched and in the present tense. It is Geoff's own voice that clearly comes through.

I'm not alone in still feeling his presence so strongly in the garden here at Barnsdale – several visitors have written to tell me that they feel it too. And just as his spirit lives on in his garden, I very much hope that it will live on in his words.

Lynda Hamilton

*T*he cheerful, optimistic Geoff on screen was the real Geoff. Even on the shortest, coldest days he would enjoy doing something in the garden, and in January it was sowing. He thrilled, he said, to the very words 'seed pan' and 'seed tray' because 'they conjured up visions of the lovely round clay pans and wooden boxes that used to contain our dreams of a flowery summer'. He was bitten by the seedling bug when he was a young boy of seven, and never understood why gardening is generally regarded as an occupation for older people. His father gave each of his three sons a plot to cultivate, encouraging them by paying for the produce they grew. The strategy worked for the twins: Geoff eventually studied horticulture at Writtle, and Tony studied agriculture. Geoff's first job was with a commercial grower of chrysanthemums, but once fully trained he went on to do landscape gardening. At more or less the same time, his love of words pushed him into writing, and out of his columns and articles grew his broadcasting career – the cameras simply recorded him doing what he was writing about.

Hard frost at Barnsdale highlights the intricate patterns of shrub and tree growth that supply varied interest all winter in a mixed border.

january

key tasks for january

ANNUALS & BEDDING PLANTS
○ Sow in modules to save time and space, page 14
○ Buy new sowing compost, page 15
○ Techniques for sowing in modules and seed trays, page 15
○ Sow sweet peas, page 16

BORDER PERENNIALS
○ Take root cuttings from dormant perennials, page 16

CONTAINER PLANTS
○ Provide alpines with perfect winter conditions, page 18
○ Sow alpines while the weather is still cold, page 18

SHRUBS, TREES & CLIMBERS
○ Stake new trees and check supports of older ones, page 20
○ Shape up young trees, page 20
○ Prune those trees and shrubs grown for their leaf colour, page 21
○ Winter-prune wisteria, page 21

LAWNS & HEDGES
○ Improve the drainage by spiking the lawn, page 21

VEGETABLES & HERBS
○ Plan now for an early start to the cropping year, page 21
○ Set up early potatoes to sprout or 'chit', page 22

FRUIT
○ Bring in strawberry plants in pots for forcing, page 22
○ Prune hazelnut trees to keep them in check, page 22

MISCELLANEOUS
○ Invest in a propagator for your first sowings, page 23
○ Continue to pull out weeds, page 23

ANNUALS & BEDDING PLANTS

It's time to sow sweet peas, and it's also not too early to make a start on the annual bedding plants like salvias, petunias, busy lizzies and lobelia. Raising your own indoors is not too difficult, and it'll certainly save you quite a lot of money.

Sowing in modules
At one time, all bedding plants were raised in wooden trays. These were replaced by plastic trays, and then by expanded polystyrene strips. Now there is another option: to raise plants in modules, which are plastic trays divided into a number of cells. This is a welcome trend as it has several advantages.

First of all, there's no need to prick out the seedlings. Modules produce very even, uniform plants which can be potted up or planted out when they are large enough. When it's time to transplant, push each cell gently at the base and the rootball will pop up intact. The trays save a lot of space in the greenhouse or cold frame, or on the windowsill. They are even self-watering if you stand them on level staging that has been covered with polythene and then capillary matting.

Modules come in a wide range of sizes, usually the best being 4cm (1½in) across and, depending on the size of tray, you can easily raise several dozen plants of any one kind. You can use the modules now for tender annuals, and then use the same system in April for raising hardier plants. Modules are ideal for perennials such as pinks and delphiniums, and hardy annuals like marigolds and nasturtiums. They are also good for sowing ferns, and for starting garlic cloves if the ground's

SOWING IN MODULES

1 Using modules allows you to sow individual large seeds or a tiny pinch of small ones which can be left to grow unthinned, or you can remove all but the strongest seedling. Disturbance at planting time is reduced to a minimum.

2 Fill the cells, making a depression in the centre of each one to hold the seeds. Bury these under a thin layer of vermiculite or compost, and germinate in the same way as for a normal seed tray.

not suitable outside for planting; offsets and pips from flowering bulbs can be grown on in this way too. They are also valuable for early vegetables grown in clusters: sow onions or leeks with 6–8 seeds in each cell and then, instead of thinning them out, plant each clump

30cm (12in) square. You'll find they push each other apart to make their own space and mature into good-sized vegetables for the kitchen. Do the same with carrots (round varieties only, such as 'Rondo' or 'Parabel') and plant them out 15cm (6in) square.

Compost for sowing

Using last year's seed composts could be a bit dodgy – they eventually go off as the fertilisers in them break down and change into other chemicals that can harm seedlings. Use up your old compost as a soil conditioner in the garden.

For years most gardeners used peat-based composts, but now that we know that digging for peat composts has been responsible for the destruction of most of our unique bogland, it is vital to find substitutes. There are several available. The one that has performed well for me is coir or coconut fibre. It needs a different watering and feeding regime from peat: it tends to hold a lot of water but the top half-inch dries out fast.

Sowing in modules and seed trays

The techniques for sowing in modules or in seed trays are very similar. It's important not to firm any soil-less compost too much. It's usually enough to fill modules, pots or trays to the brim, tap them to settle the contents, and then water well and leave to drain. Do this before sowing, which avoids washing newly sown seeds into patches; alternatively soak the containers from below after sowing.

To cover seeds that don't need darkness to gerrminate, I like to use horticultural vermiculite: it lets some light through, so all's not lost if you

SOWING IN SEED TRAYS

1 Sow on top of the compost, very thinly to avoid too much competition. Tip a little seed into one hand, pick up a pinch with the finger and thumb of the other, and sprinkle evenly in the tray.

2 If the seeds need darkness to germinate, sieve a thin layer of compost over them; otherwise cover them with horticultural vermiculite which lets in some light.

3 Keep the seeds moist by covering the tray with a sheet of glass or clingfilm. Add a layer of newspaper if they need darkness, but remove this when the first seedlings emerge.

ABOVE Undeterred by frost, evergreen *Erica carnea* 'Springwood Pink' nestles against a prostrate juniper.

TYPES OF SEED

First read the seed packet: if the seeds are F_1 hybrids, you'll end up with plants that are uniform and all in flower at the same time. But they are expensive because the seedsmen have to re-hybridise every time they want a crop of seeds. It pays to grow F_2 hybrids instead – these cost less, and are often just as vigorous, but they usually only come in mixed colours.

Primed seeds are a great advance. They've been started into growth and then dried off again before packeting, so that they are raring to go just as soon as they hit moist compost and the right temperature, which can be as much as 5–6°C (10°F) lower than for normal seeds.

Some seeds need light for germination, so check the seed packet before sowing because most failures result from burying seeds too deep.

bury the seeds too deeply. Cover with clingfilm or sheets of glass to stop them drying out, and put them where they'll get a little gentle heat. Uncover as soon as seedlings show, move them into full light, and you're on your way to a glorious summer.

Sowing sweet peas

Sweet peas are best started in mid-autumn to make strong seedlings for planting out next month, but if you missed doing it then, now's the time to catch up. They grow best in deeper pots that let them develop a good root system, and you can buy coated paper tubes at the garden centre that are made specially for them. Stack these side by side in a deep seed tray, fill with peat-free seed compost, and water well. Read the seed packet instructions carefully. Most varieties can be sown straight away, but if the seeds are black and mottled it's often best to soak them overnight first. Those that haven't swollen next morning can be 'chipped' by removing a tiny bit of the seed-coat with a sharp knife, carefully avoiding the 'eye' where the root grows.

Plant 2–3 seeds in each tube, about 2.5cm (1in) deep, and keep them at about room temperature – they don't really need a propagator. Once they are through, give them a week on the windowsill or a sunny table, and then they can go outside into a cold frame. If frost threatens, cover the frame with old carpet or sacking. For instructions on planting outside, see page 58.

RIGHT Don't be too tidy-minded with perennials. It's often a good idea to leave clearing the faded top-growth of plants such as *Sedum spectabile* until the spring, to create unexpected beauty in the depths of winter.

Taking root cuttings

Most gardeners find it hard to resist snipping off the odd shoot and turning it into a cutting to make a new plant. But at this time of year, instead of using your skill to grow roots on shoots, why not think of doing it the other way round by putting new shoots on to roots?

Plants with thick fleshy tap roots, such as Japanese anemones, are

often quite difficult to propagate by division, but grow easily at this time of year from cuttings of their side roots, as shown on the right.

Plants with thin fibrous roots can be multiplied in a similar way, but their roots are laid horizontally on compost in trays. First trim the roots to about 8cm (3in) long and coat with fungicide; then lay them horizontally, covering them with another 1–2cm (½–1in) of compost. Water well, and stand in a frost-free cold frame or heated propagator.

PLANTS TO PROPAGATE BY ROOT CUTTINGS

Acanthus, anchusa, brunnera, catananche, ceanothus, crambe, dicentra, dictamnus, echinacea, eryngium, Japanese anemones, nepeta, oriental poppies, phlox, rhus, romneya and verbascum.

Remember that root cuttings taken from variegated plants lose their variegation and their leaves will turn out green.

TAKING ROOT CUTTINGS

1 Dig up the plant to be propagated or cut a portion from one side, and wash off as much soil as possible so that the roots can be separated from each other.

2 Cut off sound roots about the thickness of a pencil and divide into sections about 5cm (2in) long. Trim off small fibrous roots. Cut the bottom diagonally and the top straight so you know which way up to plant it.

3 Insert upright in pots of cuttings compost, with the tops just buried. Water well, and stand in a frost-free cold frame, or in a heated propagator for faster rooting.

CONTAINER PLANTS

Giving alpines perfect conditions

They say that adversity brings out the best in people, and that's true of alpine plants too. They revel in spartan conditions, with next to no food, and flower all the more spectacularly for this as soon as the sun comes out. In the wild, most alpines grow high in the cold dry mountains where the weather is pretty inhospitable. They're battered by cold winds and frozen by ice, followed by a summer of merciless sun, and some of them often get no more than one watering a year when their covering of snow melts in the spring. To grow them successfully in the garden, you'll need to reproduce those conditions as nearly as possible to make them feel at home. They need perfect drainage, which means making a raised bed or digging in plenty of coarse grit and pea shingle from the builders' merchant, and they may need protection from the damp winter mists and fogs that quickly rot some species.

The best way is to grow them in gritty compost in clay pots, which breathe and drain more efficiently and so avoid too much moisture at the roots. The pots can be plunged over winter in a sand or gravel bed in an unheated greenhouse, where the plants won't mind the cold but will be protected from excess dampness. In spring you can move them outdoors if you intend using the greenhouse for things like tomatoes during the summer. Alternatively you could make a permanent miniature rock garden on top of the staging, using a well-drained compost and lightweight tufa rock – having the small flowers at nose level is really the perfect way to appreciate them.

Raising alpines from seed

Now is a good time to sow alpine pinks, saxifrages, houseleeks (*Sempervivum*), tiny primulas, stonecrops (*Sedum*) and hundreds of other fascinating species.

In the wild their seeds are mostly produced in late summer, and avoid the fatal icy grip of winter by delayed germination. But in order to trigger germination they need this cold spell, followed by rising temperatures, and you have to imitate this for success with bought seeds. You can do it artificially by putting the seeds in the fridge for 6–8 weeks before sowing, but I prefer to do mine the easy way by sowing them several weeks before the spring warmth arrives, leaving the seeds outdoors to freeze naturally.

Use a compost made with equal parts good soil, coir and coarse horticultural grit, or mix together equal amounts of John Innes seed compost and grit. Fill an 8cm (3in) clay pot to the top, and tap it firmly on the bench; firm gently and then water it well. Leave it to drain before scattering a small pinch of seeds on the surface and covering with a thin layer of grit. Stand the pots outside covered with a piece of glass or in a cold frame with the top positioned to keep off the rain but expose the seeds to the cold.

Most seedlings should be through in the spring, when they can be transplanted to individual pots and grown on. If germination occurs very early and this is followed by a cold snap, you'll have to close the frame or move the pots to a greenhouse or cold windowsill until the worst is over. In a warm season, seedlings may not appear until the second spring, so wait for at least a year before discarding any pots whose seeds haven't germinated. It's a bit of extra trouble, but the satisfaction of cracking nature's code for germinating these specialised plants makes it worth every second.

BELOW Alpines tend to be tough plants, adapted to a harsh environment, and will survive the worst winter weather provided they are grown in gritty soil in a well-drained raised bed.

RIGHT At Barnsdale, deciduous winter-flowering viburnums such as *V. farreri* shrug off the frost that glistens on the large tough leaves of evergreen *Mahonia japonica* in the right foreground.

SHRUBS, TREES & CLIMBERS

Staking trees

There's a lot at stake when it comes to supporting newly planted trees for their first few years. Allowing the top to move around freely in the wind encourages a tree instinctively to strengthen its root system. A good buffeting actually triggers a mechanism that stimulates the roots to extend quite a distance to provide further anchorage. That's why it's now recommended that the stake should come no more than about a third of the way up the trunk of a tree, and in many cases even shorter stakes are preferred.

Leaving the base of the tree moving around in the ground, however, can spell disaster. Rocking in the wind at this time of year works a hole in the ground all round the stem and allows water to sit right on the crown of the roots, often causing rotting. So check that all your newly planted trees are solid at the base, especially after strong winds and also hard frost which can make the ground heave. Make sure the tree is tied securely to its stake, but if the ties have been on for more than a season, look to see that they're not so tight that they're strangling the tree.

Shaping up young trees

If you have planted 'feathered' trees, specimens with branches starting low down on the trunk, and you want to turn them into normal standards with long clean stems, now's the time to prune them.

Juvenile trees are full of youthful vigour, with a built-in urge to grow in all directions. Sideshoots often grow almost as fast as the vertical leading stem, so that a tree will end up shaped like a pyramid. If you

SHAPING UP YOUNG TREES

A young fruit tree may have lots of sideshoots on the trunk that can be turned into fruiting spurs. Ornamental trees look best with a clean trunk, so you need to remove these 'feathers' gradually. Cut off the bottom ones completely, and shorten higher shoots in the first winter. Next year do this again, further up the trunk.

stop or reduce the sideways growth, energy is redirected to the leader and your tree will gain more height.

Don't be tempted to produce a clean trunk straight away by shearing off all the sideshoots in one go. The extra leaves these carry help to thicken and strengthen the part of the trunk where they are growing. You can also shorten some of the sideshoots higher up to about 15cm (6in) long, removing them altogether next winter when you cut back the next two or three. In this way you can guide the tree's growth without giving it too much of a shock all at once.

LEFT When supporting a tree after planting, avoid causing injury by driving in the stake at an angle so that it misses the rootball.

Pruning for good leaf colour

While you've got your secateurs handy, take a look at those shrubs and trees that produce their best leaf colour from young wood. Elders such as the lovely golden variety *Sambucus nigra* 'Aurea' and its dusky cousin 'Guincho Purple' (formerly 'Purpurea') will produce far better colour if their stems are cut back to 2–3 buds above ground level, as will the variegated maple *Acer negundo* 'Flamingo'. Others such as the purple-leafed smoke bush *Cotinus coggygria* 'Royal Purple' and the brilliant yellow *Catalpa bignonioides* 'Aurea' make much bigger leaves if pruned back hard now, although you will lose the flowers.

In small gardens pruning is a great way to keep trees and larger shrubs in check. The foxglove tree (*Paulownia tomentosa*) grows into a large tree if not cut back. But if it is pruned hard every year and the resulting suckers are reduced to just one, it will grow to about 2.4m (8ft) and produce absolutely huge velvety leaves up to 60cm (2ft) across, but you will lose the flowers.

Plants grown for their colourful winter bark can also be cut back hard, but don't be in too much of a rush. Wait another month or two, so as to enjoy the colour for as long as possible.

Winter-pruning wisteria

If you want to keep wisteria confined, and encourage flowering, this is the time to shorten the sideshoots back to 2–3 buds. Personally I prefer to take off as much growth as I feel necessary in August, but the advantage of doing it now is that you can see more of the plant's framework.

LAWNS & HEDGES

Improving lawn drainage

If you walk lightly over the lawn at this time of the year, and find areas that are actually squelching underfoot, it means that these bits need attention if the turf is not to suffer, and that means spiking.

I have to admit spiking the lawn is such a pain that I can sympathise with anyone who doesn't like the idea, and I doubt if many people do it on a regular basis. But it is a good way to remedy poor drainage. Note where the wet patches are and, as soon as the ground dries a bit, go over the area making holes at about 15cm (6in) intervals as shown below. If you don't act fast, they will simply close up again, so as soon as you have done a couple of square yards, brush in a good dressing of sharp sand (never builders' sand). Leave a shallow layer on top too, and the grass will tend to root into that in the spring.

IMPROVING LAWN DRAINAGE

A hollow-tine aerator will remove thin plugs of soil, but an ordinary garden fork, pushed in 15cm (6in) deep and wiggled about to open up holes, is equally effective.

VEGETABLES & HERBS

Planning for an early start

It's not too soon to be thinking about the vegetable plot to ensure plenty of fresh produce to harvest while shop prices are still high. But because of the weather and low temperatures, you'll need to make the first sowings indoors, and also prepare a small area of soil outdoors for planting later on.

Not only is it usually very cold at this time of year, but very often heavy rain will have turned the soil into a quagmire. Most of it will dry out over time, but the area set aside for the first sowings of the season needs special treatment. Cover it with cloches or, better still, with a sheet of thick polythene weighted down or tucked in at the edges. Not only will the cloches or sheet keep the bed dry and warmer than the air outside, but you will also be able to work the bed when you want to. (See the photo on pages 32–3.) Either prepare the seedbed first if the soil is in good condition and then cover it to keep it that way, or leave the polythene in place until the soil is dry enough to cultivate.

Meanwhile back indoors, in the greenhouse or on a windowsill, you can start sowing to produce plants that will be ready to go outside from mid-February onwards so long as they go under cloches or horticultural fleece to protect them from the worst of the weather. Sow small quantities of lettuce, early cabbage and cauliflowers in just the same way as shown for annuals on page 15. Varieties to choose include 'Hispi' and 'Kingspi' cabbages, 'Alpha Polaris' or 'Montano' cauliflowers, and fast-maturing lettuces such as 'Little Gem', 'Tom Thumb', or 'Novita' if you like the loose-leaf cut-and-come-again types. These vegetables do not need high temperatures, and will germinate easily at about 13°C (55°F). When they're big enough, prick them out to about 5cm (2in) apart if they are in trays and grow them on in plenty of light to prevent them becoming long and lanky.

Starting early potatoes

If you've never grown early potatoes before, let me urge you to try a few this year. Freshly dug, they're a different vegetable altogether from the bland, tasteless and expensive stuff you buy. (And I confess, I break all my own rules, and have my first serving obliterated with butter.) This is the time to order seed potatoes or 'sets', as they need a little preparation before planting out in March. All varieties need to be sprouted or 'chitted' to advance the date of the first harvest and also increase the size of the crop. Too many shoots on an early potato can be a disadvantage, leading to too much competition and resulting in reduced growth or smaller tubers. Overcrowded tubers tend to push themselves to the surface of the soil, where they're in danger of turning green in the light – green tubers contain poisonous alkaloids and should not be eaten. If possible choose smaller tubers for growing, as these will produce only a couple of sprouts; with the others, set them to chit, and rub off all but two sprouts as early as you can to prevent them from using up their reserves. If you are growing maincrop varieties, leave all the sprouts on as they can cope with the extra growth.

EARLY POTATO VARIETIES

Older varieties such as 'Arran Pilot', 'Home Guard' and 'Sharpes Express' are still available and worth growing. But there are more recent introductions for you to try, although you might have to buy them by mail order rather than from the garden centre. 'Accent' and 'Foremost' are two first earlies that produce heavy yields with little or no slug damage, while 'Concorde' has fine flavour. For extra-early crops, choose 'Rocket' or 'Swift' which, under favourable conditions, can be ready as soon as 8–10 weeks after planting. If you save a few tubers of these two varieties, you can plant them in August in pots under glass for Christmas.

CHITTING POTATOES

Lay the tubers out in a single layer in boxes or trays – egg boxes are ideal if you only have a few potatoes. Arrange the tubers with the ends that have the most eyes facing upwards, and stand them in maximum light in a cool but frost-free place. Very soon each eye will start to sprout a short bushy shoot, each of which is a potential plant.

FRUIT

Forcing strawberries

If you potted up strawberries last summer (see page 130), bring them into the greenhouse now, and they will soon be full of blossom, and give you fruit in May or even, if you are lucky, April. It's too late to start now if you don't have any plants potted up, but you can still push outdoor crops ahead by 2–3 weeks by covering a row with cloches or a double thickness of fleece. Tidy up the plants, taking off any leaves damaged over winter, loosen the soil with a handfork and remove any weeds. Scuffle in a dressing of general organic fertiliser, and then cover the plants with the cloches. You'll need to block the ends in order to keep out draughts, but remember to open up the flowering plants on sunny days so that bees can fertilise the blooms.

If you don't have strawberries in the garden, you can still plant maincrop varieties like 'Elsanta' even this late if you buy them pot-grown. They'll give you a crop this season, although a little later than usual. For really fast crops you can order deep-frozen runners from specialist fruit nurseries for delivery in the spring. Freezing holds them in check until they're planted, when the sudden change in temperature really boosts them into vigorous growth. In a good year they have been known to crop just 60 days after planting.

Pruning hazelnuts

Now's the time to prune mature hazelnuts. Shorten long branches by half of last year's growth. Save the trimmings to use as peasticks.

MISCELLANEOUS

Investing in a propagator

Raising your own plants still has to be the cheapest thrill of all. It's far from difficult, but you need to get geared up to the job and, at this time of year, that means providing a little heat.

Heating a whole greenhouse is much too expensive, and the few things that need starting this month can usually be raised in the house. Hardy annuals, most herbaceous plants and vegetables to be transplanted outside will germinate happily on a windowsill at ordinary room temperatures. But it will soon be time to sow the first tomatoes and half-hardy annuals, and these tender plants need extra heat.

Everyone has used the airing cupboard at some time for germinating seeds, and it is certainly a useful source of free heat. But there are pitfalls: never put seeds right on top of the hot water tank as they could cook. I find that two shelves up is about right. And remember that some seeds need light before they'll germinate, so the dark will hold these back. Finally you need to be extra vigilant, checking every day and removing the tray the instant the first seedling emerges.

All in all, a cheap propagator is definitely a better bet. The simplest are not heated at all and comprise a plastic top which fits over a seed tray, ideal for most windowsill propagation – put it near a radiator and you have the best of all worlds. But do check occasionally with a thermometer pushed into the compost to the level where the seeds are sitting, to make sure

you're near the recommended temperature.

If you've no handy heat source, you'll need to buy a similar device with an electric element in the base. Generally these reach about 18°C (65°F), which is about right for most seeds, though not hot enough for some. If you want to germinate some of the more demanding subjects, spend a little more on a thermostatically controlled model, which will normally achieve 5–10 degrees more. Remember that the temperature inside varies according to that outside, so you'll have to set it by trial and error, and for that you need a thermometer.

And, of course, you're still stuck with one temperature. I've solved that problem by using a heated mat, just like an electric blanket complete with transformer and

ABOVE At this time of year, cuttings and young plants appreciate the gentle warmth provided by a heated mat and trapped by a polythene cover.

thermostat. The mats cover about 0.75 sq.m (8 sq.ft), so you get a lot of heated space for your money. Seeds that need about 18°C (65°F) go straight on the mat; I raise those needing less heat on an up-turned seed tray, and any needing more go under a plastic cloche. It's a bit Heath Robinson, but it works.

Continuing to weed

Weeds such as chickweed and groundsel just never stop producing seeds, even in winter, so pull them out wherever you see them and you'll avoid a spring invasion of hundreds of offspring.

PLANTS FOR
january

1 Corkscrew hazel, *Corylus avellana* 'Contorta', has curiously twisted stems which spiral slowly to 3m (10ft) after 25 years and bear golden catkins in early spring.

2 Skimmias are robust slow-growing shrubs, up to 90cm (3ft) high, with evergreen leaves and fragrant blooms; the long-lasting berries appear only on female plants such as prolific large-fruited *S. japonica* 'Nymans'.

3 The spidery winter blooms of 3m (10ft) high *Hamamelis* x *intermedia* 'Pallida' are the softest coloured of all the witch hazels, but their pronounced fragrance is among the sweetest.

4 *Gaultheria* (*Pernettya*) *mucronata* is a shade-tolerant evergreen, about 60–90cm (2–3ft) high, that needs an acid soil. Heavy crops of showy berries depend on a male form growing nearby.

5 Common or English ivy, *Hedera helix*, is a hardy self-clinging evergreen ground-cover plant or climber, up to 5m (16ft) or more tall. The leaves on its climbing shoots are very variable, often deeply lobed with prominent veins, and can be very decorative.

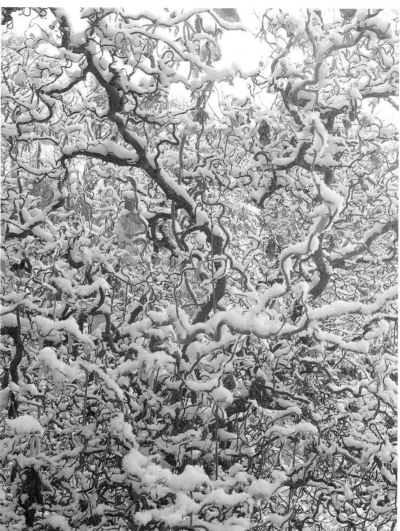

1

2

3

4

5

*F*ebruary was the month in which the television cameras moved into the garden and into our lives. From now until October, Geoff's plans were geared to the day's filming each week. A team of six would arrive in the evening to discuss details and do a 'recce'. Filming began early the next morning and went on until everyone was satisfied. It was hard work, but judging from the shouts of laughter – and the occasional uninhibited expletive when something went awry – that rang round the garden, it was obviously also enormous fun. I was the 'gofer', making tea for the show's celebrity guests, and taking endless messages since no mobile telephones could interrupt shooting. I also had to keep track of what Geoff wore, just in case any re-shooting was needed the next day. On screen Geoff wore the same type of clothes he wore off it – comfortable ones. And though he was once pilloried as the worst-dressed television presenter he remained undeterred, and continued to wear jeans and sweatshirts because he strongly believed that he should be simply part of the background, allowing attention to focus on the stars of the show – the plants.

As the days begin to lengthen, hardy
cyclamen, snowdrops, and hellebores carpet
the leafy soil beneath the bare trees in
Barnsdale's woodland garden.

key tasks for february

ANNUALS & BEDDING PLANTS
- ○ Watch young seedlings under glass, page 28
- ○ Revive stored dahlias for cuttings, page 29

BORDER PERENNIALS
- ○ Take basal cuttings from strong young shoots, page 29

BULBS
- ○ Start off tuberous begonias, gloxinias and achimenes, page 30
- ○ Force spring bulbs for early colour, indoors and out, page 30

SHRUBS, TREES & CLIMBERS
- ○ Prune late-flowering shrubs such as buddleias, page 30
- ○ Prune late-flowering clematis, page 30
- ○ Re-shape conifers after snow and frost damage, page 30

ROSES
- ○ Start pruning in the middle of this month, page 32

VEGETABLES & HERBS
- ○ Sow vegetables under cloches for early crops, page 32
- ○ Plant shallot bulbs late this month, page 32
- ○ Plan tomatoes and other tender greenhouse crops, page 33

FRUIT
- ○ Force rhubarb for early pickings, page 34
- ○ Choose and plant currants, gooseberries and raspberries, page 34

MISCELLANEOUS
- ○ Choose or make cloches to protect early sowings, page 35
- ○ Use cloches effectively by planning ahead, page 35

ANNUALS & BEDDING PLANTS

Looking after seedlings

Keep a close watch on your seedlings as they come up. They need all the light they can get, preferably on the windowsill if you don't have a greenhouse. But the problem with this is that the light only comes from one side, and doesn't encourage strong bushy upright growth. My solution is to transform an old cardboard box into a light box, as shown below. Push a table up to the sunniest window, and stand the light box there. Strong direct sunlight can scorch the tiniest seedlings so be prepared to protect them with a sheet of newspaper at midday, and remember to draw the curtains on cold nights – a little coddling now pays dividends later.

Remember that this is a dangerous time of year in the greenhouse for seedlings, so be extra vigilant. On cold nights, close the greenhouse

A LIGHT BOX FOR SEEDLINGS

The best way to deal with seedlings indoors is to cut the front out of a large cardboard box and paint the inside white to form a reflector. Line the base with aluminium foil.

early, and on sunny days be prepared to ventilate it. Standing the trays on capillary matting saves watering, but you can water and feed from above with a fine rose if necessary, but take care not to over-water.

Reviving stored dahlias

Planting time is still far away, but it's worth waking up dahlias and other stored tender perennials such as fuchsias to force some early growth for cuttings. The old tubers and stools have been kept in boxes of garden compost all winter, cool and almost bone dry. Now bring them out into full light, top up with compost so the stumps of last year's stems are just exposed, and give them a little water. Don't overdo it though: very soon the tubers and stools will start to put out new shoots, and then you can increase the watering gradually. Spraying them from the top from time to time helps stimulate the growth of those strong shoots that make the best cuttings.

BELOW *Helleborus foetidus* and *Anemone blanda* flourish in dappled shade.

BORDER PERENNIALS

Taking basal cuttings

Very soon many hardy perennials will be making short strong shoots near ground level, and these are ideal propagating material for making cuttings. This is the only way to propagate delphiniums and lupins, and is certainly the best way for many other plants.

Keep an eye on these shoots, because you need to take them before they grow too long: 5cm (2in) is ideal. There's no need to lift the plant before you take basal cuttings as shown on the right.

PLANTS TO PROPAGATE BY BASAL CUTTINGS

Achillea, border chrysanthemums, campanulas, gypsophila, lysimachia (loosestrife) and lythrum (purple loosestrife), macleaya (plume poppy), marjoram, platycodon (balloon flower), pyrethrum, sidalcea, and thalictrum (meadow rue).

TAKING BASAL CUTTINGS

1 Scrape away some of the soil to expose the base of the young shoots when they are about 5–8cm (2–3in) long, and cut them off with a sharp knife as near to the crown as possible.

2 Trim the cuttings, removing any ragged edges and older lower leaves. Dip the ends in hormone rooting powder or solution. Plant them in moist compost, 5–6 cuttings per 13cm (5in) pot, and water in.

3 Cover with a plastic bag to retain the humidity, and stand in a cold frame or gently heated propagator until new fresh growth shows the cuttings are rooted.

29

BULBS

Starting off tender bulbs

Tuberous begonias, gloxinias and achimenes can now be started off in the greenhouse or conservatory, or on a warm windowsill. Half bury the tubers in trays of compost, keep warm and evenly moist; then pot up individually once they sprout.

Forcing spring bulbs

If you potted up some spring bulbs at the same time as planting them outside (see page 140), you can now bring them indoors to force them into early flower. Move them to a sunny windowsill in a cool room until their flower buds begin to colour; then they can come into warmer surroundings. You could also think about planting some Dutch iris bulbs in the vegetable garden and covering them with cloches to produce superb early cut flowers for the house.

BELOW Snowdrops and the precocious *Crocus tommasinianus* are perfect companions for naturalising in a sunny spot.

SHRUBS, TREES & CLIMBERS

Pruning late-flowering shrubs

Most late-flowering shrubs, especially those which flower on stems they make this season, are best pruned at this time of year. Take your courage in both hands and have a really good go with the secateurs. You'll rarely do any damage, and generally a lot of good. Start now and continue whenever the weather is inviting, right up to the end of March.

Most buddleias, *Caryopteris clandonensis*, ceanothus such as *C. burckwoodii*, hardy fuchsias, *Hydrangea paniculata*, leycesteria, santolina and tamarix can all be cut back really hard to leave no more than two or three buds on last year's growth. You can leave some branches up to three-quarters their length if you want to build up the framework of a larger shrub – this works especially well with buddleias, where varying the amount of pruning will result in a strong bush covered with flowers in late summer. When you finish pruning, tidy up the soil around the plants and give them a good feed of general fertiliser to boost their new spring growth.

Mahonias with shoots that have gone woody and bare at the base can also be cut hard back as soon as the flowers fade to encourage them to produce new shoots.

Pruning late-flowering clematis

Clematis that flower after the middle of June can now be cut back to within a few inches of the ground. If you want them to flower high up though, cut back almost to the base of last year's growth.

Re-shaping conifers after snow and frost damage

Falls of heavy snow can play havoc with your conifers, especially varieties of cypress and other weak-stemmed species. Here and there the lingering weight of snow can force branches out from the main structure, spoiling their natural shape entirely. They can't be cut off as that would leave a gaping hole, but all is not lost. The answer is to tie them unobtrusively back in to the main trunk with a length of plastic-coated wire after wrapping a thick wodge of sacking round both stems to prevent the wire from cutting in. Once the branch settles back in place, the wire could be removed, although I've left it on for years with no harm to the plant.

This is also a good method of shortening conifers that have grown too tall, especially those like *Juniperus* 'Skyrocket', Irish yew, or Lawson's cypress (*Chamaecyparis lawsoniana*) 'Ellwoodii', bought optimistically as a 'dwarf' conifer and now about 6m (20ft) high – we've all done it. Prise the branches apart so that you can see the main central stem. This can then be cut down to well below where you want the finished height to be, leaving an outer ring of branches intact. You then wire these in individually to the trunk or loop a circle of wire round the outside to regain the original perfect shape – only now it will be three-quarters the size it was.

RIGHT All too often relegated to a minor role as background evergreens, ornamental conifers become important solid features in the winter garden, especially when encrusted with light snow and hoar frost.

ROSES

Starting to prune

For years now I have safely pruned my roses in mid-February rather than the recommended mid-March, when there's so much else to do.

The rose is Britain's most popular flower, and it's not hard to see why, but to get all that superb blossom and perfume plants need to be pruned every year. It's surprising how the prospect of this nearly gives so many gardeners a nervous breakdown, and yet rose pruning is not too difficult once you appreciate the ground rules. In fact there are many false assumptions about gardening that are often proved a bit of a myth. Trials by the Royal National Rose Society have shown, for example, that trimming roses with shears or a hedge

PRUNING ROSES

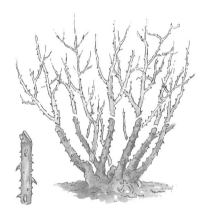

With all kinds of roses, pruning starts with the same routine. First remove dead and damaged wood, weak shoots and stems that cross the centre. Continue pruning bushy roses by shortening the strong stems by at least half. Always make a sloping cut just above a bud, as shown in the detail.

trimmer can result in better flowers than plants pruned carefully with secateurs, although I still think this is the best tool for the job.

Remember that the harder you prune anything, the stronger will be the resulting growth. So when pruning roses, you cut out very spindly shoots completely, weak ones are cut back hard and vigorous ones not so hard. But what does 'not so hard' really mean? Well, that's up to you. Bear in mind that cutting back to about 2–3 buds will induce strong growth, but fewer flowers. Pruning to, say, four or five buds will produce weaker growth but more flowers, though of slightly lower quality.

The aim when pruning should be to open up a bush and so admit light and air for strong healthy growth. You can be a bit more particular with the different kinds of rose. For hybrid tea, floribunda, patio and English roses – in other words, most bush roses – reduce the thickest stems to leave about 10cm (4in) of last year's growth, and the thinnest to about 2cm (1in), with the rest anywhere in between. Larger shrub roses such as 'Nevada' only need thinning out where they're getting congested, and then you can trim them to shape with shears. Climbers can be pruned by cutting out overcrowded shoots near the base; reduce sideshoots to about 5–8cm (2–3in) long, and then tie in all the stems to their training wires or supports.

Once you've finished cutting off all that growth, clear up the prunings as they can attract pests and diseases, and then give the plants a dose of general organic fertiliser or special rose feed to encourage them to grow again.

VEGETABLES & HERBS

Early sowings under cloches

If you got ahead and covered a patch of soil with polythene or fleece last month, and it has been in place for a fortnight, it should be warm and dry enough to sow lettuce, spinach, salad onions, cabbages, cauliflowers, radishes, turnips, broad beans and carrots.

Thinking ahead, you might also sow parsley and lettuce in small pots indoors, a pinch of seed in each; pot on the clusters of seedlings and grow on the windowsill for early cutting.

Planting shallots

It's almost possible to have a succession of onions all year round. The new crop is usually ready from August, and the onions will store

until late May or June. You can grow Japanese varieties and over-wintered onion sets to mature in July (see page 142), but that still leaves a gap, and that's where the earlier maturing shallots come in useful.

They are grown from small bulbs or sets, bought fresh or saved from last year's crop, and each one will split to form a cluster of new bulbs like small onions but with a distinctive flavour of their own. The ground needs to be well dug, with plenty of added compost and a sprinkling of general organic fertiliser. Plant the bulbs 15cm (6in) apart with 30cm (12in) between the rows, or 15cm (6in) square on deep beds. Never press the sets into the soil or the root plate may be damaged and subsequent root growth can push the bulbs out again. Instead make holes with a trowel or dibber, or take out a drill

for planting in, just deep enough to cover the tip of the set – remove any old brown skin from the tops before planting, to prevent birds from pulling them out.

Planning tender greenhouse crops

By summer most of us who own a greenhouse will want at least one side of it filled with tomato plants, even if we do then have enough ripe fruit to supply the whole road. Now's the time to be planning sowings, and perhaps using the valuable space more profitably by trying one or two plants of something else for a change.

Tomatoes

When they're grown well, a few tomato plants will produce enough to feed a family, so let me suggest that you grow fewer plants and

LEFT Warmed soil is vital when making early sowings, so cover seedbeds with polythene for a week or two.

VARIETIES OF SHALLOTS

Old traditional varieties like 'Giant Yellow' and 'Giant Red' used to be planted on the shortest day for harvesting on the longest. More recent, improved kinds that make larger uniform bulbs might bolt if planted so early, and the second half of February is soon enough for 'Golden Gourmet', 'Topper', 'Pikant' and the handsome exhibition type 'Hative de Niort'. 'Santé' produces some cracking bulbs but should not be planted until April.

---

concentrate on quality rather than quantity. Start by choosing a variety bred for flavour: 'Ailsa Craig' is still one of the best, or there's 'Tigerella' with red-and-gold striped fruits. If you like smaller tomatoes, try 'Sungold' which in my view puts all other varieties in the shade, while 'St Pierre' produces large tasty fruit perfect for slicing. Sow seeds now in gentle heat, transplant seedlings to 10cm (4in) pots when they have a full pair of seed leaves, and they'll be ready for planting in the greenhouse in April.

Other tender greenhouse crops

Sweet and chilli peppers are grown in the same way as tomatoes, but they are so prolific that you'll only need one or two plants. You can grow aubergines like tomatoes too, but finish them in 30cm (12in) pots for good root growth; they also need a longer growing season, so make sure you sow them now.

There's a misconception that you can't mix crops like tomatoes and cucumbers in the same greenhouse, mainly because older varieties of cucumber needed very high temperatures and humidity. All-female F_1 hybrids such as 'Athene', 'Petita', 'Tyria' and 'Pepinex' have changed all that, and give good crops under normal greenhouse conditions. Sow now, grow them on in 30cm (12in) pots or peat-free growing bags, and train them up strings. Unlike the old varieties, there shouldn't be any flowers to trim away, unless you let them go dry or forget to feed them regularly. Sideshoots can be trimmed after two leaves, as with older kinds, but don't remove fruits from the main stem because that's where most of them are borne.

FRUIT

Forcing rhubarb

The tartness of ordinary rhubarb is an acquired taste that many people never have the good fortune to achieve. Forced rhubarb, on the other hand, is entirely different. The sticks might look thin and anaemic but the flavour is superb – the acidity and slight stringiness of outdoor crops are replaced by sweetness and a tender texture.

Commercial growers dig up rhubarb crowns in late autumn and force them into growth inside darkened sheds to get those first juicy sticks. Outdoor forcing gives later pickings, which are just as

BELOW Cover well-fed rhubarb crowns when the buds are just about to break, tucking them up with straw for extra warmth to force those first pale tender sticks.

good to eat and much easier to manage. First feed a strong crown with a dressing of general organic fertiliser or composted poultry manure; then cover it with a large bucket, a dustbin or, best of all, a clay rhubarb forcer with a separate lid so that you can check when sticks are ready to pull. In 6–8 weeks you'll be harvesting the best rhubarb you've ever tasted. But next year you must give the forced crown a rest, so if you've only got one plant buy another now – the best variety is 'Timperley early' – and then force them in alternate years.

Planting bush fruit

Most of our gardens these days are small, and that means we have to make choices. It would be nice to be self-sufficient in vegetables and have what the Victorians called a 'fruit room' that was fully planted, but when we come back down to earth, there'll probably be space for only a few fruit bushes, so we need to select carefully.

Perhaps the most important thing is to grow fruits you like. Choose them now and get them planted as soon as possible while they are still dormant. Soft fruit like black-currants, gooseberries, red currants and raspberries are all easy to grow, and should be fitted in if possible. There are space-saving ways of training them, which I show you on pages 99–100.

Blackcurrants are packed with flavour and vitamins, but can take up a lot of space unless you go for compact varieties like 'Ben Sarek' or 'Ben Connan'. These can be grown 90cm (3ft) apart, and should be cut back hard straight after planting, down to about two buds from the ground, to encourage

plenty of vigorous new shoots that will bear fruit next year.

Older varieties of gooseberry can be badly attacked by mildew which often reduces the crop to next to nothing, so go for a disease-resistant one such as greenish-white 'Invicta' or red 'Pax' (which is also nearly spineless).

The red currant 'Redstart' and its pale cousin 'White Versailles' (now properly called 'Versailles Blanche') are popular varieties grown in the same way. These and the gooseberries should give you a small crop of fruit this year.

All bush fruit need sun and shelter from late frosts, with well-manured soil, to give of their best.

Planting raspberries

If you have no room for a row of raspberries, then grow them as a pillar (see page 100). 'Malling Admiral' is the best-flavoured summer variety, but it's not a heavy cropper, so try 'Glen Moy' which is very heavy and well-flavoured with spineless canes, or the disease-resistant 'Glen Prosen' which is also non-prickly. Plant now, and then cut each cane down to about 15cm (6in) high; the new strong stems that grow from the base are tied in and will fruit next summer. And while you're thinking raspberries, don't miss out on 'Autumn Bliss' which will guarantee you a superb crop from late August through to November. You should cut these down immediately after planting, and they'll fruit this autumn.

This is also the month to prune well-established, autumn-fruiting raspberries. Cut the old canes right down to the ground, and then tie in the new stems at waist level to support the next crop.

LEFT A planter bedded out with crocuses, primroses and dwarf narcissi, and kept under glass, supplies a splash of early spring colour.

MISCELLANEOUS

Choosing and making cloches

One of the most persuasive reasons for growing early vegetables, for me, is the joy of harvesting perfect crops when they're at their most expensive in the shops. And under cloches they really are perfect, safe from wind, rain and marauding insects. Not only that, but cloches lengthen the growing season by 2–3 weeks at each end, allowing you to get extra crops in spring and also autumn. Off-the-shelf cloches are not cheap, but even the best will pay for themselves within about two years if you use them well; it is also easy to make your own cloches for next to nowt.

If you arrange your crops in beds 1.2m (4ft) wide, with just one 45cm (18in) path each side to work from, there are three choices of cloche. The best type is the most expensive as it is built around strong tubular-steel field frames covered with polythene. It is far cheaper to bang in a few posts, staple bamboo canes

to the top to make a kind of tent arrangement and cover this with clear polythene. You can also use 'floating' cloches, which are really based on horticultural fleece or a very fine mesh netting. You simply lay a single or double thickness on top of the bed, and the plants push it up as they grow. Although not as effective as a real cloche, the plants inside can be 2°C (4°F) warmer than in the open air, and coddling them by even this much can make a difference to harvesting time.

If you prefer growing in conventional rows, you can use tent or barn cloches. The good old-fashioned glass Chase cloches are dead easy to assemble, stay together and, because they're heavy, need no anchoring to the soil. There is a polycarbonate alternative if you feel glass is dangerous to have around. It is cheap, neat and simple to make your own polythene tunnel cloche, as shown on the right, and the polythene is easily replaceable.

Making the best use of cloches

Using cloches effectively depends on planning: set them in place a fortnight or so before you need them, to warm and dry the soil ready for sowing or planting. Once a crop is covered, start another next to it so that you can just move the cloche sideways when the first batch of plants is maturing. And make full use of the room inside – if you plant two rows of lettuce, for example, sow some radishes or spring onions down the middle to fill the space.

MAKING A POLYTHENE TUNNEL CLOCHE

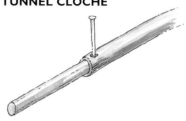

1 Cut the hoops from flexible alkathene tubing from the D-I-Y plumbing department, and plug the open ends with pieces of wooden dowel. Drill a hole at each end, then insert a nail right through the dowels and tubing.

2 Erect the hoops about 1.2m (4ft) apart and stretch the polythene over them. Loop a piece of string over the polythene and secure the ends to the nails.

3 Wedge the polythene securely into the soil at either end of the tunnel, pulling it taut and burying the ends.

PLANTS FOR
february

1 One of the brightest variegated evergreens, *Euonymus* x *fortunei* 'Silver Queen' makes a small compact shrub, but will climb to 1.8m (6ft) or more against a wall.

2 *Camellia* x *williamsii* hybrids withstand more cold and exposure than other camellias, and make handsome evergreen shrubs 4m (13ft) high. 'Debbie' bears large peony-like flowers.

1

2

3 Although individually small, the very fragrant blooms of *Viburnum* x *bodnantense* 'Dawn' are borne in large clusters from December to March, on the bare vigorous 3m (10ft) stems.

4 The 50cm (20in) tall flowers of the evergreen perennial Lenten rose, *Helleborus orientalis*, come in a range of colours from greenish-white through palest pink to deep maroon, some with upturned, saucer-shaped faces, others with nodding cups.

5 One of the winter-flowering heathers, *Erica* x *darleyensis* 'Arthur Johnson' ('Dunwood Splendour'), is a spreading 60cm (2ft) evergreen shrub, with very long flower sprays that are ideal for cutting and defy the coldest weather.

3

4

5

*T*his is the time of year when Geoff started sowing vegetables in earnest. He loved his veg. Not only did he believe that he could save money by growing his own (and one year proved it conclusively by doing a detailed experiment, costing everything that he spent), but he was also convinced that the flavour of home-grown, fresh veg was infinitely superior to any in the supermarket. We never froze any vegetables. We stored onions and root crops over the winter, but everything else was picked or dug minutes before it came into the kitchen. Geoff liked his veg best either boiled or steamed until *al dente*, and served plain, unadulterated with any sauce. From sprouts stiff with frost, through the first new potatoes to sweetcorn, runner beans, artichokes and tomatoes warm from the vine, Geoff made sure there was a never-ending supply. He and his twin brother, Tony, competed with each other to see who could have the largest selection on the table at Christmas – never minding that I ran out of saucepans. The winning number was fourteen – though each later disputed which of them had achieved this.

Early spring is a season of excess, when thick clumps of narcissi jostle with blue scillas and the bright starry blooms of wild anemones to create a carpet of colour.

march

key tasks for march

ANNUALS & BEDDING PLANTS

○ Start fuchsias into growth, take cuttings, and begin to train them as standards, page 40
○ Take spring cuttings of tender bedding plants, page 41
○ Plant sweet peas outdoors, page 41

BORDER PERENNIALS

○ Grow perennials from seed, page 42
○ Plant lily of the valley, page 42
○ Split up polyanthus after flowering, page 43

BULBS

○ Plant snowdrops in the green, page 43

CONTAINER PLANTS

○ Pot up chrysanthemums for late colour, page 44
○ Grow roses in containers, page 44

SHRUBS, TREES & CLIMBERS

○ Prune shrubs with colourful stems and grow more from cuttings, page 45
○ Revive heathers and hebes after the winter, page 45
○ Prepare large shrubs for moving, page 46

LAWNS & HEDGES

○ Give lawns early spring care by repairing damage, reviving growth and beginning to mow, page 47
○ Start to plan dwarf hedges, page 48

VEGETABLES & HERBS

○ Fit in vegetables, whatever the size of your garden, and plan a small-scale vegetable plot, page 49
○ Plant asparagus crowns, page 50
○ Plant early potatoes, page 50

MISCELLANEOUS

○ Make or buy a cold frame, page 51
○ Make the best use of a cold frame, page 51

ANNUALS & BEDDING PLANTS

Starting fuchsias into growth

Tender fuchsias are great favourites for bedding. They usually lose their leaves during their winter rest under the greenhouse staging, and end up looking like a mass of dead twiggy stems. But they'll soon be ready to spring back into life, and if you look carefully you might find tiny bright green or red buds about to break. Start them into fresh growth by treating them as shown on the right.

Keep the plants evenly moist and warm, and spray occasionally with water. New growth will soon appear, and you can then repot the plants, as shown on the right. Keep them fairly cool from now on, because you want the new shoots to be strong and short-jointed rather than long and leggy. When these shoots are about 8–10cm (3–4in) long, pinch them out to encourage bushy growth, nipping off about half their length.

The tips can be used as cuttings: leave the top pair of leaves and trim the stem just below the next pair, which should be cut off. Root as soft cuttings (see page 80).

Training fuchsias as standards

Training a cutting into a standard is not difficult, but it will take at least a season or two. When you first pot on the cutting, put a cane in the pot and tie the main stem to it at frequent intervals. Pinch out any sideshoots, but retain all leaves and keep the main stem growing unchecked until it reaches the required height, feeding every 7–10 days. It is important not to let the plant become pot-bound, so keep an eye on the rootball as it develops.

STARTING FUCHSIAS

1 Plunge the pots in water for a few minutes, then stand the plants in full light on the staging. At the same time you can prune them back quite hard, cutting out spindly lifeless shoots completely, and shortening all other shoots and sideshoots to about 2.5–5cm (1–2in) long.

2 Once new growth appears, knock the plants from their pots and tease out as much of the old compost as possible with your fingers. Then return them to their old containers with some fresh compost.

Taking cuttings of tender bedding plants

This is an excellent time to take cuttings of many greenhouse plants and tender bedding plants such as pelargoniums, marguerites and petunias. Rising temperatures and lengthening days are stimulating new growth on the plants, and the cuttings root quickly now – you might even be able to propagate the tips of cuttings rooted last autumn, so doubling your money. As a bonus, trimming off young shoot tips for cuttings encourages the parent plants to make bushier growth, so you win both ways. Treat the cuttings as shown on page 80, and root them in soil-less compost. Shade them from hot sunshine and keep them sprayed with water, and they'll get away in next to no time.

Planting out sweet peas

Seedlings started in the autumn or in January under glass will be ready to plant outside about now; those sown last month can wait until April. You'll need to train tall varieties against canes, like runner beans, so buy 2.4m (8ft) bamboo canes or some hazel sticks. In a sunny part of the garden, either arrange eight in a circle to make a wigwam, as shown on the right, or set them up 30cm (12in) apart in a straight double row. To save having to tie the stems to the canes in several places as they grow, attach a piece of pea and bean netting to the canes to form a continuous mesh; the plants' tendrils will naturally cling to this. But for the very best blooms, fit to win the village show, you will have to grow them up the canes as cordons, as exhibitors do.

Plant one sweet pea plant at the bottom of each cane. Never grow the main shoots up the canes as they quickly run out of steam and become 'blind'. Instead, tie in the strongest sideshoot from each plant to its cane and remove all the others – if there are no sideshoots, pinch out the growing tip to encourage them and then keep the best for

PLANTING OUT SWEET PEAS

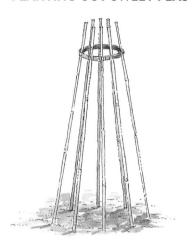

1 Space bamboo canes 30cm (12in) apart in straight rows or arranged in a circle, as above, and fasten the tops tightly to make a secure structure. Drape netting on the canes if you don't want to tie in each stem as it grows.

2 Plant a sweet pea at the bottom of each cane, and water in. If you are not using netting, hold the stem in place with a twist or wire ring to start it climbing, and continue to do this all the way up as the plants grow.

training. As the stems grow, pinch out the sideshoots and tendrils to direct all the plant's energy into flowers. Once these form you'll want to cut them regularly, not just for their sweet scent but because leaving them to set seed will stop more forming.

41

BORDER PERENNIALS

Growing perennials from seed

With a few packets of seeds, you can raise dozens of hardy perennials like lupins, delphiniums, pinks and many others, and you don't have to be an expert to do it. What's more, if you sow them now some could be in flower late this summer.

If you want to try and have plants that will flower this year, sow now in trays or modules (see page 15) of moist seed compost, very thinly and only just covered with a fine layer of compost. Put the trays in the greenhouse or on a not-too-sunny windowsill – they don't want a lot of heat, and 13°C (55°F) is usually ample. Cover with opaque polythene initially, but take a peek underneath every morning, and as soon as you see the first green shoots move them into full light.

Keep them watered but don't overdo it: it's much better for the shoots to be too dry than too wet.

Don't force them along in high temperatures either. What you're after is short bushy seedlings, so as soon as they're about 1cm (½in) high transfer them to about 5cm (2in) apart in seed trays and, after a day or two, move them outside to the cold frame. When they're about 5cm (2in) high, they can be grown on in 9cm (3½in) pots until they're planted in their flowering positions, or they can be planted outside in rows in a nursery bed.

If you're not in a hurry for plants to flower, sow the seeds in shallow drills in a corner of the garden. Water down the drill before sowing in dry weather, cover the seeds with dry soil, and pack this in place gently with the back of the rake. Once the seedlings are big enough to handle, water well and then transplant them about 15cm (6in) apart. By autumn or early next spring, they'll be big enough to plant in the border where they'll give you a stunning display next year, all for next to nowt!

MY TOP DOZEN PERENNIALS

I wouldn't want be without any of the following: *Achillea*, with its large flat heads of yellow, pink or lavender shades; *Aquilegia* – more commonly known as columbines; one of the *Campanula* family with blue or white bell-shaped flowers; *Coreopsis*, which provides brilliant yellow flowers all summer – try 'Sunray'; blue, white and purple *Delphinium* spires; *Dicentra*, or bleeding heart, with its gracefully arching stems of pink and white lanterns; the thistle-like leaves and globe flowers of steely blue *Echinops*; *Geum*'s cup-shaped flowers in a range of bright colours; *Heuchera* for its excellent green or reddish foliage; *Lupinus* and *Nepeta* are old favourites; and finally *Rudbeckia* for late colour, with its masses of bright yellow or gold daisies.

Planting lily of the valley

These are supremely attractive spring perennials with their graceful sprays of scented white blooms, but don't be misled by their ladylike appearance. In some soils they are virtually thugs: plant a crown or two and, if they're happy, they'll romp far and wide. In fact some experts recommend digging up and dividing plants every three years. If you do so now, it will give you the

LEFT *Magnolia stellata*, which flowers while still young, is a good choice for small spaces; and crown imperials, *Fritillaria imperialis*, either in yellow or orange, are the aristocrats of the spring border.

RIGHT Blue *Scilla sibirica* spreads freely and makes a bright background to the checked inverted cups of native snakeshead fritillary, *Fritillaria meleagris*.

opportunity to pot some up to make early, highly perfumed houseplants.

They love shade, and grow contentedly under shrubs or fruit trees. They need well-dug soil with plenty of compost or rotten manure added, and make sure you take out any perennial weeds as these will be hard to get at once the lily of the valley plants are growing well. Plant the crowns about 5–8cm (2–3in) apart, with their growing points uppermost and just below the surface, and then mulch the surface with compost or leafmould.

You can plant them in September or now, but this month is certainly the best time to divide and replant if they're spreading where they're not wanted. Simply attack them with a spade, digging up the crowns in small lumps like miniature turves. Replant in freshly prepared soil, and keep a few clumps back for potting. Trim these to fit into 15cm (6in) pots of good potting compost, water well, and then stand them in the greenhouse or a cold frame until they start to bud up. Then you can bring them indoors to fill the house with their seductive perfume.

Splitting up polyanthus

The best moment to split up polyanthus is just after they have flowered. Each plant will make several more if you dig it up, divide the roots using two handforks, and then grow on the separate small plants 8cm (3in) apart in a spare corner until autumn.

BULBS

Planting snowdrops

There is something specially fascinating about bulbs: each of them is a prepacked plant with an embryo flower inside. These days there's a huge range available in garden centres in the autumn and most are excellent value, but there are some exceptions.

In my experience, for example, there is little point in buying dry snowdrop bulbs as they will often have dried out so much that many will have become completely useless and you'll be lucky to get a 50 per cent success rate – those that do grow often take a whole season to establish themselves. I think it's quite wrong that they should be sold in this way at all. Leave them alone, and instead buy pot-grown plants from a specialist or a garden centre that stocks them at the right time, which is now. They're a bit more expensive than dry bulbs, but they're almost guaranteed to grow.

PLANTING SNOWDROPS

Snowdrops, like winter aconites and hardy cyclamen, are best moved and planted during or just after flowering – in fact any time while they're making growth is fine as long as their roots aren't allowed to dry out. They'll appreciate some compost or leafmould worked in before planting if the ground is dry and sandy, or if you're growing them at the foot of hedges, shrubs and trees. Add a little bonemeal when forking over the soil, and then plant the whole clump or potful a little deeper than it grew before, and water in if dry.

CONTAINER PLANTS

Potting up chrysanthemums

Chrysanthemums can easily become a glorious obsession that just keeps on growing. I got hooked on them about thirty years ago.

Old hands like me will have overwintered their plants in a frost-free greenhouse, and will now be taking cuttings which usually root within days. If you're just starting though, you'll need to send away for some rooted cuttings. When they arrive, pot them up immediately in 9cm (3½in) pots of soil-less compost. They're tough customers and need no heat at this time of year so they'll be fine in a cold frame, but it's worth keeping an eye on the weather forecast – if a hard frost threatens, throw some sacking or a bit of old carpet over the frame to be on the safe side.

Mid-season and late-flowering varieties must be potted on into 23cm (9in) pots where they stay until flowering. They make big plants, so you'll need some kind of support – each plant needs a strong cane to tie the brittle stems to as they develop. If you've got several plants, rig up a couple of horizontal wires on the fence or between two posts to tie the support canes to. These varieties all need greenhouse protection from the beginning of October onwards, so they're ideal for following on from tomatoes.

If you don't want to go to so much trouble, grow early-flowering kinds which can be planted outside in late April or May about 38cm (15in) apart to bloom outdoors, but the plants will need digging up and bringing indoors for the winter. There are some really good ones that are bone-hardy for growing in the border, particularly the Pennine varieties. They are potted up in the same way as rooted cuttings when they arrive, but they can go straight out in the border as soon as they're big enough, and there they stay. For all these outdoor kinds, prepare the soil now with plenty of manure, compost or spent mushroom compost, and if your soil is heavy, dig in a barrowload of coarse grit because the one thing chrysanths object to is bad drainage.

Growing roses in containers

If you love roses and can't wait to have them in flower, get a head start now. Ground-cover roses, patio roses and the miniatures are all perfect for pots and containers.

Ideally they should be bought in threes to make a knock-out show in a big tub, but single plants look fine in 30cm (12in) pots. It's the depth that is important, to give plants a good root run, so allow 25cm (10in) for the smallest varieties, and up to 40cm (16in) deep for ground-cover roses. Use a soil-based compost such as John Innes No. 2 – although soil-less compost is fine if moving heavy pots might be a problem – and set the plants a little deeper than they grew before.

Prune them hard, cutting thicker shoots back to about four buds and thinner ones to two, always cutting to just above a bud that faces outwards. You can then stand the plants in a sunny cold frame until next month, or put them straight in a cool greenhouse or conservatory where they'll grow a little taller than normal and flower several weeks earlier. Water them regularly but don't let them get waterlogged, and give them a good feed after 6–8 weeks and then every fortnight.

There's a huge choice of varieties: 'Anna Ford', 'Festival' and 'Pretty Polly' are prize-winning patio roses; 'Baby Masquerade', 'Fire Princess' and 'Starina' are some of the best miniatures, while the County series of ground-cover roses, such as 'Avon' and 'Kent', are hard to beat.

LEFT Roses and small shrubs such as *Skimmia japonica* and *Euonymus fortunei* form centrepieces in outdoor containers, here edged with ivies and ornamental cabbages.

SHRUBS, TREES & CLIMBERS

Pruning shrubs with colourful stems

A number of shrubs, including willows, dogwoods and even one or two of the bramble family, are often grown for the attractive colours of their winter bark. Of the willows, *Salix alba* subsp. *vitellina* has brilliant orange-yellow bark; that of *S. × rubens* 'Basfordiana' is a red-orange which really glows in the spring sunshine, while that of *S. acutifolia*, especially 'Blue Streak', is damson-coloured with a white 'bloom'. Of the dogwoods, *Cornus alba* 'Elegantissima', which has the bonus of leaves that are edged and splashed with white, has ruby-red stems though these are not as bright as those of the green-leafed variety,

PRUNING SHRUBS WITH COLOURFUL STEMS

To ensure brightly coloured new shoots, cut back the old stems to within 2.5cm (1in) or so of their base, then feed the plant well. If you want flowers as well, cut out between one and two thirds of the stems each year to leave some older ones which will bloom later this year.

ABOVE Firm annual pruning is the key to a regular display of vivid red dogwood stems.

C. a. 'Westonbirt'. And the purplish stems of the brambles *Rubus cockburnianus* and *R. thibetanus* become covered in an eye-catching white bloom in winter. They're all looking so good now, it seems a pity to prune them. It's the youngest growth which gives the most vivid display, however, and cutting the stems back to within 2.5cm (1in) of their base about now keeps the plants in check and helps produce new stems with the best bark colour for next winter.

Don't throw the cut stems away – if they are trimmed into 15cm (6in) lengths and stuck in the ground they will root easily. If you push quite large branches into the soil they'll still root, and a row can make an attractive hedge. I've even seen them woven together to make a very attractive living screen which looks almost as good in winter as it does in summer.

Reviving heathers and hebes

As soon as winter-flowering heathers are past their best, clip them lightly over the top with shears as this ensures that they remain compact and sturdy.

At the same time, have a look at any hebes. Many of the best hebes are slightly tender, and are only really reliable grown outdoors in sheltered or coastal areas or kept in containers for bringing inside in winter. Elsewhere they can often look tattered and damaged after hard weather, and sometimes there's no saying if they're alive or not. They will grow out from the base, however, if the roots are still alive, so cut them back almost to the ground and keep your fingers crossed. If the weather looks like

LEFT This month is truly blossom time, with magnolias and flowering cherries competing for attention.

being as bad next winter, you can always cut them back before the worst sets in, and protect them with a thick layer of bark mulch.

Preparing to move a large shrub

Although the job might look daunting at first sight, a large shrub in the wrong place can be transplanted to another position quite successfully if you get it ready well in advance to reduce the inevitable shock to the plant. The best time to move it is the autumn (see page 156), but start preparing it now by severing the long side roots. This gives the plant the rest of this season to recover and make a compact fibrous rootball.

PREPARING TO MOVE A LARGE SHRUB

Reduce the shock to a shrub by trimming its roots now. Simply slice down with a spade all round the plant, or dig out a trench the width of the spade, cutting roots as you go, and refill it with a blend of soil, compost and general fertiliser to encourage new fibrous roots by the autumn.

LAWNS & HEDGES

Britain's climate allows us to grow the very best grass in the world. Compared with warmer drier countries it's really hard to go wrong, but to keep your lawn in top condition it needs a bit of regular care, starting now. So if it isn't quite up to scratch, here's my three-point plan for success: repair, revive and mow.

Repairing damage to lawns

This is an ideal time for covering up bare patches. On hard compressed soil, scratch the surface of the patch with an old kitchen knife to form a fine but shallow tilth. Mix a little seed with some soil, and spread it over, and then cover the patch with clear polythene held down with wire pegs. Cut a few slits in the plastic to let in air and water, and the seed should germinate in a matter of days.

Cut and repair the edges. This is best dealt with by cutting out a section of turf: turn it around with the ragged edge towards the centre and then you can repair this with a handful of seed and fine soil. No amount of rolling will remove bumps, because the flattened areas simply rise up again after rain. Instead make up a top dressing of sieved soil, garden compost and sharp sand in a 3:2:3 ratio. Spread this over the area, levelling it into the depression and leaving the high areas uncovered.

Reviving lawn growth

Old dead grass or 'thatch' builds up at the base of the grass, choking it out where amounts get bad. It should be raked out at the beginning of the season with a spring-tine rake or a hired electric machine. If you've got moss in the lawn, spread a special moss killer first and then, after it has gone black, rake out the dead stuff with the thatch. Organic gardeners don't use chemical moss killers, and just rake the worst out or learn to live with it. It's too early to do any weeding just yet – wait until the grass is growing vigorously, and then either water on a lawn weedkiller or combined weed and feed product, or dig the weeds out individually. You can give the grass a feed of nitrogenous lawn fertiliser as a spring boost at the end of this month, in which case you will need to give it another in June. Alternatively, you can apply a slow-release fertiliser just the once in May (see page 81).

Mowing

Sometime this month or next, when the grass starts to look ragged, you can begin the mowing regime. Avoid slashing grass close to the ground for the first cut, as this can set growth back if the weather turns cold again. It's much better to set the mower at its highest and just trim the top. Then you can lower the cutters a little each time each time you mow over the next few weeks until you leave the grass at its summer level. During the season, aim to mow a minimum of once a week, and 2–3 times each week for the finest lawns. If you can, mow diagonally in the opposite direction each time as this ensures that you pick up long grass flattened by the roller last time, and makes for a finer finish. And never kill worms: just brush their casts into the grass with a broom before mowing.

Starting dwarf hedges

Plant breeders are forever recommending pygmy versions of taller plants as 'ideal for small gardens'. But even if your plot is small, this doesn't exclude you from growing tall plants here and there, with a few larger drifts for more impact. And one of the ways to make ambitious ideas work in a small space is to tie the scheme together with dwarf hedging. If you edge borders or paths with a continuous run of the same plant the effect is to bind all the various plants together into a coherent scheme, and the last thing it looks then is bitty or boring. One of the traditional features of cottage gardens was a hedge of catmint or lavender running down both sides of the path that led to the front door. Although both sides of the path were largely planted with vegetables, this didn't look out of place or ugly. Dwarf box is a more formal, evergreen alternative.

The trouble is that a long run of hedging needs a lot of plants, and that could just break the bank. But if you have a bit of patience you can do it for next to nothing, because many of the best hedging plants can be raised from seed or from cuttings. Take catmint, for example: sown early in warmth, it will actually flower in its first year; otherwise sow it this month or next in a cold frame. Go for *Nepeta mussinii* (now called *N. racemosa*), or *N. nervosa*. Lavender can be raised in the same way. It's a superb traditional hedging plant, with greyish foliage all year round and scented blue flowers. Most of the popular varieties like *Lavandula* 'Hidcote' or 'Munstead' are available as seed. Cotton lavender (*Santolina chamaecyparissus*, also called *S. incana*) is another excellent hedger with silver filigree foliage. It also produces yellow flowers but is best cut back before these appear, to keep the hedge neat and compact.

ABOVE A framework of neatly clipped dwarf box provides a disciplined surround for small beds of spring bulbs.

Pot up the seedlings individually when they are large enough or line them out in a spare bit of the garden, and then plant them finally 15–20cm (6–8in) apart in the autumn. The one thing to bear in mind is that seed-raised plants are not as uniform as those grown from cuttings, but for hedging I don't think that matters at all. Since it's going to be clipped regularly, any difference in height won't show and slight variation in leaf or flower colour is to be welcomed.

Dwarf box needs the most patience but, once established, is disease-free and will last a lifetime. One decent-sized plant bought now could give you dozens of semi-ripe cuttings later in the year. These root easily, (see page 125), and in a year or two will provide yards of hedge.

VEGETABLES & HERBS

Fitting in vegetables

Some gardens are just too small to accommodate a kitchen plot. If you are in this position and haven't the time to rent an allotment locally, don't despair. You can always grow a few vegetables in your flower borders. Many vegetables are very attractive and, far from spoiling a flower bed, will enhance it. And by camouflaging vegetables among other plants you'll confuse many insect pests, so there's no need to cover your food with chemicals.

Leave a few spaces, ideally near the front of the border so that you can reach them from the path. Dig 15–20cm (6–8in) deep with a border fork, preferably working in garden compost, well-rotted manure or spent mushroom compost at the same time. Add a handful of organic fertiliser, and then rake the surface with the back of the fork to bring up a fine tilth. Scratch shallow rows about 15cm

(6in) apart using a bit of garden cane, and then this month you can sow radish, lettuce, carrots, spinach, turnips or summer cabbage. Later on you can add courgettes, bush cucumbers, tomatoes and sweetcorn.

Herbs, of course, are even easier to fit into a border scheme because most have very decorative leaves or flowers. Try chives or parsley as an edging, or plant thyme, marjoram and pennyroyal to tumble over the sides of a path, while giants like angelica, lovage and bronze fennel look great at the back of a border.

Planning the small-scale plot

If you do have a small plot, you'll have some hard decisions to make about what to grow and how to get maximum yields from every square inch. If your plot is small and your freezer's big, it's worthwhile growing things like spinach, Swiss chard and beans to stock up for the winter – frozen peas are the one exception though, because commercial growers do them so much better than we can. Try some

roots like carrots and beetroot: you can store all you can grow by putting them in boxes of garden compost in the garage. Then there are the vegetables that are expensive or hard to come by. I certainly wouldn't be without things like asparagus, globe artichokes, sweetcorn and courgettes, which are all very much cheaper to grow and taste a million times better when harvested minutes before cooking.

Above all, make the most of your space. Grow plants close together, perhaps in a deep bed (see page 117), and sow just the right amount and no more. That means crops grown in succession – lettuces, summer cabbages, radishes, carrots, beetroot – must be sown in short rows at frequent intervals. It all depends on how fast you eat them, but I'd suggest sowing a short row

BELOW Hardening off early vegetable sowings or tender plants is easy with a simple cold frame, equipped with a clear lid that can be opened a little more each day (see page 51).

MARCH SOWING LIST

In a small bed try: lettuce 'Tom Thumb'; carrot 'Early Nantes'; turnip 'Purple Top Milan'; salad onion 'White Lisbon'; radish 'Sparkler'; beetroot 'Boltardy'; spinach 'Medania'; cabbage 'Kingspi'; pea 'Douce Provence'; broad bean 'The Sutton'; parsnip 'White Gem'. The only tools you'll need are a border fork, a stick and a bucket for as much compost or manure as you can spare. Sow rows at close spacings, thin seedlings early and pick while crops are young.

of radishes once a week and a longer one of lettuces every fortnight: thin the lettuces when they're large enough, and use the thinnings for another, slightly later, row.

Turnips, carrots and beetroot are tastiest when they're pulled small, so I get them in once a fortnight too, but the winter storage varieties are sown just once, of course. If you like a succession of summer cabbages and cauliflowers, sow those once every three weeks – bear in mind, though, that when beans, sweetcorn and tomatoes come in, you might lose interest in cabbages.

If space is really scarce, you can always try growing 'mini-veg', specially bred compact varieties (see page 182).

Planting asparagus

Now is a good moment to make an asparagus bed, which I suggest should be about 1.2m (4ft) wide and as long – or short – as you like. Dig it deeply and add plenty of compost. On heavy soil also add some coarse pea shingle for better drainage. Mound the bed 15cm (6in) higher than its surroundings to improve drainage. For heaviest yields order crowns of an all-male variety such as 'Franklim', 'Lucullus' or 'Dariana', and when they arrive soak them for a couple of hours. Dig out shallow trenches about 15cm (6in) deep and 45cm (18in) apart, and mound up the centre of each trench to make a gentle ridge. Rest the crowns on the top, 45cm (18in) apart with the fleshy roots spreading down each side of the ridge, and replace the soil over them. You won't be able to cut any spears this year, and will have just a taste next season. But after that, gastronomic bliss!

Planting early potatoes

Potatoes can be put in now, although if the sprouts are still small there's plenty of time. Provided the sprouts are healthy, the potatoes can last unplanted until early April, but yields begin to decline after that.

If the ground is well prepared in advance, you can plant potatoes with a trowel. Otherwise dig out planting trenches about a spade deep and 60cm (2ft) apart, and put manure or compost in the bottom. Don't use spent mushroom compost as this contains lime which could encourage unsightly potato scab.

Plant the tubers on top, 30cm (12in) apart. Since they're gross feeders, add about 136g/sq.m (4oz/sq.yd) of pelleted chicken manure or Growmore to the soil you dug out, so that it's worked in when you refill (alternatively scatter the dressing down the rows after planting). You'll find the soil naturally mounds up slightly over the top of the rows, and they'll need a further mounding later when the shoots have grown about 15cm (6in) high. Once these appear, watch out for frost and if this is threatened cover the plants with horticultural fleece.

For extra-early crops, prepare the ground in the usual way and then ridge the soil into mounds 30cm (12in) high and 60cm (2ft) apart. Plant an early tuber in each mound, as deep as possible. Cover the area with clear polythene held down with bricks or pieces of timber, and when the foliage appears cut slits to let it through. It is even easier, because the potatoes are grown on the surface, to use black polythene, as shown above. If you protect the plants with fleece in the event of

PLANTING POTATOES

1 Prepare and level the bed, and cover with a sheet of black polythene tucked in all round. Cut a small cross for each potato, large enough to push the tuber into place just below the surface.

2 The foliage will grow through the slits and then, at the end of the season, it's simply a matter of peeling back the polythene to expose the crop, right at the surface and ready to harvest.

frost, you should be harvesting new potatoes in mid- to late May.

Maincrop varieties can also go in now, planted in the same way, except that they're spaced 38cm (15in) apart with 75cm (30in) between the rows. Frankly though, there's not such a huge difference in taste over shop-bought supplies so, unless you have plenty of space or want to clear new ground, perhaps maincrops are not so worthwhile.

MISCELLANEOUS

Make or buy a cold frame

You'll soon find the greenhouse overflowing, or your windowsills so full of young plants that you can't see out. What you need is a cold frame, a fairly modest but worthwhile investment that's sure to reap dividends.

Frames come in all shapes and sizes, in wood or aluminium, with a glass or plastic lid, and either with solid sides or fully glazed right down to the ground. Naturally, all-glass frames let in more light but can be colder – in early spring it's a good idea to line one of these with bubble plastic or even insulate the sides with sheets of polystyrene. Some frames are glazed with twin-wall polycarbonate, which lets in almost as much light as glass does, and is warm and completely shatterproof. Wooden frames look attractive and they tend to retain more heat than aluminium ones.

Alternatively, it's very easy to make your own. In fact, a wooden apple box with a piece of rigid plastic on top, held down with a bit of string and an elastic band, served me well for years. You can make a more elaborate version from old timber, as shown above. A cast-off window frame or even a surplus car windscreen would do for the lid.

You could paint the inside of the frame white for maximum light, and treat the outside with a couple of coats of timber preservative.

There's no need to make a solid floor, indeed, a frame is better without one at all. It will be more use if you can stand it on the soil, partly because bare soil provides better drainage for trays and pots,

MAKING A COLD FRAME

A sturdy and durable frame can be made from strong recycled timber that has been treated with preservative. Make sure the lid slopes to shed rain and collect maximum light. If you make the frame to fit one of your vegetable beds and add a handle at each end, it can be placed over growing plants to protect them out of season.

especially if you cover the ground with a layer of capillary matting; but also because you can actually sow and grow plants directly into the soil inside the frame.

To make maximum use of the frame, cultivate the the ground it stands on as a seedbed, forking in plenty of compost and then levelling the surface. Cover this with the matting while you are hardening off your pots of plants – once they're safely out, remove the matting and the seedbed will be ready.

Using a frame

Site your new frame in a sunny spot and it will deliver enough light to allow you to grow good short bushy plants in complete safety from frost and wind. Right now its main use is to 'harden off' tender plants. Any you've raised on the windowsill will be desperate for full light to keep them sturdy. Put them inside the frame, close the lid and cover it with a bit of old carpet or a blanket if frost threatens at night. In April you can open the lid a fraction during warm days, gradually giving the plants a bit more air each day. Then start opening it at night, depending upon the temperature. By late May you should be able to leave the plants exposed day and night – they should be hardy enough by then to take anything the weather can throw at them.

During June you can use the frame for soft-wood cuttings, or for a batch of self-blanching celery. In the autumn it can be used to help to root semi-ripe cuttings, and then in winter it could house November-sown sweet peas, or you could plant crops of winter lettuce, endive and chicory in the ground. In a well-run garden a cold frame should never be empty, and will earn its keep over and over again.

PLANTS FOR
march

1 The hardy evergreen lesser periwinkle, *Vinca minor*, is more restrained than its large cousin *V. major*; the 20cm (8in) gold-splashed stems of 'Aureovariegata' spread 60cm (2ft) after three years.

2 'Rose Queen' is one of the finest varieties of hardy perennial *Epimedium grandiflorum* (*E. macranthum*). Its 30cm (12in) high clumps of richly tinted leaves last all winter. Trim them off in spring to reveal its crimson-pink blooms and the newly emerging shoots.

1

2

3 The flowering quince, *Chaenomeles*
× *superba* 'Knap Hill Scarlet', is a dense
spreading deciduous bush, eventually 90cm
(3ft) high and 1.5m (5ft) wide, with a long
season of brilliant blooms.

4 As its name implies, *Daphne odora* has
intensely fragrant flowers which stud the
1.5m (5ft) evergreen shrubs from late winter
onwards. *D. o.* 'Aureomarginata' has creamy-
yellow edged leaves and is slightly hardier.

5 Perennial double primroses are often sold
unnamed in collections of mixed colours. At
15cm (6in), they are ideal highlights for small
beds and containers in March and April.

OVERLEAF Parrot tulips have large heads of
fringed petals, and provide an extravagant
display both in the garden and as cut flowers.

3

4

5

G eoff would complain loudly at this time of year about lack of sleep, having frequently been woken at first light by what he called the 'twittering cacophony of lustful birds'. In truth, of course, he loved the dawn chorus, and it was one of the reasons why planting a variety of mature trees was among his first priorities at Barnsdale. Now there are finches, wrens, robins and owls in the woodland; we have bird boxes for blue tits, house martins have nested in the eaves, and we have to leave the barn doors open all summer for the swallows. Geoff loved their songs — even the bullfinch's, which he said sounded like a squeaky wheelbarrow. But he also loved them for being allies in the fight against greenfly, slugs and caterpillars.

Geoff felt passionately about encouraging these garden pests' natural predators, and never, ever used pesticides or slug pellets. He was even known to have 'hardened off' the ladybirds which hatched in his office by gently scooping them up and taking them into the garden where he installed them under a cloche to get them used to the lower temperatures outside.

The popular weeping willow-leafed pear,
Pyrus salicifolia 'Pendula', takes centre-stage
as its young foliage opens above a border
packed with tulips and hardy perennials.

april

key tasks for april

ANNUALS & BEDDING PLANTS
○ Sow hardy annuals outdoors where they are to grow, page 58
○ Sow annual climbers early in the month, page 58
○ Buy summer bedding as plugs for growing on, page 59

BORDER PERENNIALS
○ Clean up borders now growth is well under way, page 60
○ Start to plant borders, page 60
○ Make a scree garden for alpines and drought-tolerant plants, page 60

BULBS
○ Pinch off spent bulb heads, page 63
○ Plant gladioli corms, page 63

SHRUBS, TREES & CLIMBERS
○ Plan climbers to add height to the garden, page 64
○ Support and tie in climbers, page 64
○ Prune quinces after they have flowered, page 65

ROSES
○ Feed and mulch roses, page 65

LAWNS & HEDGES
○ Assess your mower at the start of the season, page 65

VEGETABLES & HERBS
○ Sow French beans in pots under glass, page 66
○ Sow maincrop leeks outdoors, page 66
○ Sow peas, and keep on sowing at regular intervals, page 66
○ Make plans for late crops and winter supplies, page 67

FRUIT
○ Choose fruit trees for training into compact shapes for small gardens, page 68

MISCELLANEOUS
○ Feed outdoor plants to stimulate growth, page 69
○ The benefits of organic fertilisers, page 69
○ Grow your own manure, page 69

ANNUALS & BEDDING PLANTS

Sowing annuals outdoors

Hardy annuals can produce probably the cheapest and most cheerful flower borders possible, and they're also useful for providing flowers in new beds while slower plants are still settling in. A sprinkle here and there will help to fill gaps in established borders, and many annuals will also attract a lot of bees and butterflies to the garden.

At this time of year annuals can be sown direct into the soil, but don't start before the ground is warm enough as the seeds won't germinate until the temperature has reached about 7°C (45°F). Wait until the soil is dry enough to rake down to a fine crumbly tilth – there's no need to add any fertiliser, because most annuals flower much more prolifically in poor soil.

Although they are great for filling in gaps in borders, annuals always look most impressive in big bold blocks of colour. The easiest way to mark these out on the ground is to fill a wine bottle with fine dry sand and then use this to outline planting areas for each variety. Then sow as shown on the right.

For early flowers, or if your soil lies wet and cold until late in spring, sow early this month in the greenhouse. Fill seed trays with moist soil-less compost, sow the seeds very thinly and allow them to grow on without thinning. Harden them off when they're about 5cm (2in) high, and plant them out in small clumps – just lift the whole block of seedlings out of the tray and cut it into 4cm (1½in) squares with a knife.

SOWING ANNUALS OUTSIDE

1 Mark the outlines of planting areas with dry sand trickled from a wine bottle; then make parallel drills for sowing within each patch with a cane.

2 Sow a different variety in each patch, arranging heights and colours to produce a balanced design. Water and weed the area until the seedlings are through.

3 When the seedlings are 5cm (2in) high, thin them to about 15–20cm (6–8in) apart, depending on the variety. Water them with a diluted feed after you've finished.

Growing annual climbers

A little social climbing will do you and your garden no harm at all, and it needn't cost a fortune. There's a small range of annual climbers that are easily raised from seed.

Sweet peas (*Lathyrus odoratus*) should have been planted earlier (see page 16), but there are three other annuals that will flower from late summer onwards if you get the seeds in early this month. Morning glory (*Ipomaea*) has large blue or pink trumpets with white centres; cathedral bells (*Cobaea scandens*) has large bell-shaped flowers that are violet and purple on the outside and green inside; and climbing nasturtium (*Tropaeolum speciosum*) is a knock-out in brilliant reds, oranges and yellows. All three need to be planted in a sunny spot with some support, such as a pergola or fence. They are also ideal for growing through evergreen shrubs.

Buying bedding as plugs

These days most seedsmen offer more than just seeds in their catalogues. There are all kinds of accessories, plus an increasing range of half-hardy bedding as plants, which could save you a lot of worry if you haven't the time or space to raise your own. The trouble with the more tender kinds of bedding like petunias, busy lizzies and begonias is that they usually need heat early in the year to get them to germinate. New F_1 hybrids are getting quite expensive and if the seeds don't grow, or only a few do, that can prove far too costly. Buying plants at bedding out time can work out expensive too, but there is a way to grow the best bedding ever, while leaving all the early risks to someone else.

Growers now tend to raise all their bedding by precision-sowing large trays divided into dozens of tiny tapering cells, and these produce 'plug' seedlings. At this stage they have got past all the hazards of germination, and don't need such high temperatures. When you buy plugs from a seed catalogue or garden centre they'll be ready for transplanting, each with its own perfect root system.

With no disturbance to the roots, they're off and away before you can say 'petunia', and they are comparatively easy to grow on until you plant them out when the danger of frost has passed in late May or early June. They should be in flower when you plant them, and considerably bigger and bushier, so you might need fewer of them than

BELOW Violas and winter-flowering pansies are favourite choices for spring bedding and for combining with low-growing bulbs.

if you'd raised your own. They could work out cheaper too.

When they arrive, pot the plugs up in 9cm (3½in) pots of soil-less compost and put them in a cool greenhouse or a cold frame. Although no extra heat is necessary from now on, they must be kept frost-free, so keep an eye on the weather forecast and, in the unlikely event of very hard frost, cover the frame with a blanket or a bit of sacking. Start to feed the plants with a general liquid fertiliser a fortnight after potting.

They should be pinched back two or three times by nipping out the tips of leading shoots with your thumbnail. This encourages them to bush out and produce big fat flowering plants to brighten up your summer borders. Make sure that you harden them off thoroughly for a fortnight or so before planting, by gradually opening the top of the frame a little more every few days until they're used to outside conditions.

BORDER PERENNIALS

Cleaning up the borders

Some time this month you'll find just about everyone outside in the fresh air, both fair-weather gardeners and those of us who are at it all year round. If your garden hasn't been worked on since the winter, the first job is a general clean-up of the borders.

Cut away any old dead growth from last year's herbaceous plants, pull out the weeds and then give the soil between the plants a light forking over, just the top couple of inches or so. I like to spread a layer of compost on the surface first, and tickle this in as I fork. If you have no compost or manure, spent mushroom compost is the next best thing, except around acid-loving plants. Never, of course, use peat.

Add a sprinkle of rose fertiliser or a general organic one if you are moving plants or planting new ones. Check for any herbaceous plants that are overcrowded or have become old and tired. It's getting a bit late to lift and divide them, and I prefer to do this in the autumn anyway (see page 138), but I'd still do it now if it's really necessary. (Though this is the best time to divide sweet violets, which will have flowered by now, and move them to a shady spot for the summer.) Make sure you water in any newly divided plants well.

LEFT A raised scree bed, like this one constructed for alpines at Barnsdale, is an attractive and practical alternative to a rock garden for displaying arabis, alyssum and other compact alpines that need perfect drainage to do well.

Starting to plant

This is the perfect time to put in new herbaceous plants, and it's worth paying a visit to the garden centre or nursery if you have any bare spaces in the border. But please don't buy everything that's in flower now or you'll have a garden that only flowers in the spring. Look for summer-flowering plants, such as achilleas, delphiniums and lupins. They'll produce masses of colour year after year, are generally soil-tolerant and easy to grow.

Before you buy, check on heights, spread, required position, colour and flowering time: this is where a good book becomes essential. But many books encourage you to plant three, five or even seven plants in a group; that can be mighty expensive and, if you have patience, could be completely unnecessary. If you wait until next year, you'll be able to lift most of your new plants about this time and split them up to produce the extra plants you need, all for the cost of just one plant.

Although we expect spring to start with buckets of rain, don't be lulled into a false sense of security. The plants will need watering in and, if the weather remains dry, watering again in a week or so.

Making a garden for alpines and drought-tolerant plants

As I said in January, alpines can withstand most extremes of weather, but the one condition they can't abide is excess wet, a condition they share with drought-tolerant or Mediterranean plants. Efficient drainage is a must.

While a full-scale rock garden will provide the right drainage conditions, it will also take up a lot of space. Instead, you could always

ABOVE As well as being a wonderful aid to drainage in alpine beds, gravel can be added to the soil and spread as a mulch, as here at Barnsdale, to provide the conditions that drought-loving Mediterranean shrubs and perennials most enjoy.

make yourself a small scree garden which will re-create the gravelly conditions found at the bottom of mountains, where some of the best alpines grow, or the dried-up river bed typically colonised by heat-loving plants.

You can make a scree garden as large as you like and with a natural appearance, or do what I did and make it small and formal. Mine is a circle edged with bricks and looks good all year round. Simply mark out the area you want to plant, and dig a lot of grit into the soil: a barrow-load per square yard is certainly not too much. Make sure the grit is at least 0.25cm (⅛in) in diameter; never use sand, which is too fine. Pea shingle from builders' merchants is ideal, and you can also incorporate about half as much well-rotted garden compost. Mix all this in thoroughly.

If you want to make a rock garden, position a few groups of rocks here and there, burying them about one-third of their depth to make them look natural. And always put them in random clumps, rather than spreading them around evenly like currants in a bun. But please be careful that you don't buy water-worn limestone for the rocks – it is robbed from rare and irreplaceable limestone pavements in the countryside.

After planting mulch with more pea shingle or coarse grit, tucking it under the plants where you can to keep their leaves off the damp soil. I like to mix the sizes of the gravel to make an interesting texture, and find that larger pebbles deter cats from scratching it about. The mulch will greatly reduce water loss and

61

suppress most of the weeds – any that do blow in and germinate will be a lot easier to control. Water and feed your plants only if they look as though they are not growing well.

CHOOSING ALPINES

Start with one or two taller plants like dwarf conifers, but make sure they are truly dwarf: slow growers like the little Noah's Ark juniper, *J. communis* 'Compressa', are ideal. When you buy the smaller plants check that they're not too rampant – too much arabis or aubrietia will soon swamp the garden. There are hundreds to choose from, so go for the tougher customers like saxifrage, thrift, rock pinks, houseleeks, sedums, miniature aquilegias, thymes, raoulias and dwarf hypericum.

CHOOSING DROUGHT-TOLERANT PLANTS

I would start with lavender and rosemary, the many varieties of *Cistus* or rock rose that thrive on sun-baked hillsides, and smaller hebes like *H. pinguifolia* 'Pagei' and *H.* 'Red Edge'. You can grow yuccas, cordylines and sea-hollies, and some kinds of osteospermum and penstemon; in summer interplant with tender perennials such as marguerites and cannas, as well as annuals like Livingstone daisies.

LEFT This bold grouping of yellow and orange crown imperials (*Fritillaria imperialis*), with blue pulmonaria and muscari at their feet, is one way to illuminate a border of summer-flowering perennials still in their early stages of growth.

BULBS

Treating flowered bulbs

April is the prime month for bulbs. Daffodils are at their peak, with tulips coming on fast and many smaller bulbs such as fritillaries also making a show. In order to channel the plants' energy into building up flowering bulbs for next year, prevent them from forming seedheads by pinching off the flower heads as soon as they fade.

Planting gladioli

Although there's no doubt that the large-flowered hybrid gladiolus deserves its reputation as a 'mega-star' of the border, there are few better flowers for cutting, so a row or two in the vegetable plot is a must. If you cut them when the first floret is just opening, the flowers will continue to develop in water and last for ages.

A good mixture is perhaps the best choice for cutting. That way you should get a superb range of colours, from delicate pastels to flaming scarlet, often with exotically frilled petals and contrasting markings. If you decide to go for individual varieties to fit in with your border scheme, choose them from a good catalogue that lists them according to season because there are early, mid-season and late kinds. Not only that, but if you plant a few every fortnight between early April and late May, they'll flower in succession through the summer and autumn months. If there's a choice of sizes, I'd recommend the '14cm (5½in) upwards' grade, as these are the largest corms and produce the best flowers – for the biggest spikes, peel

the corms before planting and nick out any shoots coming from the sides with a knife, to concentrate all the energy in the spike at the top.

Gladioli can look a bit ungainly in borders if you grow them singly or in rows, so group about five or six in a circle to make a stunning column of colour. That way you can also stake the lot with one unobtrusive cane in the middle. Straight rows often fit in better among vegetables – set up a couple of strong stakes and a horizontal wire or two for tying them to, or simply tie each stem to a cane.

Prepare the soil well with plenty of manure or compost, and a handful or two of pelleted chicken manure. If you are on heavy soil, plant the corms on a layer of coarse grit, just to keep the base-plate dry and free from rot. Space large-flowered kinds 15cm (6in) apart each way, or with 30cm (12in) between rows if you're growing them in this way. The corms need to be 10–15cm (4–6in) below the surface, a little deeper on very light soil because the tall stems are more likely to topple over if they're not well supported at the base.

For me, the smaller Butterfly hybrids have a special charm and come in a range of superb colours with bright patches on the lower petals – try white and scarlet 'Bizar', pink and yellow 'Jackpot' or violet 'Pop Art' with its brilliant white markings. My own favourites are the *Primulinus* hybrids with flowers more loosely arranged and in slightly more restrained colours. Try potting some of these smaller types, about 8cm (3in) apart and 10cm (4in) deep in 20cm (8in) pots of John Innes No. 2 compost with about 25 per cent added grit.

SHRUBS, TREES & CLIMBERS

Planning for climbers

Cover the boundaries of a tiny new garden with climbing plants and you'll transform a confined space into a secret haven. Even in large gardens, climbers will give height and increase your growing space three- or four-fold. They can be used to clothe the walls of the house and hide ugly features such as a central heating oil tank. And don't forget, many climbers will also provide a home for all kinds of wildlife.

Everyone would like a climber that is evergreen, fast growing, loaded with flowers all year long and thrives on a freezing north-facing wall. Well, I have to tell you

BELOW Early-flowering *Clematis armandii* scrambles through a white camellia, making a perfect partnership.

that such a plant doesn't exist. For a start, you'll miss a lot if you insist on evergreens. There are certainly some very good ones (pyracantha and garrya, for example) but to be without clematis, most of which are deciduous, would be a sin. Don't get hung up on their speed of growth either, for the faster a climber grows, the bigger the problems can be later on – choose a Russian vine, *Fallopia* (*Polygonum*) *baldschuanica*, and although it will clothe your garden shed in two years, it will bury it in five. And although there are climbers for every wall, it's the east- and north-facing ones that really sort the men from the boys, because lack of light and the possibility of biting winds make these positions suitable for only the hardiest climbers. It's no good putting wisteria, for example, on an east- or north-facing wall: it will certainly grow perfectly well, but the flowers will be as rare as hen's teeth.

There is no need, however, to be satisfied with just one climber. Walls can actually be gardened just like borders, allowing one less vigorous plant to scramble through another. A favourite combination of mine, for example, is a climbing or rambling rose with a clematis growing through it, but be careful which kind of clematis you choose. A vigorous species such as *C. montana* will swamp anything smaller than a large tree. The best bet is to use a less rampant variety and, if you go for one that flowers late, you'll be able to cut it to the ground after flowering and pull out all the shoots to give the rose a chance. The following year the rose will flower well, and the clematis will grow back again to flower

afterwards. The best kinds would be any of the *C. viticella* or *C. texensis* varieties.

Supporting climbers

There are a few climbers that will cling to a fence or wall without any support at all. If you grow Virginia creeper, one of the ivies or a climbing hydrangea, all you need do is plant it and then point the growing tip towards the fence. But there are many more that need some support. The best method is to staple wires to fence posts. If you want to grow plants on an old wall, you should be able to drive 'vine eyes' into the mortar – these are small hardened steel wedges with a hole in one end for the wire. On modern walls with strong mortar, you'll have to drill and plug holes for screw-in eyes. Horizontal wires set 30cm (12in) apart will be enough for tying in most perennial climbers with woody branches, but for twiners such as honeysuckle or clematis, you should add thinner vertical wires at 15cm (6in) intervals to make a wide mesh.

Don't be afraid to plant restrained climbers in the middle of a border. You can support climbing roses by tying the stems in to an upright pole; for self-clinging climbers, wrap a couple of thicknesses of chicken wire or dark-coloured plastic netting round the pole to help give them a grip. Alternatively, you could build a wigwam like the structure you'd make for sweet peas or runner beans (see page 41). You can use garden canes for lighter climbers such as a late-flowering clematis that is pruned to ground each spring, or stronger poles for heavier climbers like roses or early-flowering clematis that keep a permanent framework of branches.

Finally, don't forget that walls, especially house walls which are protected by the eaves, are some of the driest places in the garden. Dig in lots of manure or compost before planting, position the climber at least 30cm (12in) away from the wall, and give it a good soak from time to time in its first year or two, at least until it has been able to root out into moister soil.

Pruning flowering quinces

Flowering quinces can be wall-trained as well as grown as free-standing specimens. If they are wall-trained they must be cut back annually to keep their shape and hug the wall, but even free-standing quinces will become choked with growth if they are left to their own devices. They are best pruned as soon as the flowers fade: cut back the flowered shoots to 1–2 buds.

CLIMBERS FOR SHADY WALLS
Akebia quinata; camellias – though not on an east-facing wall; some clematis such as *C. × jackmanii;* flowering quince (*Chaenomeles*); silk tassle bush (*Garrya elliptica*); most ivies (*Hedera*); climbing hydrangea (*H. petiolaris*); winter jasmine (*Jasminum nudiflorum*); honeysuckles such as *Lonicera americana* and *L. tellmaniana*; Virginia creeper (*Parthenocissus quinquefolia*); firethorn (*Pyracantha*); flowering currant (*Ribes speciosum*); some roses such as 'Golden Showers', 'Mme Alfred Carrière' and 'Zéphirine Drouhin'; and *Schizophragma.*

ROSES

Feeding and mulching
A large part of the enjoyment of gardening is the actual doing, but reducing work in certain areas will allow more time for the most agreeable jobs. Growing plants well will greatly reduce labour, and one of the most important ways is to get the soil fertile in the first place and then keep it that way afterwards so that plants almost look after themselves. Nowhere is this more critical than for roses, which really enjoy good living.

After pruning and cutting back roses earlier in the year, it's a good idea now to show you care by giving them a liberal feed and a heavy mulch to sustain all that new growth and flowering. Some gardeners mulch straight after pruning, but the soil is still cold and will take longer to warm up under a blanket of manure so wait until this month when temperatures are rising. And before you mulch, give the plants a feed so the fertiliser is in direct contact with the soil.

You can use a standard rose fertiliser at the rate suggested on the packet, or spread an organic feed such as blood, fish and bone or pelleted poultry manure at about 136g/sq.m (4oz/sq.yd). Then dress the plants with a good mulch of garden compost or well-rotted manure all round, 5–8cm (2–3in) deep and covering the same area as the spread of the branches. This will help keep the soil moist in summer and stop annual weeds in their tracks. About mid-summer, after the first main flush of bloom, you can give the plants another feed to encourage later colour.

LAWNS & HEDGES

Assessing mowers
If you haven't started mowing yet, the first job is to drag the mower out of the shed where it has been rusting all winter. With a bit of luck, it will start. If not, get it down to the repairer pronto because there's bound to be a queue by now.

If you are a keen lawn-keeper but have an old mower, and want to be popular with your neighbours, let me diplomatically suggest that you consider renewing it. Manufacturers have made great efforts to tackle excess noise recently, and not without cause: noise is regularly listed as the biggest complaint levelled by neighbours who like to live in peace. Apart from noise level, the type you buy depends on the kind of lawn you want.

I'm not a great believer in bowling-green lawns in gardens. They are a lot of work and can make the plot look too neat and precious for my liking. I'd go for a good green hard-wearing lawn that sets off borders well but can also be used by the family and requires minimum labour. I encourage grass to grow as strongly as possible, and learn to live with a daisy or two. If you do dream of the perfect finish, you'll need a cylinder mower with as many blades as possible. It will give the finest cut and tend to remove the coarse grasses.

If you cut the grass less frequently or need a good general-purpose lawn, a rotary mower is fine. I always insist on a mower that picks up the cuttings, which look ugly and tread into the house if they're left to lie in swathes. On the other hand, there are mulching mowers which cut the grass very fine and blow it evenly downwards so that it is re-incorporated into the soil, improving its structure and returning the nutrients, thus saving many trips to the compost heap.

The best source of power depends on the size of your garden. Electric mowers are cheap, as easy to use as a vacuum cleaner and quieter than most, but have the disadvantage of a trailing cable which can be dangerous unless you use a residual circuit-breaker.

Battery models are a good choice for small lawns, now that the rechargeable batteries are smaller and lighter than earlier kinds and run for longer on a single charging. For bigger gardens, petrol power is the best choice and much more versatile, if more expensive and not as quiet as electricity; and some have electric ignition, which can save a lot of back-breaking effort when starting the engine.

Don't despise the good old-fashioned push mower if you have a small lawn and you're under 80. They're as cheap as electric models, up-to-date designs are a million times easier to use than the rusty old job father had, and the exercise is as life-enhancing as gardening itself. And they're the only type that are pleasant to listen to.

Trimming formal hedges

A formal hedge of box, yew, lonicera or santolina, needs clipping more often than other kinds and can begin to look shaggy and neglected if you don't start trimming it as soon as the danger of heavy frost has passed. Use a taut line if necessary as a guide to get a precise finish. It will need clipping again in August (see page 128).

VEGETABLES & HERBS

Growing French beans in pots

Dwarf French beans hate having cold feet, and if you put them outside a bit early or sow them too soon they will quickly turn up their toes. Even if they survive, they will stop growing and be reluctant to start again for several weeks.

They can be started in the greenhouse, however, with a few potted on to give the earliest pickings. Sow a variety like 'Daisy', two seeds to each 8cm (3in) pot of John Innes No. 1 compost, and give them a little bottom heat if you can, although this isn't essential. If both seeds germinate, remove the weaker seedling. Space plants as they grow to give plenty of light and to make strong bushy plants for hardening off and planting out in late May.

If you want to grow them to maturity in the greenhouse, transfer four or five of the young plants to a 20cm (8in) pot when they've made their first true leaf, or sow half a

BELOW Gentle heat is enough to ensure a spring crop of dwarf French beans in pots.

dozen seeds direct. Keep them in good light, and support them as they develop with some twiggy sticks or a few thin canes and raffia. Feed them every week once they come into flower, and you'll be picking tender beans well before outdoor crops are ready.

Starting leeks

If you have a greenhouse, it's always worth growing an early variety of leek such as 'King Richard' by sowing indoors in March and then planting outdoors in early May. Sowings of maincrop leeks, such as 'Musselburgh' and 'Giant Winter' are usually made now in a seedbed outdoors. Any earlier, and you risk the plants running to seed later in the season.

Fork and rake the soil until you've got a nice fine tilth, and then make shallow drills 15cm (6in) apart. Sow the seeds thinly 1cm (½in) deep, and thin them to about 2.5cm (1in) apart as soon as they're large enough to handle. When they are as thick as a pencil, they're ready to transplant into holes made with a dibber, 15cm (6in) apart and the same in depth. Water the seedlings well before lifting, separate them and just drop one in each hole. Then pour water into each hole to settle the seedlings, but don't refill with soil – the stem of the plant will fill the hole as it grows and develop a pure white blanch where it is buried beneath the ground.

Sowing peas

If you cover a strip of ground with polythene or cloches you can sow peas as early as the beginning of March. Otherwise start this month, and make further sowings at three-week intervals up to the beginning of June. Always use a first-early wrinkle-seeded variety, which will take about 12 weeks to mature compared to the 16 weeks for maincrop kinds; the sweetest early pea I've yet found is 'Douce Provence', although 'Hurst Beagle', 'Hurst Greenshaft' and 'Kelvedon Wonder' are almost as tasty.

You can take out a single drill for a narrow row of plants if space is limited, although I prefer to make a wide drill the width of the spade and about 5cm (2in) deep. Scatter the seeds in this, aiming to get each one about 5cm (2in) from its neighbours – the actual distance isn't critical, but it's always worth taking a bit of time to space the seeds out as plants dislike overcrowding. Cover with soil, tamp down lightly and, if the weather's cold, cover with polythene. You'll have to keep an eye open though, so that you can remove the cover as soon as the first seedling shows through. If you use horticultural fleece instead, this can stay over the seedlings until they make their first tendrils, when it is time to remove the cover and push in a few twiggy sticks or stretch some netting between canes to provide support.

Planning late crops

As the month progresses you can really get going with sowing summer vegetables outdoors, and right now I would sow spinach, carrots, turnips, radishes, kohl rabi, lettuces, spring onions, summer cabbages and cauliflowers. But don't forget to look ahead, even though it seems crazy to be thinking about Christmas before spring is really under way.

If you want big cauliflowers, savoy cabbages and Brussels sprouts for your Yuletide dinner, you'd better get to it because the seeds need sowing this month. You'll produce plenty of seedlings for the average garden from seedbed rows 60cm (2ft) long and 15cm (6in) apart. Sow autumn and winter cabbages, Brussels sprouts, winter cauliflowers, curly kale and sprouting broccoli, all at the same time, and add a few calabrese for eating in late summer too.

I like to transplant all these when the seedlings are still quite small, about 10cm (4in) high or when they've made 2–3 true leaves –

ABOVE Pliable stems from willow, hazel and other shrubs can be recycled as decorative pea supports.

never leave them until the stems darken and become woody, as they are unlikely to grow well then. The trouble is that autumn and winter varieties need quite wide spacings, anything from 45cm (18in) to 60cm (2ft) apart, but you can arrange some catch-crops of quicker maturing stuff in between. Fast carrots, beetroot, lettuces, radishes and salad onions, for example, should have plenty of room within 60cm (2ft) rows of transplants.

67

FRUIT

Choosing trained fruit trees

Fruit trees are at their most appealing now, when they are covered in blossom. More traditionally, apples and pears are planted in November, and early winter is the best time for bare-rooted trees (see page 170), but a good range of varieties is available in containers now. This means that you can plant them straight away, and may even get an apple or two this year (though you shouldn't count on it!).

The great thing about apple and pear trees is that you can do just about anything with them, short of growing them upside down. So even if you have a postage stamp of a garden, you can still grow your own fruitful orchard by training the trees in special ways. A hedge of cordons, or a fan or espalier against a wall, for example, will take up a strip of soil about 15–30cm (6–12in) wide and look terrific.

Of course, what puts most people off trained apples and pears is the thought of all that complicated pruning. But a fruit-farmer I know prunes his apples with an electric hedge trimmer and still gets a bumper crop, so you see it needn't be difficult. It's mostly done in the summer and is easy to understand (see page 130). Most container-grown trees are sold ready-trained, however, because it is the first year or two's training that needs the most care. All you need do now is decide on the tree shape.

To restrict growth and reduce the amount of pruning you need to do, trees are grafted on to a special rootstock. If you want a very dwarf apple tree and your soil is fertile, go for the rootstock M27. If you need a slightly more vigorous tree to cover a larger space, or your soil is not as good as you would like, stick to MM106. There's less choice with pears, and most are grafted on the semi-dwarfing Quince A rootstock. If your nursery or garden centre can't identify the rootstock, go to one where they can.

BELOW This dessert apple 'Sunset' has been grown as a single espalier or 'step-over' tree on low supports.

TRAINING FRUIT TREES

1 An espalier is a neat productive shape, perfect for growing beside a path. A fairly vigorous rootstock is best, together with tight wires or a timber framework to support the horizontal tiers of branches.

2 Cordons take up the least room, and several different varieties may be grown in a confined space to spread out the harvest. Sloping them at an angle increases the length of the single stem and encourages heavier crops of fruit.

3 A perfectly trained fan, normally used for plums, cherries and pears trained on walls, is very decorative and easy to manage. Choose a vigorous rootstock and train the branches from an early stage, tying them to long bamboo canes to keep them straight like the ribs of a fan.

MISCELLANEOUS

Feeding outdoor plants to stimulate growth

Signs of renewed growth in the garden means that plants will be hungry after their long winter's sleep. You have to speculate to accumulate, and now's a good time to shell out on fertiliser – and reap the benefits later in the year.

All plants need three main nutrients – nitrogen, potassium and phosphorus. Nitrogen helps to produce leaves, so it's especially important for leafy plants like spinach and hostas. Potassium is needed by all flowering and fruiting plants, while phosphorus helps root growth so is essential for all plants.

The chemical symbols and their percentages in the mix are marked on a bag of fertiliser. N is the symbol for nitrogen, P is for phosphorus and K for potassium. So Growmore, which has equal amounts of each, is marked N7:P7:K7, although the letters are sometimes dispensed with. A 'balanced' or 'general' fertiliser like Growmore is ideal for routine use, and if you want to buy only one kind, this is the one to go for. As an alternative you could use rose fertiliser, high in potassium, for most flowering plants in spring, and bonemeal (high in phosphorus) when planting in the dormant season.

Organic fertilisers

As a 'natural' gardening freak, I prefer to use organic fertilisers, and they are generally much easier to use. Because chemical feeds are concentrated, they must be applied in precise amounts, whereas organic kinds release their nutrients

slowly so it's hard to overdo it and cause damage. Generally I use two handfuls of pelleted chicken manure per square metre before sowing or planting. Bear in mind that, because this kind of feed must be broken down in the soil before it can be used by plants, your soil needs plenty of it, which is why organic gardeners use so much manure and compost. Either dig the fertiliser into the soil before planting, or apply it as a mulch on the surface afterwards – or even better, do both, especially for fruit.

Growing your own manure

If you can't buy manure or make compost, why not grow your own? Wherever you have a bit of ground

ABOVE All fruits, particularly greedy kinds such as blackberries, benefit from a rich mulch of manure or compost this month.

bare for six weeks or more, try growing a crop of 'green manure' such as clover, mustard, lucerne (alfalfa), lupins or beans. When you need the ground, cut down the plants and dig them in to recycle the nutrients they've brought up from below. They also improve the soil structure, making it more water-retentive. Field beans and winter tares can be left uncut to keep the soil covered in winter, preventing rain damage and erosion. Try a crop or two and see the difference they make to your soil.

PLANTS FOR
april

1 *Clematis alpina* 'Ruby' grows to 3m (10ft) tall by about 1.5m (5ft) wide, with slender climbing stems and elegant foliage. The pendent four-petalled blooms have a central tuft of stamens.

2 In mid-spring the vigorous arching stems of *Berberis* x *stenophylla* are wreathed in dense clusters of golden-yellow blooms. The hardy evergreen shrub can reach 3m (10ft) high.

3 The double wild cherry or gean, *Prunus avium* 'Plena', is a medium-sized deciduous tree with peeling mahogany bark on older specimens, and masses of drooping blooms.

1

2

3

4

4 The 10cm (4in) wide blooms of perennial pasque flowers, *Pulsatilla vulgaris*, range in colour from light mauve to deep red and sit snugly in a bed of ferny leaves and silky hairs.

5 Doronicums are dependable hardy perennials for supplying a bright splash of colour early in the season. Growing to about 60cm (2ft), they revel in full sun and also do well in partial shade in light soils.

5

As it did for many gardeners, 'Chelsea' – the Royal Horticultural Society's main annual show held in London – tended to dominate May for us. Geoff loved it. Because he fronted the *Gardener's World* filming, we could spend Monday there, before it was open to the public, feeling very privileged. One of his dates that week was lunch with the *Daily Express*, for which he did dress more formally. Seeing my nod of approval, he grinned: 'I clean up nice, don't I?' But he also did stints answering questions at the *Daily Express*'s garden. He enjoyed meeting what he called 'real' gardeners, hearing their views and finding out what they were doing, and spent several weekends each spring and autumn at various garden centres and at our own nursery doing just this. Some customers demanded to see his hands – just to make sure they had all the scratches and calluses working gardeners can't avoid, especially if, like Geoff, they don't wear gloves. But most knew instinctively that he was a hands-on gardener. They would comment on the way he'd pour soil and compost through his fingers, glad to see this earthiness.

The double late tulip 'Mount Tacoma' makes
a strong impact in a cool green and white
border with white violas and the prettily
edged foliage of *Hosta crispula*.

may

key tasks for may

ANNUALS & BEDDING PLANTS
○ Plan and plant out summer bedding, page 74
○ Plant out dahlias and take cuttings of their young shoots, page 75

BORDER PERENNIALS
○ Support tall herbaceous plants while they are small, page 77
○ Plant hardy chrysanthemums for autumn flowering, page 77

BULBS
○ Feed daffodils to build up next year's flowers, page 78
○ Dig up and store tulips after flowering, page 78

CONTAINER PLANTS
○ Deal with the first signs of vine weevils, page 80

SHRUBS, TREES & CLIMBERS
○ Take soft cuttings of garden shrubs, and make a cuttings frame for them, page 80

LAWNS
○ Feed lawns for good summer growth, page 81

VEGETABLES & HERBS
○ Plant tomatoes under glass, page 82
○ Sow some extra root crops for winter storing, page 82
○ Sow and plant tender vegetables outdoors, page 82
○ Beware of frosts and blackfly, page 83

FRUIT
○ Nick and notch fruit trees to control growth, page 84
○ Prune plums and cherries now the sap is rising, page 84

MISCELLANEOUS
○ Make a compost container for home-grown fertility, page 85

ANNUALS & BEDDING PLANTS

Summer bedding

Towards the end of this month there's a busy week or two in store for bedding plant enthusiasts. The sooner the salvias, petunias, alyssum and begonias go in, the quicker they'll fill their spaces and cover themselves with flowers.

I know there's a sensitive school of design that claims annual bedding is brash and gaudy, while devotees hold that no other group gives as much joy all summer long. But gardening is about doing your own thing, so take no notice of what others think – thank goodness we all have different tastes. For sheer colour, bedding plants give maximum value until the first frosts consign them to the compost heap.

I wouldn't be without half-hardy bedding like petunias, busy lizzies and salvias, but I plant them in large informal drifts among the shrubs and herbaceous plants, and under roses – not too close, though, because you don't want to impede the growth of the shrubs. Towards the back of the borders, I leave a space for taller annuals like the sweetly scented white tobacco plant (*Nicotiana affinis*). And I find that cosmos, with its ferny foliage and constant succession of flowers, and tall mallows like *Lavatera* 'Silver Cup' are indispensable.

For later in the season, don't forget the taller asters and annual delphiniums, which start flowering in July. Annual nemesias are ideal in the middle of the borders, producing flowers in an amazing mixture of colours from crimson through pink, white and yellow, to blue. The shorter tobacco plants

are terrific there, too: many of the newer varieties have the advantage of presenting their flowers facing upwards instead of hanging down.

Then there are all those annual poppy mixtures, such as 'Summer Breeze', which produce a good succession of silky flowers in shades of yellow, orange and white, and also poor man's orchids (*Schizanthus*) with a range of fantastic shades and markings.

If you want a few special plants to catch the eye in a large expanse of low-growing bedding, buy a few tender perennials like cannas, marguerites, pelargoniums and fuchsias to use as 'spot' plants in the middle. At the front of all these, I grow bedding petunias – these incidentally are not affected by the virus that tends to hit the trailing types. And there are always new varieties of phlox and annual pinks, none of them to be missed.

BEDDING PLANTS FOR SHADE
Most summer bedding is best in the sun, but I've found a few plants that are excellent for deep shade. Mimulus, busy lizzies and lobelia do well, as do foliage plants such as the silver-leafed *Cineraria maritima* (*Senecio cineraria*), all kinds of coleus and the fibrous-rooted begonias, especially *B. semperflorens*. But don't expect quite so many flowers, and allow for most plants to grow slightly taller than they would in full sun.

Planting out summer bedding

First fork over the planting area, remove all the weeds and work in a little compost – the nutrients in this should be enough, but if you don't have any compost or your soil is very poor, a little organic fertiliser or a tomato base feed is needed. But the operative word is *little* – too much nitrogen will result in large plants with lots of green leaves and few flowers. Most summer bedding plants thrive in poor soil, so I try never to feed them at all. Plant them 15–23cm (6–9in) apart according to size, with 30cm (12in) between the very largest varieties.

You've nothing to gain by planting out too early. In cold conditions plants simply stand there waiting to get warm, and any check to their growth takes a while to get over so they lose the race against those planted a little later. Look for plants that are not yet in flower. Growers know that a few flowers will seduce you into buying, but a precocious start to flowering often means that plants will go out of flower sooner.

So bide your time, plant strong young specimens when the weather's warmed up, water well and then stand back. If you can find time to deadhead plants as they go out of flower, they'll produce even more colour. The very last job is to reckon up what you've spent, and resolve firmly that next year you'll raise your own!

Growing dahlias

From the land of the sombrero and the hot chilli pepper comes the dahlia, and it is no surprise that this can be one of the most dazzling, flamboyant flowers we grow. They'll give sunny life to the dullest border, but they're not all brazen hussies and some varieties are as demure as a vicar's daughter. All can be invaluable for a number of garden uses.

If you see them in flower you'll almost certainly want them all now, but bear in mind that they are the tenderest of plants which can be knocked back by the slightest frost. You can plant dormant tubers towards the middle of this month,

LEFT Hardy perennials such as *Euphorbia characias* and the young spring foliage of spiraeas and hardy geraniums begin to make an impact in the border this month, while tulips are still in full bloom.

them into 8–10cm (3–4in) pots of soil-less compost. Put a plastic bag over the top of each pot and put it in a warm spot out of bright sun. The cuttings should look quite perky after 7–10 days, when you can remove the bag. A week later separate and pot the cuttings up individually in 9cm (3½in) pots. Grow them on until the first week in June, when you should be able to plant out two or three extra plants from each tuber. These will flower, then make tubers of their own.

but growing plants must wait until the first week in June because a late cold snap could see them off altogether. Buy tubers now by all means, and pot them up in 13cm (5in) pots of soil-less compost. Keep them in a warm place such as the greenhouse or a sunny windowsill, provided you can avoid cooking them in the mid-day sun. Water them so they're just moist and you'll find they'll shoot in next to time, usually producing at least 2–3 strong young growths. These shoots could provide propagating material for cuttings, or you can simply start hardening plants off in a cold frame for planting out early next month.

The soil needs to be dug thoroughly, with a good dressing of compost or manure worked well in and a rose or general organic fertiliser raked in the surface just before planting. All tall varieties will need strong stakes or canes, so knock these in position before planting giant varieties 75cm (30in)

apart, other kinds 60cm (2ft) apart, using a trowel and firming them in with your fingers. Cover with 8cm (3in) of soil. Water them after planting and regularly afterwards, and tie in the stems as they grow. If you want enormous blooms for shows, you'll need to thin stems and remove all but the central bud; otherwise pinch out the shoot tips in June to encourage sideshoots and plenty of slightly smaller blooms.

Taking dahlia cuttings

Bought tubers planted in pots this month, together with your own stored tubers started earlier in the year, can all be used for propagation once their shoots are about 8cm (3in) long. Cut them off the plant with a sharp knife, leaving just one or two shoots on each tuber to carry on growing. Trim the shoots just below a leaf joint, and remove all but the top three leaves.

Dip the ends of the cuttings in hormone rooting liquid, and dibble

CHOOSING DAHLIAS

For me, the real worth of dahlias is as cut flowers and I always grow a row or two of mixed types in the veg plot for this.

When it comes to size and flower shape, they are a mixed bunch, so choose carefully. They range in height from 15cm (6in) to 1.8m (6ft), and the shapes vary tremendously. Perhaps the most popular are the fully double, flat-petalled decoratives, and the narrow-petalled cactus and semi-cactus types. Then there's the almost too perfect pompon and ball types. My own preference is for the open-centred singles, broad-petalled daisies in a whole range of wonderful colours. Even more beautiful are the collarettes, perfectly shaped singles with a central fringe of smaller petals, often in a contrasting colour.

76

METHODS OF SUPPORTING BORDER PLANTS

Large clump-forming plants such as peonies benefit from a stout support set in place well before the foliage develops.

You can buy interlocking wire stakes which can be joined together to make variably sized enclosures to surround the plants.

Tall-stemmed plants such as dahlias, delphiniums and hollyhocks are best secured to single bamboo canes or stakes with string, plastic twists or wire rings.

Thin canes and string is a perfectly adequate method for supporting bushy plants, but don't have the string so tight that it makes stems look trussed.

A panel of wire netting attached to a few canes is ideal for supporting plants with tall slim stems or flower stalks – border carnations, for example.

Twiggy sticks cut from hedges or left over after pruning provide what must be the simplest support method of all, and one that costs nothing.

BORDER PERENNIALS

Supporting border plants

Taller perennials need some kind of support, a job you cannot leave until the last minute. Once delphiniums or hollyhocks, for example, fall over, the stems will kink and never straighten again.

Choose a method of support that suits the particular plant. Just remember that the stems should not be too constricted – they need to spill outwards a little to look natural. Craftsmen gardeners used to support plants with peasticks. They'd put a few in around the plant, break the twiggy bits near the top, bend them in towards the centre and weave them together. It's a skill that, along with the peasticks themselves, you see only rarely these days, but you can make natural supports of this kind from your own prunings – a few twiggy sticks of philadelphus or deutzia, say, can be shoved into the middle of a border plant to support it; and dogwood and willow stems are pliable enough to be woven or tied together to make a sort of wigwam for climbing plants.

Planting out hardy chrysanthemums

My first job ever involved growing chrysanths for cut flowers and, for nostalgia's sake, I wouldn't be without a few in my garden every year. They provide a splash of colour in the borders during late summer and autumn. And now's the time to plant them.

Chrysanths hate wet feet but need a steady supply of moisture throughout the season, so dig the soil very thoroughly and add plenty

77

of well-rotted manure or garden compost before planting, together with a light dressing of general fertiliser. They like slightly limy conditions, so if the soil's on the acid side use a little lime, but not if you've only just manured.

Plant cut flower varieties 45cm (18in) apart with 90cm (3ft) between rows, tying each plant to a strong 1.2m (4ft) cane. Then 'stop' the plant by pinching out the growing tip just above the first fully developed pair of leaves. This encourages more sideshoots that will bear the flowers. If you want cut flowers for the house limit the sideshoots to the six strongest, but if you want to win the show leave just four stems. Spray varieties should not be disbudded and can be left to their own devices to produce large sprays of smaller flowers.

Plant 'cushion' chrysanths in the same way but without the cane. Pinch out all the growing points until late July or early August, and you'll get big bushy plants which, by September, will be a mass of blooms.

BELOW The Welsh poppy, *Meconopsis cambrica*, in its desirable double form 'Flore Pleno', is happy in full sun or partial shade.

BULBS

Feeding daffodils

Daffs look wonderful in spring and no garden can afford to be without them. But when they've finished flowering, they're nothing short of ugly. The last thing you should do, though, is cut the leaves off or tie them into neat knotted bunches: the plants need the foliage for at least six weeks after flowering to give them a chance to build up their bulbs for next year.

For this reason you should give them a boost by feeding them as soon as the flowers fade, using a fertiliser high in potash – a rose or tomato feed is ideal. Do this whether you leave the bulbs in the ground or move them somewhere else. If your garden's small you may need the space for planting bedding, and in that case it's best to dig up the daffs carefully and replant them close together in a sunny corner, in a trench at the same depth as before. Mix the feed in the soil as it is replaced, and leave the bulbs until the foliage has died down. Then you can dig them up for drying. Store in a cool dry spot, and you'll have top-quality bulbs to plant again early next autumn.

If your garden is large enough, or you can't spare the time to shift bulbs each year, you can plan the planting scheme around them so that something covers the daffs after flowering. It's hard to time this exactly, but you can make sure that you see the dying leaves for only a short while. What you need are herbaceous plants that die down in winter and then produce lots of good leafy growth in late spring. Hostas are excellent, though they

may be a bit too late in colder gardens. Try bleeding heart (*Dicentra*), which has superb foliage and grows fast, as does the forget-me-not-flowered brunnera. For shade you could use evergreen *Tellima grandiflora* or *Tiarella cordifolia*, two similar foliage plants that cover a lot of ground quickly and produce attractive sprays of small flowers.

Digging up tulips

Once tulips are over, it is a good idea to deadhead them to prevent them from setting seed. Most then need warm dry conditions – something our summers can't guarantee – while they are dormant. There are a few species, including the soft yellow *Tulipa sylvestris* and dwarf *T. tarda*, which survive happily in sunny well-drained spots. Some of the hybrids will too, if they are planted deeper than normal in gritty soil. Most tulips, however, are better if they are dug up and stored indoors. Start by lifting and heeling them in close together in a trench where they can get the benefit of full sunlight. If you haven't space in the garden, pack them in pots of compost and stand these in a sunny place. When the leaves have died down lift the bulbs and dry them in the sun, outdoors or under glass. After a week or so you can rub off the dry foliage and roots, and store the bulbs in a dry place until November.

RIGHT Flowering onions such as *Allium aflatunense* and its richly coloured hybrids are superb bulbs that need a little shelter; here they are imaginatively partnered by the profuse blooms of a wisteria trained horizontally on low supports.

CONTAINER PLANTS

Controlling vine weevils

The dreaded vine weevil is on the march across the country. The first sign it's arrived is when your plants suddenly wilt or keel over. Lift them up out of the pots and you'll find the roots eaten away and the compost full of creamy-white grubs.

They especially seem to like cyclamen, primulas and begonias, but their tastes are expanding. The adults, which are dark grey beetles about 2cm (¾in) long, are rarely seen as they are nocturnal. They do little damage, but if you see notches chewed from the edges of pot and container plants be on your guard. It's the grubs that are difficult to control. They hatch out in late spring, and then munch away underground until they emerge as adults in the autumn under glass, or the following spring outdoors. They resist most chemicals except some ludicrously expensive and dangerous kinds used by growers. The most effective control available to amateurs is a biological one, sold under several trade names. Basically it is a microscopic worm called a nematode, which attacks and feeds on the grubs. This can be bought packaged in granules for adding to a measured amount of water. You simply pour this in the infected pot, or apply once or twice as a precaution to all your container plants. The nematodes only work when temperatures are higher than 10°C (50°F), however, so there's no point using them before this month, and once they've cleared an infestation they'll die out. So get some this month, and another batch in late summer for total control.

SHRUBS, TREES & CLIMBERS

Taking soft cuttings

Even after all these years of gardening, I'm still amazed and delighted at the astonishing way shoots, lumps of root and even leaves are so ready to put out roots and produce another generation of plants. It's something you should be taking full advantage of towards the end of this month.

Most shrubs are becoming fine and bushy, with lots of sturdy young shoots that have grown this year and can be used for soft cuttings. You've got from now until the beginning of July to select them from somewhere on the shrub where the loss of a shoot or two won't be noticed. Normally you'll want just one plant, so take about six shoots to be on the safe side, and cut them off the plant just above a leaf joint so that each cutting is about 8–10cm (3–4in) long. Have a polythene bag with you and pop them inside; keep the bag closed and out of the sun. When you've finished, the sooner you can get back indoors the better – if you can't work on the cuttings straight away, put them in the main compartment of the fridge.

Prepare the cuttings with a sharp knife or razor blade. Start by trimming just below a leaf joint, where most of the root-forming hormones are located, to leave cuttings about 5–8cm (2–3in) long. Remove all but the top 2–3 leaves, then immerse them in a solution of copper fungicide, and dip the cut ends in hormone rooting powder or liquid. Dibble 4–5 cuttings to half their depth in an 8cm (4in) pot of cuttings compost or a 50:50

TAKING SOFT CUTTINGS

1 Cut off the soft tips of main stems and sideshoots, and keep all the cuttings fresh in a plastic bag until you are ready to prepare them for potting.

2 Trim the shoots to length, cutting the base just below a leaf joint or 'node'. Remove all the lower leaves, together with any stipules and flower buds.

3 Dunk in fungicide and then dip the cut ends in rooting hormone. Insert the cuttings, to the lowest leaves, in compost and seal in a thin polythene bag.

RIGHT A greenhouse packed with pelargoniums, coleus and gerberas, all competing for space with young begonias and carnation cuttings, would be a favourite target for vine weevils, so do beware.

mixture of peat-free compost and vermiculite, and water them in with more fungicide solution. Cover the pots with thin polythene, making sure this is resting on the top of the cuttings and held in place with an elastic band, and then put the pots in a shaded cold frame. They should root without further watering in 6–8 weeks.

Making a cuttings frame

I get a great deal of enjoyment from propagating plants, so I've made a special frame to take softwood cuttings rooted straight into the ground. Mine is made from an old wooden box with the bottom removed, but it'd be easy to knock up a simple frame about 60cm (2ft) by 45cm (18in), and 30cm (12in) deep to hold about 100 cuttings.

Start by cultivating the soil and working a good quantity of horticultural grit into the top 5cm (2in); level the soil and then spread a layer of grit over it with a layer of sharp sand on top of that, before putting the box in place. The cuttings are dibbled in about 2.5cm (1in) apart and watered in with a fungicide solution. Cover with thin polythene resting lightly on the cuttings and then use a piece of glass or rigid plastic for the lid, shading it with a couple of old onion bags from the greengrocer. You'll soon see rooting taking place when the cuttings perk up generally. Leave them 6–8 weeks, and then lift them for potting up or lining out.

LAWNS

Feeding the lawn

There's one plant in the garden we really take for granted. We tread all over it, we prune it every week, we kick it and scuff it, use it and abuse it, and yet it still comes up smiling. Grass is pretty hard to offend, but it'll repay you if you look after it: the energy removed by mowing, for example, needs to be replaced.

As I suggested in March (see page 47), a feed in spring and again in summer can work wonders. Alternatively, if you use the type of slow-release fertiliser that supplies nutrients over a long period, one feed early this month should normally be enough – autumn feeds are really only for deficient soils. As with any other fertiliser, the important thing to remember is to measure the amount you spread and stick religiously to the maker's instructions. Don't add a little extra for luck, because too much causes scorching, so it's always worth hiring or buying a special spreader to apply just the right amount. You can buy 'weed and feed' dressings that contain a herbicide, and for these it is even more important to keep closely to recommended application rates.

Most lawn feeds are very much of a muchness in terms of quality, and the only real choice is between liquid and granular feeds. Liquids act a bit faster, they're cheaper and they generally allow a greater margin for error, but it can be a fag going backwards and forwards with the watering can. Granular or powdered types last a little longer and are more easily distributed, but must be watered in afterwards. They always say apply just before rain on the pack. But that can't be guaranteed, and if it hasn't rained two days after spreading you'll have to water the lawn well in order to avoid scorching.

VEGETABLES & HERBS

Planting tomatoes under glass

If you have a greenhouse, you'll find that there's plenty to do in it from now on. Perhaps the most important task is to plant tomatoes and other tender crops as these will be safe now without any extra heat. You can grow them direct in the soil after digging in plenty of garden compost and a base fertiliser. There is a risk of attack from soil-borne virus diseases, although the chances are small – many gardeners have used the same soil for more than twenty years without a problem.

If a virus does strike, and you will recognize it from yellow streaks or mottlings on the leaves, the crop won't be wiped out, but next year you should use 'grow bags', or you can grow tomatoes individually in 25cm (10in) pots of soil-less compost, and save the cost of bags.

When you put in the plants, run a strong nylon string from a wire

BELOW When planting a tomato in the greenhouse, secure one end of the support string under its rootball.

fixed to the glazing bars above each plant down to the ground. Leave enough string for the loose end to be 'planted' by passing it under the rootball. The tomato stem can then be twisted round the string as it grows. I feed at every watering after the first truss has set, but try to use as little water as possible because that will improve the flavour. And don't shade the plants unless the heat becomes extreme.

You should remove any sideshoots that grow in the leaf joints. (If you need more plants, the shoots can be rooted as soft cuttings under a plastic bag.) When the plants are flowering, spray them over at mid-day with water or tap the stems sharply with a cane to help pollinate the flowers. And then you just keep picking the fruit, pound after pound of it, well into the autumn.

Root crops for winter

There are two important vegetables for winter storing that are often forgotten at this time of year, probably partly because it seems too early to be thinking of winter: swedes and salsify. The swede's now a completely different vegetable from the one you hated at school. The flavour and texture of modern varieties has been improved no end, and swedes are as sweet and nutty as anyone could wish. Try a variety like 'Marian', which is resistant to mildew and club root – don't forget swedes are a form of brassica and share the same pests and diseases as cabbages. 'Ruby' has very large roots and a flavour rating second to none, while 'Lizzy' resists root cracking and bolting in a dry season. Sow direct in rows 23–30cm (9–12in) apart, thin the seedlings to

20cm (8in) apart, and grow on until lifting time after the first frosts.

Salsify and scorzonera are usually grouped together because they need the same treatment. Salsify roots are white and scorzonera black, but they taste much the same with a subtle, though superb, flavour and they're rich in minerals. They are gourmet crops which are unfairly neglected these days, partly I suspect because they take a little extra trouble to prepare for cooking. But they're very easy to grow in deeply dug soil, in rows 30cm (12in) apart with the seedlings thinned to 15cm (6in). Either lift them for storing in autumn, or leave them in the ground until needed.

Growing tender vegetables

Courgettes, French and runner beans, tomatoes and cucumbers are the aristocrats of the kitchen garden, and yet they're as easy to grow as radishes. If you've got young plants in the greenhouse or on the windowsill, you're laughing, but if you haven't, there's still time to catch up.

If frost is no longer a threat all these crops can be set out in their final places, but keep a few large flowerpots handy for covering them up, just in case. In colder areas, you'll have to wait a couple of weeks before planting out, but you can sow seeds outdoors now with a bit of protection to warm the soil. All these crops are moisture-lovers so, since you only get out what you put in, it's worth piling on the compost or manure – dig it in the top spit, together with a handful of general fertiliser such as pelleted poultry manure, and they'll be set up for the season.

Courgettes and bush marrows can be sown direct if you didn't manage to sow them last month under glass. Sow two seeds per station about 60cm (2ft) apart, and cover each station with a jam jar or cut-off plastic bottle. Take this off when the seedlings show through, and remove the weaker seedling. But if the weather is still cold, leave the jar on for a while to create a warm humid atmosphere and also to protect against slugs.

Treat French beans in the same way, sowing two seeds at stations 30cm (12in) apart. They crop better than runners in a really hot dry season, and are usually a better bet if there's a hose-pipe ban. But personally I think it's always worth growing runner beans, whatever the season, as I could happily eat them

at every meal. Sow the seeds for runners in twos, each pair at the base of a 2.4m (8ft) cane. You'll have to slit a plastic bottle up the side to get it round the cane, and then leave it in place over the best seedling until it is large enough for the leaves to touch the sides.

It's too late to sow tomatoes for outdoors, but you can usually buy plants if you haven't started any under glass. If you go for a bush variety such as 'Red Alert', you can grow them 60cm (2ft) apart without any support, and they'll produce excellent crops if you mulch the plants with straw to keep the fruit clean; alternatively plant them through a sheet of black porous matting, which will also suppress weeds as well as stopping the soil from drying out.

ABOVE Early broad beans are here in full bloom, with rows of young lettuces, onions and peas well advanced for harvesting later in the summer.

Guarding against frost and blackfly

Don't let thoughts of summer crops lead you into thinking that all risk of frost has passed. If frost threatens, earth up potatoes or cover them with fleece; keep cloches handy for other early crops; and be prepared to cover cold frames at night.

Broad beans will be safe from frost, even though they should be flowering well by now, but their soft growing tips are a prime target for blackfly. Discourage these by pinching out the tips as soon as the lowest pods have set.

FRUIT

Nicking and notching fruit trees

Sometimes the buds on apple and pear trees can be infuriating. Varieties differ, but some can produce quite long lengths of bare shoot where the buds refuse to grow out. And without sideshoots, of course, you'll never get fruit.

One of the reasons is that the bud at the top of the tree sends down hormones which retard the growth of others. This is to ensure, in natural conditions, that the tree reaches up for the light as quickly as possible. The growth hormones are carried just below the bark so, if you nick out a tiny bit of the bark just above the reluctant bud as shown on the right, the retardant is diverted and the bud will grow into a new shoot.

The experts call this method 'notching', and it's particularly useful if you are training an apple

NICKING AND NOTCHING

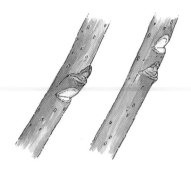

This simple method of switching sideshoots on or off depends on knowing what goes on under the bark of a stem. Removing a tiny bit of bark and the green cambium layer underneath it interrupts or diverts the upward flow of nutrients and hormones. So nicking below a bud stops it developing, while notching above it makes it grow.

or pear tree to a formal shape and happen to have a shoot missing just where you want one. There's also 'nicking', which is making the same kind of cut just below a bud to stop it growing. In practice, it's usually much easier to simply rub off a bud before it can grow, which you often have to do to wall-trained trees to stop shoots growing towards or away from the wall.

Pruning plums and cherries

The regular pruning for plums and sweet cherries is straightforward, and all done in spring and summer. This is when the sap is rising and cuts heal quickly to reduce the risk of fungal spores entering the wounds. As soon as a new shoot has made six leaves in the spring,

LEFT Turning fermenting compost heaps once or twice helps to accelerate their decomposition.

pinch out the tip. Then after the fruit has been picked, take out any dead or overcrowded shoots and shorten by half those you pinched back earlier. That's all there is to pruning plums and sweet cherries.

Acid cherries such as the self-fertile 'Morello' are quite different, though. These make their fruit on two-year-old wood, so you always have to look forward. Select a shoot for fruiting this year, but also allow a replacement for next year to grow alongside it. Then, instead of shortening the fruited shoot after harvest, cut it out altogether and tie the new one in its place.

You can prune flowering cherries at the same time, especially if you've just planted a weeping cherry, which has to be butchered now – you need a lot of courage but you'll get a much better tree in the end. Inspect each branch and discover where the new wood grew from last year: it'll be a lighter brown and the joint will be quite easy to see. Then cut back to leave 2–3 buds of this new wood, cutting back to an upward facing bud. That bud will be the one to grow out and, by the end of the year, you'll get a wider, and more graceful tree.

If you have fan-trained plums or cherries against a wall or fence (see page 68), you will simply need to tie in sideshoots wherever you have a hole, and in spring remove any shoots that are growing directly towards or away from the wall. Ready-trained fans are well worth their rather high cost because they'll save two years of careful pruning and shaping. As they grow, tie in the main branches to canes arranged in a fan shape on horizontal wires fixed to the wall and spaced 60cm (2ft) apart.

MISCELLANEOUS

Compost heaps

As well as providing food for all those soil organisms that are vital to a healthy, colourful and productive garden, organic matter is the first line of defence against drought. Once the soil starts to dry out in summer, it'll be very noticeable when you fork over the garden that the areas which have received a heavy dose of manure or compost are still satisfyingly moist; those which haven't will soon be in need of water.

So, if only because most of the ingredients are free and readily available, it's important to get a compost heap working overtime. Compost is second only to good farmyard manure, and it's easy to make. Of course, we've all made some pretty repulsive compost at some time, either wet and slimy or as dry as straw, but making good compost only comes down to the right technique.

Compost containers

It's best to have two containers, one for compost that is rotting down while the other's filling up. They don't have to be elaborate or expensive, and the cheapest way to make one is to bang four posts into the ground and then staple on wire netting to make an enclosure about 90cm (3ft) square and the same high. Then beg a large cardboard box or two, and line the enclosure with the cardboard. Cover the compost material with a bit of old carpet or cardboard, and you're on your way to making perfect compost.

If you'd like something a little more decorative, there are any number of wooden and plastic designs available. Make sure that there are no holes or spaces in the sides, and that there is a lid of some sort as it is important to keep in all the heat you can.

It is also possible to construct a fairly basic wooden container using old floorboards, as shown below.

Compost material

Almost any vegetable matter that has once lived can be composted, from weeds, vegetable waste and grass cuttings to woollen or cotton clothes and paper. But avoid roots of weeds such as ground elder or couch grass, weeds that are seeding, and cooked food which might attract rats. Leathery evergreen leaves will take longer to decompose, and the stems of shrubs and trees will take longer still.

Grass clippings are the very best composting material because they heat up quickly, which helps break down the rest of the contents. Unfortunately, because they're small and soft, they tend to pack down tightly if you put a lot in together, and they'll push out the air. Then they'll be rotted down by a different type of bacteria which can turn your heap into a vile smelly mess. What's needed is air within the heap itself, so mix the grass cuttings with coarser material such as large weeds or straw. Good gardeners don't have large weeds, so I keep a bag of fresh strawy manure by the container to mix in when coarse stuff is scarce.

After you've filled the container and the contents have been working for a month or so, turn them by throwing them out of the container and back again, fluffing them up as you go. You might have to do that twice, and it does need some energy, but it'll make sure you stay young and beautiful, and you'll produce compost fit almost to eat – within six months over the summer, and within eight or nine over the winter.

MAKING A COMPOST BIN

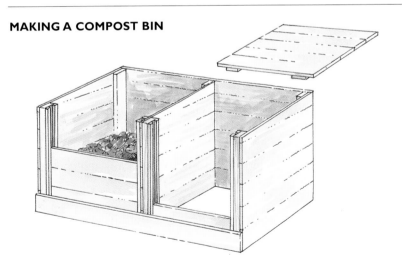

Strong boards and a few uprights can be transformed into a double bin with channels at the front, for slats to slide in and out so you can reach the compost at the bottom when it is ready. Completely fill one bin, cover its contents with an old blanket and the wooden lid, and leave it to rot down while you fill its neighbour.

PLANTS FOR
may

1 'Nora Barlow' is an old cottage garden variety of hardy herbaceous perennial *Aquilegia vulgaris*, with fully double flowers on strong leafy stems 60cm (2ft) tall.

2 *Allium aflatunense* is one of several ball-headed flowering onions and the source of various richly coloured hybrids such as 'Lucy Ball' and 'Purple Sensation'. The large

1

rounded heads are carried on 75–90cm (30–36in) stems, and are excellent for cutting.

3 The best known of a small group of yellow-flowered peonies, *P. mlokosewitschii* (affectionately known as Molly the Witch) is a small herbaceous perennial, often less than 75cm (30in) high, but its cool yellow blooms make a strong direct impact in any border.

4 Viridiflora or green-flowered tulips are a great favourite with flower arrangers for their unusual colour combinations: 'Spring Green' is also a fine garden variety, with shapely blooms on sturdy 40–45cm (16–18in) stems.

5 *Viburnum sargentii* 'Onondaga' is a vigorous deciduous shrub, up to 3m (10ft) high, with maple-shaped leaves which are rich red when young and again in autumn. In the large lace-cap heads of flowers deep red fertile buds are surrounded by a ring of clear white sterile flowers.

2

3

4

5

*G*eoff genuinely felt that each month was the best one in the garden. But perhaps June was his favourite. 'Gardening is half achievement and half optimism,' he said, 'and in June we really have the best of each. The foliage is at its finest, borders are awash with flowers, with plenty to come; strawberries have started, raspberries are on their way and the vegetable plot is at its most mouthwatering.' June was also the month when he finished pruning the spring-flowering shrubs. He was quite convinced that this shouldn't be done without the aid of a large teapot – a more vital tool, he once joked, than secateurs. 'You should take off a branch, then step back with a cup of tea and weigh up the consequences before you take off another.' Cups of tea were always an important part of gardening to Geoff. If possible, he liked to have them every hour, on the hour. Often I would carry two mugs down to meet him where he had said he would be, only to find that he had moved on – and because the layout of the garden is such that you can't see or hear far, the tea would be cold by the time I found him!

Poppies, campanulas and roses of all kinds
are essential ingredients of the summer
border, which begins to make a colourful
impact this month.

june

key tasks for june

ANNUALS & BIENNIALS

Sowing biennials

With summer only just under way, we gardeners are already thinking about next spring, because if you want a colourful display then, you'll have to act soon. Forget-me-nots are so prolific that you can just pull them up after they have flowered and shake the dead heads over a bit of ground to produce a mass of seedlings for transplanting in the autumn. Biennials like wallflowers, sweet williams and Iceland poppies need a little more care. Sow them either in a nursery bed in the garden or in pots if you haven't the ground to spare. Use plastic pots of soil-less compost, and sprinkle a pinch of seed in each; stand them on a hard surface, on a porous mat like a piece of carpet underfelt, and keep them moist. When the seedlings are large enough, prick them out 5–8cm (2–3in) apart in the open ground or in seed trays, and grow them on until the autumn when they can be planted out where you want them to flower. Polyanthus and pansies need slightly different techniques.

Sowing polyanthus

These seeds need a little gentle heat – 15°C (60°F) should be sufficient – and at this time of year a cold greenhouse or frame will provide that. Sow them on the surface of very moist soil-less compost and cover with a little vermiculite. Put clear polythene over the pots and keep them in full light as this is essential for germination.

Once the seedlings are through, transfer them to plastic modules, trays of small pots about 4–5cm

(1½–2in) in diameter (see page 15), and grow them on by standing them on a piece of capillary matting to make sure they never dry out. After three weeks start feeding them with a general fertiliser, and by October they should be large enough to plant outside. For this, of course, you need a tough strain, and I can recommend 'Crescendo' for real winter hardiness.

Sowing pansies

The way to germinate pansies is just about as different from that for polyanthus as it could be. The seeds are sown in the same way and covered with vermiculite or a little seed compost sieved over the top. But they must be dark and cool to germinate, so cover the pots or trays with black polythene or kitchen foil to exclude light, and put them in a shady place outdoors. Seedlings take about a fortnight to

ABOVE Campanulas, clematis and lady's mantle congregate round *Choisya ternata* in a mixed border of hardy perennials and shrubs.

emerge, so check them regularly after about ten days. Once they are large enough, transfer to modules or transplant them outdoors 15cm (6in) apart in rows. Grow them on until early October, when you can finally plant them out 15–20cm (6–8in) apart where you want them to flower.

Winter pansies are popular for good reasons: hardy types give a little colour during the winter and then, in spring, they really shine with masses of blooms. The Universal strain is well known, and is available as a fine mixture or in separate colours, but 'Allegro', an S_1 mixture and cheaper than the slightly more uniform F_1 hybrids, is an excellent alternative.

BORDER PERENNIALS

Increasing violas

By this time of year, the chances are that some of your violas will be getting a bit straggly and untidy. You can simply trim them back, but if you would like to increase the number of your plants, try taking 'Irishman's cuttings'. This process is also called 'mounding' or 'mound-layering', and is a logical short cut to propagating perennials that produce long stems.

Make a compost mix using equal parts of good soil, well-rotted garden compost and sharp sand (make sure it isn't builder's sand which will go rock hard). Add a little organic fertiliser, but no more than a handful, to a large bucket of the mixture. Then work the compost into the clumps of violas so that the straggling stems are well covered. Water occasionally, and in a few weeks you'll find the stems have rooted into the compost. Cut them off the main plant and then either pot them up or plant them in a corner where they won't get swamped by other plants.

Sowing hellebores

If you look at any catalogue of hellebores, you'll find that many of the varieties are in fact strains or seedlings. This is because the plants set seed quite readily, and most of the seedlings are worth growing – and will give you a whole range of fine colours. But they're best sown just before the seeds ripen, so you'll have to be quick off the mark.

Check your plants and remove any capsules from the flowers before they dry and split. Crack the capsules open and take out the

LEFT This arbour at Barnsdale is surrounded by a riot of roses, foxgloves and campanulas, as well as lilies on the point of opening – summer is in full swing.

RIGHT Vivacious but fleeting single scarlet oriental poppies complement the lavish longer lasting perennial flowers of valerian (*Centranthus ruber* 'Coccineus').

Tidying oriental poppies

The huge blowsy blooms – either brilliant red or in varied shades of pink, orange and white – of oriental poppies (*Papaver orientale*) make them irresistible. But like several other early-flowering herbaceous plants, once they finish flowering they become a nuisance. The large, rather rank foliage looks good in early spring but begins to flop after flowering, smothering anything else in its path and looking untidy and ugly. Be ruthless and cut it off right down to the base. The foliage will always regrow, returning to its early spring freshness, and if you're lucky you may benefit from another blooming in late summer.

This is also a good time to sow oriental poppies in pots outdoors. Prick out the seedlings when they are small into separate 9cm (3½in) pots, and plant them out 30–38cm (12–15in) apart in the autumn or next spring, disturbing the roots as little as possible when you do so.

A full-grown oriental poppy is a huge plant, often up to 90cm (3ft) or more in diameter, so if you haven't room for this classic giant try the modern dwarf mixture 'Pizzicato'. Although this is a much smaller plant, the blooms are just as glorious, more than 10cm (4in) across with at least a dozen per plant in a range of colours.

seeds. Sow them on the surface of deep 15cm (6in) pots filled with moist soil-less compost, and cover with a thin layer of coarse grit. Put the pots in a cold frame on a layer of sand or grit, and cover them with slates or something similar that will keep them moist, humid and cool.

Check the pots from time to time to make sure they don't dry out. The seeds should germinate from October to the end of the year, although this often depends on

which species their parents have come from. The stinking hellebore (*Helleborus foetidus*) and the Corsican kind (*H. corsicus*) are fairly quick to appear, and can even flower the following year. But Lenten and Christmas roses (*H. orientalis* and *H. niger*) are slow growers and may not appear until next spring, after which they need growing on for 2–3 years before they'll flower. Once in final position, they prefer not to be moved.

BULBS

Planting anemones

Growers have got anemone production to such a fine art that the cut flowers seem to be available for most of the year. This is partly because the tubers are not too fussy about when they're planted. You can start them at various times to flower about three months later: plant them in April for summer flowers, in June to bloom in the autumn, and early autumn for late winter or spring flowers.

Anemones are particularly welcome towards the end of the season, so this month plant as many of the small dry tubers as you like, some in groups near the front of the border to flower there, and others in rows in the vegetable garden for cutting. Start some in pots at the same time, for windowsills or outdoors on the patio. There are two main kinds, both forms of the poppy anemone (*A. coronaria*): De Caen or Giant French make huge single flowers up to 8cm (3in) across in a range of bright colours with dark centres, while St. Brigid is similar but semi-double.

Soak the dry knobbly tubers overnight to give them a good start, and then plant them 5cm (2in) deep and 8–10cm (3–4in) apart. They were traditionally grown for cutting in the kitchen garden, where the soil was rich and well-manured, and this gives a clue as to the diet they enjoy. Work plenty of compost into the soil, especially if it is light and sandy, and add a handful of pelleted chicken manure before planting. Water well and then stand back for a glorious display.

Some growers lift the tubers after the leaves have died down and store them for replanting, but you can leave them in for another season. After that they tend to deteriorate, so plant some more every other year for a continuous supply. They can also be raised from seed, taking about 18 months to flower, but there's an F_1 hybrid mixture called 'Cleopatra', with blooms up to 10cm (4in) across, which takes just a few months to come into flower and can be grown outdoors like a hardy annual.

CONTAINER PLANTS

Growing tender plants in pots

All too often when I buy plants I don't know, I find, when I come to look them up, that they are too tender for my cold garden. And I wouldn't mind betting you do too. If a book says a plant is on the tender side, my solution is to grow it in a pot – then you can bring it inside in October and take it out again late the following May to give a repeat performance each year.

I always use large pots at least 30cm (12in) in diameter or small tubs, filled with a soil-based compost because that provides enough weight to anchor them down on windy days and also offers a buffer against forgetting to water them. I also include a slow-release fertiliser to save the job of fortnightly feeding. It helps to prolong flowering if you pinch off faded blooms, and if a plant is outgrowing its position, just pinch back the shoot tips to keep it in check.

You'll need to repot the plants each year, gradually moving them on into larger containers until they reach maturity. Then all you need do is revive the soil in the containers each spring by replacing the top 5cm (2in) of compost with a fresh supply. Alternatively, most plants root readily from cuttings taken in late summer, so you can replace the old ones after 3–4 years with younger ones.

There are some tender plants that I risk growing outside, but only if I have taken cuttings as an insurance policy. These include willow-leafed jessamine (*Cestrum parqui*), which has great spikes of yellow flowers (deep blue in 'Cretan Purple') and is

93

ABOVE Containers of all kinds can be adapted for summer bedding plants, as here at Barnsdale where florists' buckets are packed with pelargoniums, marguerites and petunias.

94

Plants I've grown successfully in pots, taking them outside for the summer, include angel's trumpets (*Datura* or *Brugmansia*); abutilon hybrids (which need pruning back quite hard in spring to induce new growth), with their bright yellow, red or orange chalice-shaped blooms; perennial cherry pie (heliotrope), which can be grown as a pyramid or standard – its fragrance is unique, so grow it near where you sit; oleanders, shrubby evergreens with heavy clusters of double flowers in various shades of peach, pink and crimson as well as white; pineapple sage, an attractive evergreen with mouthwatering fragrance and scarlet flowers in winter; and the Chinese hibiscus, an evergreen with spectacular trumpet-shaped flowers all summer.

too good to miss, and several fuchsias of borderline hardiness. I take cuttings in the plant's first or second season and, once they're growing well, I plant the youngsters in a well-drained gravel bed under my warm south-facing wall. They remain outside, while the parent stays in the pot and comes inside when the first frost threatens. That way I can find out just how hardy a tender plant can be, while keeping the big plant safe in its pot.

Planting up patio containers

Most gardeners need no encouragement to buy pots and plants to decorate patios and the paved areas outside the back door. Most of us have some hard areas of paving in the garden, and they can all be softened and brightened up with a real splash of summer bedding; after that's cleared, replant the containers with small evergreen shrubs and bulbs to continue the colour through winter into spring.

There are hundreds of different plastic containers available these days, most of them reasonably priced, although it must be admitted that some of them come in quite obnoxious colours. But it's

easy to respray these with the colour of your choice by using aerosol spray paint sold for cars. Plastic is fine unless you want a more traditional look or intend keeping permanent plants outside in winter, when plastic offers little protection to roots in freezing weather. In this case you'll have to buy clay, stone or concrete containers, which often look much more attractive anyway.

The compost in containers always dries faster than the garden soil, so you'll need to water regularly. Soilless composts are much more demanding than soil-based ones, although you can mix water-holding crystals into the compost to help delay drying out. Perhaps because I'm old-fashioned, I prefer to use soil-based John Innes composts because I find it easier to control the watering. It's really a case of getting used to it, but whatever else you do, never use ordinary garden soil, which will not grow good plants in containers.

Planting is a very personal thing, but I like to plan a bright medley of colours in the summer using pelargoniums, marguerites, felicia, fuchsias, verbena and bacopa, plus half-hardy annuals such as petunias, salvias and lobelia.

If you think mixing all these colours can be a bit garish, stick with just a few shades such as pale blue, pink and white. Try something like the pink marguerite 'Vancouver' in the centre, surrounded by the much shorter marguerite 'Sugar Baby' with its masses of white daisies. Mix that with mauve *Nemesia* 'Elliott's Variety' and pink *Diascia* 'Joyce's Choice', and you'll have a display guaranteed to soothe any savage breast. If you feel in a gaudier frame of mind and have a sunny spot, plant something brilliant like vivid 'Vista Red' pelargoniums in the middle, with *Verbena* 'Pink Parfait' – a delightful pink and red – and the brilliant orange-red *Arctotis* 'Red Devil'. Trail a bit of blue lobelia down the sides, and you won't be able to resist a quick samba round the patio every sunny morning.

At the end of the season you can lift all these, shake off most of the soil, cut back the straggly tops hard and pot up afresh. Water and bring them indoors into full light. Give them a weekly feed at half strength, and they'll reward you with more flowers within a couple of months.

SHRUBS, TREES & CLIMBERS

Pruning spring-flowering shrubs

Many shrubs that flower early in the year – weigela, mock orange (philadelphus), kolkwitzia and deutzia, for example – are best pruned immediately after they have flowered. In warm areas and seasons, that could be the second half of this month, but in colder parts they may not be over for another week or two.

Obviously you don't want to remove wood that has grown this year and will flower next. So look for older branches that have flowered and cut those out, either right at the base or down to a good sideshoot near the bottom. Lilacs, for example, should be carefully pruned down to the two new shoots below the flowers – these will carry next year's blooms. As a rule of thumb for spring-flowering shrubs, you should remove about a third of the branches to open up the bush to light and air, and to encourage the growth of new young shoots for future flowering. If space is precious harder pruning will not harm the plant, but you may sacrifice some of next year's blooms.

One exception to this is broom, both *Cytisus scoparius* and *C. praecox*. These won't grow out of old wood, so they should be cut back to leave about a third of the current season's growth. Bear in mind that these are short-lived shrubs and, however well you prune them, they're bound to become untidy and exhausted after 7–10 years. Then it's best to bite the bullet and throw them away, but only after first taking some cuttings, of course, or buying a new plant.

ROSES

Training climbers

Keeping on top of training climbing roses can be a painful and frustrating battle at this time of year, although it's worth it in the end. The trouble is that you have to get the thorny branches into the

CLIMBING ROSES FOR NORTH- AND EAST-FACING WALLS

The main difference between ramblers and climbers is that ramblers are more vigorous, producing very flexible stems that are generally longer than those of climbers, but they normally only flower once, while many climbers will repeat flower all summer. My recommendation would be to choose climbers for walls or fences, and leave ramblers for training up posts or to ramble through trees. A great many varieties will be happy on a south- or west-facing wall, but east- or north-facing walls can be difficult. For scarlet try 'Danse du Feu' or the darker red 'Guinée' or 'Etoile de Hollande'; for yellow try 'Maigold', 'Gloire de Dijon' or the perfumed 'Golden Showers'; for pink I'd recommend 'Madame Grégoire Staechelin' or the thornless 'Zéphirine Drouhin'; the best white is undoubtedly 'Mme Alfred Carrière'. Roses on walls are susceptible to mildew because of the reduced air circulation, so avoid disease-prone varieties such as 'Crimson Glory', 'Dorothy Perkins', 'Handel' and 'Mrs Sam McGredy'.

TRAINING CLIMBING ROSES

ABOVE The Seven Sisters rose, *R. multiflora*, and *Clematis* x *durandii* are companion climbers behind white foxgloves.

The best way to train climbers growing on a wall is on horizontal wires 60cm (2ft) apart, or on trellis. Make sure the wire is strong, since there could be quite a weight of leaf and stem to hold, especially in wet and windy weather. When you tie the branches in, aim to pull them down more or less horizontally – this will encourage new shoots from the top of those you've tied in, and lots of bloom low down on the wall.

place where you want them, and hold them there while you tie them in. If you've tried fiddling with thin string while wearing thick gloves, you'll know what I mean.

My answer is to use sweet pea rings. These are small wire rings used to hold climbing sweet peas in place on their canes – they're easy to handle with gloves on, and will hold the branches in position long enough to enable you to tie them in with string after taking your gloves off. But even if I had to do it with my teeth, I'm sure I would – there are surely no better climbing plants.

VEGETABLES & HERBS

The warm weather doesn't just wake up plants and get them going. It also sends a signal to all the pests that might be lurking, telling them there could be rich pickings in your vegetable garden. There're two pests in particular you need to keep an eye open for this time of year.

Carrot fly

The female cruises around just above soil level, looking for the tell-tale smell that attracts her to lay her eggs at the base of the carrot foliage – and not just on carrots, but on parsnips, parsley and celery too. The eggs hatch out into tiny grubs that make brown tunnels in the tops of the roots. There are chemical treatments you can use, and a few carrot varieties such as 'Fly-Away' and 'Sytan' are 90 per cent resistant, but the best way to foil the fly is to hide its target. You can alternate rows of carrots with onions, which have a stronger smell that confuses the fly, or plant them among flowers, or you can cover or surround them with a sheet of horticultural fleece.

I prefer to grow all the susceptible crops together in a block, and surround this at planting or sowing time with a wall of fleece or clear polythene supported on short posts – the low-level carrot fly will bump up against this and then fly round. But remember that the larger your block of plants the higher the barrier needs to be, or gusts of wind could carry the fly up and over to drop inside. Panels 45cm (18in) high work for a block 1.2m (4ft) square, but you might need to go 60cm (2ft) high for anything bigger.

Cabbage root fly

Another kind of root fly attacks young brassicas such as cabbages, cauliflowers and Brussels sprouts, causing them to collapse completely. If you see a small transplant wilting and then dying, pull it up and you'll probably find the root has been invaded by tiny fat white grubs. By that time it's too late to take action, and it's best to take precautions at planting time by preventing the adult fly from getting to the soil near the stem, where she lays her eggs. Use a piece of old carpet or underlay, and cut this into 15cm (6in) squares. Make a cut to the centre of each square, where you make another small slit at right angles so that the square will sit neatly round the brassica stem. Then plant in the usual way, simply slipping a square round the base of each plant so that it fits tightly all round the stem and lies flat on the soil.

Planting cauliflowers

Although they're very popular for summer and autumn use, there's no doubt that cauliflowers are a difficult crop to grow well. For a start, they're some of the greediest plants and need transplanting to soil that has been deeply prepared with as much compost or manure as you can spare, not just to feed the plants but also to keep the roots moist at all stages of growth.

One of the most common problems is that the flowers – the bit that you eat – sometimes start to mature too early. They come to a tiny head and refuse to develop further. This is called premature curding, and the biggest frustration is that, by the time you see it, it's too late to do anything. The secret

PREVENTING CABBAGE ROOT FLY

It doesn't matter whether you buy special planting mats or make your own from old materials. They can be round or square, but the important thing is that they fit snugly round the plant to stop the adult fly laying her eggs at the base of the stem.

is to give the plants a good start: thin them early, water them well in dry weather, and keep them growing smoothly.

One of the great danger periods is about now when the plants are being moved from the seedbed to their final rows. There's no way to eliminate stress, but you can reduce it greatly by transplanting when the seedlings are still small. Move them just as soon as they're big enough to handle, and certainly before they're six weeks old. Make sure that the roots are kept covered while they're out of the ground, water them in thoroughly with a little feed added to the water, and then ensure they are never short of water afterwards.

Sowing chicory for forcing

Round about Christmas I always like to have my own chicory roots for forcing to produce the best winter salad available. There are, of course, two distinct types of chicory. One is like a lettuce but with a slightly bitter refreshing flavour, and that's sown this month for eating fresh in late summer and autumn – 'Sugar Loaf' is a fine variety, or there's the red 'Rossa di Verona'. The other is the Belgian or Witloof kind, also sown now but in this case to produce roots for forcing in winter. Make sure you have the right one!

Start by sowing an up-to-date variety such as 'Apollo' or 'Zoom', which can be forced without blanching the shoots with soil. You'll need a fairly sunny position, and rich soil to fatten up the biggest roots, so add plenty of manure and a couple of handfuls of pelleted chicken manure per square metre. Sow in shallow drills 30cm (12in) apart, and thin the seedlings to 15cm (6in) apart. All that's needed before you dig the roots up in October or November (see page 170) is to water them in dry weather.

BELOW The decorative ferny foliage of carrots blends successfully with colourful multiflora petunias, a combination which hides the crop from the carrot root fly.

FRUIT

Controlling fruit pests
Many common fruit pests are difficult to control by conventional methods such as spraying because they arrive on the wing and are gone in seconds after laying their eggs. But trapping is a modern way that uses the flies' own lifestyle to lure them to their doom.

Take codling moths, for example. They're flying around on warm nights this month and next, looking for apple trees where the females can lay their tiny single eggs on the immature fruits and leaves. These hatch into those disgusting little maggots you generally bite in half if you haven't noticed the hole that they make at the top of the apple.

Trapping the females doesn't have much effect, but pheromone traps use the typical smell of the females to attract amorous males, which then get ensnared on panels of sticky grease. With reduced fertilisation, the females are unable to lay eggs and you'll cut the problem by 85 per cent. Just one trap for every five apple trees is enough.

There's a similar device for controlling plum fruit moth, which is a close relative of the codling moth and does the same amount of damage – the little blighters tunnel into ripening plums, causing them to drop prematurely or making them inedible at harvest time. In a poor season when a cold spring has thinned the crop, almost every plum can be ruined, so it makes sense to invest in a few of these tent-shaped pheromone traps and leave them suspended all summer from the tree branches to save the fruits of all your labours

RIGHT A wide selection of lettuces, including cos and loose-leaf types, promises a succession of colourful summer salads. Behind them is a bank of diascias for cutting, and a gooseberry trained as a standard.

Training in bush fruit shoots
If your garden is small and lack of space is a real problem you can, if you're canny, fit in a whole range of bush fruit by training the bushes into restricted shapes. These can be very decorative and no less productive than normal bushes.

A gooseberry, for example, can be grown as a standard, which is nothing more than a gooseberry bush grafted on a 90cm–1.2m (3–4ft) stem. These look great, even in a border and, since you can grow flowers or vegetables underneath, they really take up no room at all.

You can also grow gooseberries and red and white currants as cordons. These consist of single, double or triple stems, grown vertically and trained on canes tied to a post and wire support or on wires against a fence or wall. Kept neat, they can take up just 15cm (6in) of your valuable border. The main pruning is best done later, in August (see page 130), when sideshoots made this year are cut back to two leaves. But at this time of year new shoots are extending fast, and need to be tied back and into shape while they are still young and pliable.

Growing raspberries in a retricted space
If you're beginning to pick raspberries and find that you haven't got room for as many canes as you'd like, my solution is to grow them as a pillar. When the

canes grow they're tied to wires to form a column of foliage and fruit, as shown below. This arrangement produces a slightly lower crop than is normal in traditional rows, because the light only reaches the outside of the canes. But it looks neat and decorative, and takes up much less room. And, as with all these training methods, the fruit is more easily covered with netting or fleece to protect it against its two biggest enemies – frost and birds.

At the same time as you're harvesting the fruit, take along your secateurs and cut out late suckers that are congesting the plants at ground level.

GROWING RASPBERRIES AS A PILLAR

Drive a 2.4m (8ft) stake about 45cm (18in) into the ground; then nail six 60cm (2ft) 'arms' to the stake, in pairs to make a cross shape, one at the top of the stake, one in the middle and another about 60cm (2ft) from the ground. Staple wires to the ends of the arms to tie the canes to. Plant the raspberries 45cm (18in) apart in a circle around the pillar.

MISCELLANEOUS

Tackling weeds

I've proved that organic gardening is not just good for the environment: it works better too, filling your garden with wildlife, fine sturdy flowers and excellent crops of fruit and vegetables – all without chemical fertilisers or pesticides. But what about weeds?

Annual weeds such as chickweed and groundsel are no problem and certainly not a reason to spray, because you can pull them out easily by hand or use the hoe regularly. Awkward weeds like stonecrop (*Sedum*) in a drive would resist chemical control anyway, with the waxy waterproof coating to their leaves. The solution here is to use a flame gun, which works on portable gas cylinders and is simplicity itself to use – you can get one from a small tool-hire shop quite cheaply. The job might need doing every month for a while, but eventually you'll manage to get rid of the stuff.

Weedkillers won't touch tough customers like marestail and oxalis, which are particularly difficult, and here you must rely on that other well-known preparation, elbow grease. By hoeing regularly before the shoots are more than 1cm (½in) tall, you'll deprive the plants of light and without that they'll eventually die.

If you're starting with a new garden, however, and find it is smothered in pernicious weeds such as couch grass, bindweed or ground elder, then it's worth making an exception to the organic rule and spraying with a total weedkiller. One containing glyphosate will kill everything green that it touches, so do be careful, but it is inactivated when it hits the soil and is harmless to animal life.

For tough perennials like nettles and ivy the best bet is to spray now, and again in late summer. The weedkiller is taken down to the roots, but these can sometimes regrow so the second application, just when the plants are beginning to slow down, should complete the job. For weeds growing in borders among plants, you'll have to paint the weedkiller on the leaves – wear rubber gloves and diligently avoid the leaves of other plants. To treat bindweed growing among plants, try putting a cane near the weed and allow it to scramble up: this makes it easier to treat safely.

And finally, why would this hardened old reactionary advise using a chemical weedkiller? Well, otherwise you'd get thoroughly discouraged and just give up. And that does no one any good at all. But promise me you'll throw the sprayer away afterwards.

Watering techniques

Whatever the reasons and whoever's fault it is – and believe me, I've shaken the bones and danced round in circles a bit – we have to face the fact that water is likely to be in short supply in the foreseeable summers ahead. So it is vital to manage those resources we have as efficiently as possible.

The first and most obvious measure is to catch rainwater. A lot comes off the house and greenhouse roofs, so water butts are essential. You can buy little plastic inserts which fit to the down pipe, fill the butt to the top and then divert the rest to the drain. Better still, link

other butts to the first with a series of simple connector pipes and fill them as well.

Next, it's worthwhile directing water just where it is needed. A sprinkler is very inefficient with big losses to evaporation: bear in mind that one hour's sprinkling uses as much water as an average family in a whole day. Much better to target plants that need it most – young transplants, leafy plants and vegetables or fruit that are in flower or ripening their crops. Use a hose which oozes water along its whole length so that, when laid among the plants, it delivers water straight to the soil with minimum evaporation. A soaker hose – a flat hose with rows of tiny holes along its length – can be turned upside down to do the same job.

Watering's best done in the evening, when the heat has gone out of the sun, by soaking a few plants thoroughly and then leaving the rest for the following evening. And make sure they are soaked: lightly sprinkling the ground makes matters worse by bringing roots to the surface where they'll dry out even quicker. Mulch the plants after watering. One way to trap water is to work plenty of organic matter such as compost into the soil, and then add more to the surface while it's still moist. Anything organic will help – grass cuttings, shredded prunings, compost, manure, leafmould, bark and so on.

Even your newspaper can make an effective and inexpensive mulch. When you've finished reading it, don't throw it away. Instead, get out in the garden with it, rake away a little moist soil, lay three sheets of newspaper on the surface and cover them with a thin layer of soil. You can even lay the paper in place and then plant through it when transplanting: the paper barrier will last all season and can be dug in afterwards to add a bit more organic matter. Black plastic between rows of vegetables is excellent and also inhibits weeds, cutting down on work and reducing competition for moisture. But ideally you should use one of the porous woven plastics that will allow the rain through when it eventually does come.

Proper gardeners never go away in summer – life's one long holiday already – but if you do, watering precautions become critical. First, chat up a neighbour who can come round and water hanging baskets, containers and plants in the greenhouse; or, alternatively, fit up one of those automatic trickle devices that deliver drops of water direct to the plants through individual nozzles. Weed the garden as much as you can, soak essential plants and then mow the lawn the morning you depart.

Indoors or in the greenhouse, take all the house- and pot plants and stand them in the bath or in large bowls. Lay a blanket or wet towels on the bottom with one end resting in a bowl of water. The towels will stay wet for a couple of weeks, drawing up water from the reservoir bowl as necessary, and the plants will have enough to drink while you're away. And remember to draw the curtains and shade the greenhouse to exclude hot sunshine.

PLANTS FOR
june

1 The large-flowered jackmanii type clematis 'Comtesse de Bouchaud' is a versatile variety. It grows to 1.8–2.4m (6–8ft) and blooms profusely even on a north-facing wall.

2 *Digitalis purpurea* 'Alba', the white-flowered form of the common foxglove, is a coveted hardy border biennial or short-lived perennial up to 1.8m (6ft) high.

3 The popular hardy deciduous mock orange, *Philadelphus coronarius,* makes a vigorous bushy shrub 3m (10ft) high, even on light dry soils. In early summer it's smothered with creamy-white, richly fragrant blooms.

1

2

3

4 Bearded irises are classic early summer flowers, very often flamboyantly bi-coloured, for growing in mixed borders or in beds to themselves. Although their flowering season is somewhat short, they are very hardy plants with hundreds of varieties that are divided into tall, medium and dwarf categories.

5 Available in a number of brightly coloured mixtures easily raised from seed, the sun-loving Iceland poppy, *Papaver nudicaule,* can be treated as a biennial or short-lived perennial; the 30cm (12in) blooms are produced over a long season.

OVERLEAF Many lovely plants combine well with roses, whether as ground cover or as edging, a role for which lavender is traditional. Here *Campanula lactiflora* 'Pritchard's Variety' complements glorious old-fashioned shrub roses.

4

5

With the heat of the summer came perhaps my least favourite – but also my most favourite – times in the garden. At weekends, when there was no extra help, the job of watering fell to me. It was time-consuming and fiddly: there were seven greenhouses, three tunnels, two conservatories and an alpine house to take care of, as well as all the individual gardens. Some had water butts, so cans had to be filled and carried, others needed what seemed like miles of hose. But it was an educational task; I learned a lot about plants as the weeks and years went by.

On the other hand, hot summer evenings, when we had the whole place to ourselves, were blissful. We'd walk through the garden at twilight, relishing the peace and quiet, the sights and the scents. The white flowers stayed visible the longest, seeming almost luminescent as darkness fell, while the scents of the flowers were at their strongest after sundown. Geoff would never grow scentless roses or sweet peas, however beautiful they were; he just couldn't see the point.

The well-known rambler rose 'American Pillar' flanks a stone path leading through mid-summer borders where hollyhocks and white mallows provide elegance and height.

july

key tasks for july

ANNUALS & BEDDING PLANTS
○ Harvest flowers and dry them slowly, page 108

BORDER PERENNIALS
○ Divide and plant flag irises, page 109
○ Take cuttings of pinks and carnations, page 109
○ Cut back flowered perennials to encourage a second flush,
page 110

BULBS
○ Divide congested clumps of daffodils, page 111

SHRUBS, TREES & CLIMBERS
○ Prune clematis, take cuttings and watch out for wilt, page 112
○ Propagate short-lived shrubs by taking soft cuttings, page 112

LAWNS & HEDGES
○ Keep lawns in top condition, page 114
○ Control leylandii hedges and take cuttings, page 114

VEGETABLES & HERBS
○ Watch for tomato disorders, page 115
○ Ripen and harvest shallots and garlic, page 115
○ Plan for plenty of autumn vegetables by sowing now, page 115
○ Cut back herbs for further young growth, page 116

MISCELLANEOUS
○ Make the best of limited space with a deep bed, page 117

ANNUALS & BEDDING PLANTS

Harvesting flowers for drying

True everlasting flowers, such as helichrysum, helipterum and rhodanthe, hardly need drying because their flowers are naturally papery and long-lasting. They need picking just as they reach their best – which is fractionally before they're fully open.

Hang them upside down in a cool airy place to dry them slowly with plenty of circulating air. Whatever you do, don't try drying them in the kitchen or greenhouse as they quickly shrivel up.

Many other flowers can be preserved in the same way. The translucent white seedpods of honesty are always popular, but it's also worth having a go with achillea, amaranthus, delphiniums, gypsophila, golden rod, zinnias and, of course, lavender.

BORDER PERENNIALS

Planting flag irises

Every cottage garden used to have its stand of blue 'flags' making a splendid show each year. While they've lost none of their hardiness or vigour, irises have come a long way since then and they're now available in almost every colour from deep purple through smoky browns to white and yellow, with many bi-colours too.

Given the right situation, they are among the easiest plants to grow. I don't remember ever having a single pest or disease attack mine, and they never fail to flower their hearts out. Their one demand is for a dry well-drained sunny spot. Their fleshy rhizomes form clumps that need to be baked in the sun to ensure a crop of flowers.

Before planting, dig in some compost or manure and, if your

DIVIDING FLAG IRISES

1 Irises branch each side of the thick original main rhizome, which is sometimes rotten at its oldest end. Use these young laterals or side pieces for propagation. Cut each one off with a fan of leaves, using a sharp knife.

2 Throw away the old root. Reduce the leaves on the young rhizomes by half their length, and replant the young segments in groups of three or four to make good-sized clumps. Make sure they're not completely buried, especially on heavier soil.

soil's heavy, add plenty of coarse grit; if this raises the soil above its surroundings, so much the better – it all improves drainage. A good dressing of general fertiliser completes the job. Scrape a shallow depression in the soil, and make a ridge in the centre so that the rhizome can rest on it with its roots lying either side. Plant it so it is half buried and water once. In windy sites it pays to support the leaf fans with short canes. Then leave the plants to their own devices.

Dividing flag irises

Plants increase rapidly and should be divided every 3–4 years because the centres produce fewer flowers as they age. But the job's not difficult, and the best time for it is

LEFT A combined display of hardy perennial white leucanthemums (shasta daisies) with annual *Godetia* 'Grace'.

about five weeks after flowering ends. Start by cutting off the old flower spike, and then lift the clump and shake off the soil – you might want to wash the roots to see where to cut. Then cut the rhizomes and replant as shown above, planting in groups of three or four to make a good-sized clump.

Propagating pinks and carnations

There's little point struggling to grow plants that don't like the conditions in your garden, when there are lots of others that will grow there happily and unaided. If your soil's chalky, for example, you should be growing lime-lovers – and there are plenty of real beauties, few finer than garden pinks and border carnations. But be warned: they soon get thin and straggly unless replaced every 3–4 years.

I've never understood why so many gardening books recommend

PROPAGATING CARNATIONS

You can cut off the tips of shoots with a sharp knife, or more simply just pull out the end with the last few pairs of leaves. Peel off the lowest of these carefully so as not to break the base of the soft stem, and dip the cut end in rooting hormone. The 'pipings' will root in pure sharp sand or perlite if this is kept moist, but I like to use cuttings compost with extra grit for drainage. Cover pots with plastic bags to stop them drying out.

propagating them by layering, a method I find very fiddly, time-consuming and rarely successful. Taking stem cuttings or 'pipings' at about this time of year is so much quicker and more reliable. Just pull the top 8cm (3in) of the stem away from the plant. It'll come out quite cleanly, and then you can dip the end in rooting hormone and dibble it into a pot of soil-less compost. Cover the pot with a clear plastic bag and stand outdoors in the shade. If you have the space, you can even make a shallow depression in the soil in a shady part of the garden, fill it with sharp sand, and strike the cuttings in this.

Cutting back perennials

Raising a family is an exhausting business, and since plants produce offspring by the thousand it's little wonder they tend to flop a bit. Many of the early-flowering herbaceous varieties are now getting on with the job of making

seeds but, unless you intend raising more plants this way, you'd be well advised to teach them a bit of family planning.

It's especially important with notoriously short-lived plants such as lupins, which last only a few years anyway and much less if you let them run to seed every year. As soon as the last flower has faded, cut the spikes off to allow the plant to put all its strength into enlarging itself, with the help of a little general fertiliser. Just leave one or two stems to produce seeds so that you can replace short-lived varieties every few years.

Early-flowering geraniums, violas and delphiniums can be sheared off right down to the crown, just above ground level. If you leave them the foliage will collapse and swamp other smaller plants around them. Take the old leaves to the compost heap, give the plants a sprinkling of fertiliser and a good soak of water if necessary, and they'll soon produce fresh young leaves. In warmer parts of the country, many will also produce a second, smaller crop of flowers as a bonus.

One disadvantage with this drastic method is that it leaves a bare patch in the border at a time of year when it should be completely overflowing. Obviously you can't plant anything permanent because the space will soon be filled again. So I keep a few pots of tender perennials or mixed hardy annuals which can be put in the empty spaces as temporary fillers.

LEFT There is a huge expanding range of modern double pinks, all supreme edging plants for sunny well-drained positions, and good for cutting too.

Not all perennials benefit from cutting hard back, and the simple test if you are not sure is to part the old leaves and look down at the base of the plant. If you see new leaves at soil level, the old ones can go. But plants that tend to have a single stem at the base with branches above, such as penstemons or perennial cornflowers, also known as knapweed (*Centaurea*), should be just trimmed lightly.

Another example of this is the perennial wallflower (*Erysimum*), which can die out in two or three years on heavy soil – trim it lightly as I've suggested, and take some cuttings from the prunings to make sure you have replacements.

BULBS

Dividing daffodils

The bulbs in old clumps of daffodils multiply over the years, and eventually begin competing with each other to the point where they go 'blind' and refuse to flower. So split them up before this happens. Early in the month, when the foliage has died right down but while you can still see where the clumps are, lift large ones and split them into individual bulbs. Then either dry the bulbs off and store in a cool dry place for replanting in late August or September, or replant them immediately.

ABOVE Some osteospermums, such as this *O. ecklonis*, are reliably hardy perennials, whereas the marguerite behind needs over-wintering indoors.

If daffodils that were planted last year failed to flower this spring, they might be too small, of course, and need another season to build up to flowering size. But they could also be planted too shallowly, and it's worth digging them up now for replanting either straight away or at the usual time in early autumn. Aim to cover the bulbs with at least twice their own depth of soil, more on light soils where they can go 5–8cm (2–3in) deeper.

111

SHRUBS, TREES & CLIMBERS

Looking after clematis

Nothing gives such a startling display of large flowers or masses of smaller ones over as long a period as clematis. But there are two factors which put gardeners off.

First is the dreaded clematis wilt. This is a fungal disease that makes clematis wilt from the top, progressing gradually downwards until the whole plant is affected. It is most noticeable in the summer, especially after humid weather. Chemical control is not much good, but there are measures which can help. Always plant clematis deeply, with about 15cm (6in) of soil above the top of the rootball. The fungus doesn't attack below ground, so even if you lose the top there will still be plenty of buds below the surface to replace infected growth. If you do see any signs of wilt, such as limp, drooping shoots, prune back immediately to healthy wood.

Pruning is the other big deterrent for some gardeners, because the rules can sound complicated. But I have found that there's a much simpler approach that works. If your clematis flowers before the end of June, prune it immediately after flowering by shortening sideshoots back to 2–3 buds off the main framework of branches. If it flowers after June, prune in the autumn or, in colder areas, in February by cutting hard back to just above a good fat bud within 15cm (6in) of the soil.

Propagating clematis

You can often take advantage of pruning to propagate clematis from cuttings. I've no idea why I have little success layering it: the books tell me that all I have to do is pin the shoots to the ground in autumn or late spring and they'll root in no time, but they never seem to. I find that taking cuttings any time in spring or summer is usually far more successful.

Unlike most plants, clematis are propagated by 'internodal' cuttings, as shown below – several can be cut from a single stem, since each needs only one pair of leaves. Once potted, cover the cuttings with very thin polythene, which should rest lightly on the leaves, and tuck it under the pot to make a good seal. Put the pots in a shaded frame or even outside in a shady spot, and the cuttings should root in 6–8 weeks.

Propagating short-lived shrubs

There's still time to take soft tip cuttings of shrubs and herbaceous perennials, and very often they root fast at this time of year while the temperatures are high. I try to make a point every season of propagating anything that seems to be short-lived or doubtfully hardy. Plants

RIGHT The rose garden at Barnsdale where mat-forming edging plants, such as stachys, soften the angular paving, also includes border perennials and lilies in a framework of shrubs and trees.

like lavender, which soon becomes gaunt and leggy, or grey-leafed shrubs like artemisias and euryops that often don't last long in heavy soils or cold gardens, all benefit from replacement every 3–5 years.

There's never a problem finding a home for surplus young plants – friends and relatives often welcome them or you can donate batches to local fund-raising events – so keep on taking cuttings whenever there's space in a frame or you see inviting young shoots. Soft tips just 5cm (2in) long are all you need. Remove the lower leaves, immerse the cuttings in fungicide and dip their ends into hormone rooting powder. Then insert them in pots of soil-less compost and keep them in a shaded frame. It takes no time at all, and ensures a continuous supply of young plants to replace any losses.

PROPAGATING CLEMATIS

1 Cut between leaf joints to leave a long stem below the leaf.

2 Dibble the cuttings into soil-less compost so that the leaves are resting on the surface.

LAWNS & HEDGES

Keeping lawns in top condition

A hot dry summer will usually show up the inadequacies in your lawn. It's often the nicely manicured lawns made of the very finest grass species that suffer first in a drought and start turning brown, while those composed of tougher grasses, clover and even moss still look refreshingly green.

If your lawn regularly and quickly turns brown in dry weather it's a sure sign of stress, and you're not going to cure it just by watering – all this will do is waste water and stop the symptoms from showing for a little bit longer. The real cause is more likely to be a combination of poor soil preparation and over-enthusiastic mowing, and the best way to start putting things right is to raise the cutting height of the mower. Aim to mow less frequently, leaving the grass 2.5cm (1in) high or a little more, and it won't look so parched and scalped. Leave the grass box in the shed and allow the cuttings to fall on the lawn where they'll act as a thin mulch and gradually return humus and nutrients to the soil – if you invest in a mulching mower, this will chop the clippings very finely so they are virtually invisible and won't tread into the house. Then resolve to add some organic matter to the soil in the autumn, and again in the spring, by spiking the lawn and raking in some sieved garden compost to help retain moisture at the roots. If the season continues to be dry, give the lawn an extra feed in the autumn just before rain is forecast, and it'll soon look immaculate again.

Controlling leylandii hedges

Conifer hedges are much maligned these days, mainly I suspect because they tend to be of Leyland cypress, × *Cupressocyparis leylandii*. This is often sneered at because it's so widely grown, but if the truth be told, the reason that it's common is that it's such a good hedging plant.

It is, of course, a fast mover, putting on 60–90cm (2–3ft) of growth in most seasons, and you can't afford to let it get away from you. The plants won't produce new growth from old wood, so it's essential to begin trimming the sides as soon as they start to exceed the width you want. Plants can be as narrow as 15cm (6in) each side of the main stem if you clip them twice a year – early this month and again between late August and October.

You can trim the sides while the plants are still young, but leave the main leader at the top until it has reached about 90cm (3ft) higher than you want it. Then cut it back to 15cm (6in) lower than the required height. This will allow it to form a thick bushy top, which you'll be able to cut to a neat flat finish. By trimming it regularly you'll have a hedge that's almost as aristocratic as yew but a lot quicker.

LEFT An immaculate grass path emphasises lavish plantings in the Barnsdale borders and creates an illusion of distance.

Taking conifer cuttings

Whenever you're trimming any conifers at this time of year, decide if you want to grow more of them because the prunings will often supply perfect semi-ripe cuttings. These are the little sideshoots, about 5–8cm (2–3in) long, growing from the main stems and branches, and just becoming woody at their base. Pull them off, as shown below. There's no need to remove any lower leaves, but otherwise root them like other semi-ripe cuttings (see page 125).

TAKING CONIFER CUTTINGS

1 Pull sideshoots off downwards so that each has a little heel of tissue at its base.

2 Trim the ragged end of the heel with a knife and root like other semi-ripe cuttings (see page 125).

VEGETABLES & HERBS

At this time of year, when the vegetable garden is overflowing, one of the main jobs is to keep harvesting. Don't forget that the more you pick summer vegetables such as courgettes and runner beans, the more they'll produce.

Looking out for tomato disorders

In order to help the fruit finish ripening before the frosts, it's a good idea to stop tall outdoor tomatoes after three trusses. Keep an eye on greenhouse tomatoes too. Black marks at the flowering tip of fruits is not a disease but a physiological disorder called blossom end rot, and is the result of irregular watering. It's hard to stop completely, especially in hot weather, but it helps if you can shade the greenhouse lightly and keep the compost evenly moist at all times. Another problem is halo blight, which shows as small spots on the fruits, surrounded by a lighter ring. This is a water-borne fungal disease and can be prevented if you avoid splashing the fruits when you water or damp down.

Harvesting shallots

Shallots need to be ripened well in the sun. This helps ensure that the bulbs keep for a longer period in store, and I'm convinced it improves their flavour too.

In a warm dry season the bulbs can be left to ripen in the ground, especially if you draw a little soil away from the clusters to expose them to the sun. Otherwise lift them carefully with a fork when the leaves turn yellow, making sure you don't break the clusters up before

they're ready or you'll leave wounds open to disease. If you make a temporary 'table' with a piece of wire netting nailed to four posts, you can spread out the clusters clear of the ground and surrounded by free circulation of air – but keep a piece of polythene handy to cover them over if it rains.

When the skins are papery and dry, you can separate the bulbs in each cluster and clean them up by removing the old leaves and scaly skin and rubbing off any clinging soil. Pack the bulbs in onion or Brussels sprout bags begged from the greengrocer, and store them in a frost-free place.

Harvesting garlic

Like shallots, garlic also needs to be ripened in the sun, but there's no need to wait until its leaves turn completely yellow before you harvest the bulbs. These can be dug up as soon as the tips start to turn colour. Dry them in the same way as shallots, or hang them in bunches in the sun until the skins are dry and flaky. Cut off the dead foliage and rub the bulbs clean before storing them in the same way as shallots. If the crop is good and the plants were healthy – their leaves free from the yellow spots and stripes of virus – save a few bulbs for replanting this autumn.

Planning vegetables for autumn

Despite the fact that the vegetable plot is yielding masses of delicious fresh produce every day, we can't afford to rest on our laurels and rely on a never-ending supply of runner beans. Control the euphoria for a bit, because autumn will be upon us sooner than you think. As soon as a bit of ground becomes available, revitalise it with a dressing of compost and a light dusting of organic fertiliser so you can bung in a follow-on crop.

Lettuces are welcome at any time, and you should be trying to aim for an unbroken succession of supplies. At this time of year they're quick to mature provided they get enough moisture – if you're unlucky enough to have water restrictions in your area, dig in as much compost, rotted manure or spent mushroom compost as you can to hold the moisture in the soil. And if you can sow in a shady place, that'll help too. This month I continue sowing 'Saladin' and 'Lakeland', which have large crisp iceberg-type heads.

For beetroot I stick to quick maturing 'Boltardy' because I find

BELOW A neatly sculpted mophead bay tree crowns a bed of fennel and echoes the formality of annual herbs in rows.

it's just as good for winter storage as for pulling young; sown now it'll provide delicious baby beet for autumn use. For rapid germination it pays to wash the seed capsules in a flour sieve under the tap to remove the germination inhibitor in the seed-coating.

Carrots will also produce delicious young roots this season, and any not needed immediately can be stored. For some years I've used, and been pleased with, the variety 'Berlicum Berjo', even if it does sound like a music-hall song.

Let me say a word for kohl rabi. It's a funny looking customer with leaves sticking out all over the swollen stem, the part you eat. Despite mouthwatering claims in catalogues, it's not the best flavour in the world eaten raw, but it makes a superb soup. Old-fashioned varieties tend to get pithy when they're bigger than tennis-ball size, but modern types like 'Rowel' and 'White Danube' stay sweet and fibre-free even when they become large – not that they'll have time to get enormous if sown this month. Sow them in a seedbed and transplant next month or, better still, sow direct and thin to final spacings of 23cm (9in) each way.

Turnips are so quick to mature that they can be left until the last week of this month or even early August, if you sow 'Golden Ball', a fast-maturing variety that can also stand some frost in autumn. There's still time to sow Florence fennel, which is delicious with roast meat and lasts well into winter if covered with cloches: use a modern variety like 'Zeva Fino' or 'Cantino'. Keep the plants well watered and if you're sowing in dry weather, water down the drill before you sow and

then cover the seeds with dry soil – this prevents the surface crust that forms if you water after sowing.

Sow some spinach beet (perpetual spinach) in a shady spot, and also its close relative, Swiss chard, which happily stands the hardest frost.

Finally, one crop I wouldn't be without is land cress, sometimes called American cress. It has a delicious watercress flavour, but without the need for a running stream to grow in. Sow it in the coolest, moistest part of the vegetable plot where it's less likely to run to seed, and transfer a few spare plants to the frame or greenhouse in September to make the most delicious and nutritious winter soup you could ask for.

Rejuvenating herbs

Years ago I used to wonder why gardeners bothered to grow sorrel, one of the ugliest herbs there is. It tends to run to seed quickly, and when it does the leaves seem to become tougher and more bitter. But I discovered that if it's cut back hard as soon as it starts to bolt, reducing the whole clump in fact to nothing more than a stump, a wealth of tender new leaves soon appears from the base, and these have a wonderful flavour.

Marjoram, mint and tarragon respond to a good haircut about now by producing new young leaves. When you cut them back, sprinkle some general fertiliser around the plants and give them a good watering to encourage faster regrowth. The new leaves are much tastier than the old ones, and by the time they're ready to be harvested you might have enough to lay up a good store of preserves such as mint jelly for the winter.

MISCELLANEOUS

Building a deep bed

If you're serious about growing vegetables and you haven't got unlimited acres at your disposal, you'll naturally want to maximise your harvest per square metre. One of the best ways to do this is to grow your crops on the deep bed system, which can double or even treble yields. And if the mention of beds starts you thinking of snoozing, I'd better explain that there's nothing cosy about these. They need a bit of hard graft at first, but after this initial slog they get easier to work each year. They're cleaner, more encouraging to work on and, if they're well maintained, they look terrific.

This is what you do. Mark out a bed 1.2m (4ft) wide, with access from each side. You can make it as long as you like, but if you make more than one, leave a 60cm (2ft) path in between. It will repay you in dividends if you manage to double-dig the bed. Ideally you should break up the subsoil but avoid turning it over or bringing it up to the top. As you dig, work in manure, compost, spent mushroom compost or some other humus (but not peat, of course). Make sure you mix it throughout all levels of the soil and not just in the bottom of the trench.

That part is hard work, but you only need to do it once because afterwards you'll single-dig the bed each year, working a bit more compost or manure into the top spit. After a while the soil becomes so easy to work that, for example, I don't have to put my foot on the spade at all – a gentle lean is all that's needed to slice into the soil. If you can't double-dig, initial single-digging is the next best thing and will still yield dividends.

ABOVE Deeply dug organic vegetable beds are easily managed and protected when they are narrow and framed with edging boards.

There are several reasons why deep bed culture works. Except for the annual dig, you never tread on the soil because you do all the work from the side paths. That way the soil never gets compacted. Also, because it's deeply dug the plants' roots can get right down instead of competing with each other near the surface. This means you can space crops more closely together, and so grow more. Growing them close together has more advantages: there is less evaporation, so you need to water less, and there will be less room for weeds to grow. And on top of all this, if you edge the bed with 8 or 10cm (3 or 4in) treated boards and gravel the paths, it'll delight your eye every time you go out to pull a carrot.

PLANTS FOR
july

1 The vigorous woody twining stems of *Lonicera* x *brownii* 'Dropmore Scarlet', a hardy honeysuckle, will reach 4m (13ft) on a sunny wall or large host shrub. It is very long-lived, and produces an abundance of 5cm (2in) trumpet-shaped blooms in dense whorls from mid-summer until autumn.

2 This month and next are the peak season for *Phlox paniculata*, the hardy herbaceous perennial border phlox. It has tall stems 90cm (3ft) or more high and flowers in a range of colours, from purple and crimson through to the pure white blooms of 'White Admiral'.

1

2

3

4

5

3 There are several lovely forms of knapweed or perennial cornflower, with *Centaurea hypoleuca* 'John Coutts' among the finest. The hardy herbaceous plants are 50–60cm (20–24in) tall and, with their handsome long-lasting blooms, spread steadily without being invasive.

4 The common morning glory, *Ipomoea purpurea*, is a half-hardy annual climber up to 2.4m (8ft) high, with numerous large funnel-shaped flowers in shades of blue, white, pink and red. Each bloom lasts for a single day.

5 In full sun and well-drained soil, alstroemeria hybrids derived from *A. ligtu* and *A. aurantiaca* are reliable hardy perennials, easily raised from seed. They produce strong-stemmed flowers in a range of prettily marked colours.

August was birthday month — mine, one son's, Geoff's and, of course, his twin's. And the obvious place to celebrate with friends and family was in the garden, with a barbecue. Here Geoff took command of the cooking. He used a 50-gallon drum that he had cut in half, with reinforcing mesh as the grill, to do the job. But though he liked the idea of relaxing in the garden, he almost never managed actually to do so. The moment he sat down, he'd spot something that needed attention — a weed to be pulled up, a long stem to be tied back.

This was the time of year when the allotment bulged with rows of flowers that could be pillaged for the house. The rest of the garden was more tricky. Because I didn't always know which area was to be filmed in any one week, I could never simply go and pick where and what I wanted. But even though the finer arts of flower arranging were rather lost on Geoff — he really did prefer to see his flowers in the garden — he always made sure that he grew enough in the allotment for me to pick all through the summer.

There are many fine crocosmia hybrids, but few can match 'Lucifer' for bold foliage and dramatic intensity of colour in the late summer border.

august

key tasks for august

BORDER PERENNIALS
○ Weed borders but watch out for self-set seedlings, page 122

BULBS
○ Plant Madonna lilies to bloom next year, page 123
○ Plant autumn crocuses and nerines, page 123

CONTAINER PLANTS
○ Sow tender perennials for a late display, page 124

SHRUBS, TREES & CLIMBERS
○ Summer-prune vigorous shrubs and climbers, page 124
○ Take semi-ripe cuttings, page 125

ROSES
○ Deadhead roses to stimulate more flowers, page 125

LAWNS & HEDGES
○ Prepare lawn sites for sowing or turfing, page 126
○ Seed a new lawn, page 126
○ Trim hedges before growth slows down, page 128

VEGETABLES & HERBS
○ Protect late sowings from sun and then from frost, page 128
○ Sow Chinese vegetables for autumn and winter use, page 129

FRUIT
○ Make new strawberry beds and propagate from old plants, page 129
○ Summer-prune trained fruit, page 130
○ Cut down spent raspberry canes, page 131

MISCELLANEOUS
○ Take steps to discourage slugs, page 131

BORDER PERENNIALS

Looking out for seedlings

When you grow old-fashioned cottage garden plants, weeding ceases to be a chore and becomes a treasure hunt. It's essential that you do the job by hand or you may be guilty of hoeing out hundreds of free bonus plants.

Many flowering plants will seed themselves in the borders without your having to lift a finger. That has nothing to do with plants having developed a good aim; it's simply that, to be sure of success, they have been equipped with the ability to produce seeds by the thousand. Most of these will land in places that are unsuitable – sun-lovers land in the shade or vice versa, or small seedlings lose the battle against competition from larger plants. But just a few will finish up right on the perfect spot and thrive.

So when you're weeding, look out for seedlings of plants like aquilegias, Jacob's ladder, opium poppies and foxgloves. They may take a bit of recognising at first, but you'll soon get used to it. Some plants are renowned for their self-seeding: hellebores (see page 91), red valerian (*Centranthus*), sweet rocket (*Hesperis*), English or pot marigolds (*Calendula*), the prolific fried egg plant (*Limnanthes*) and Welsh poppies (*Meconopsis cambrica*) which tolerate fairly dense shade. Bowles' Golden Grass (*Milium effusum* 'Aureum') also seeds all over the place and always looks good wherever it falls, like a spring gloss of bright yellow between other plants in sun or shade. They're all worth saving.

ABOVE Bushy branching sunflowers such as these 'Sungold' are a perfect backdrop for late lilies and free-flowering marguerites.

My advice would be to collect everything and anything, provided you're prepared for a few disappointments. Most plants grown from seed are unique, like fingerprints, so there's always the chance you might find something new and exciting. Well-established annuals, hardy perennials and shrubs usually come fairly true to type every time, resembling the parent plants with only minor variations. But others, like aquilegias, poppies and hellebores, are very promiscuous and will cross-pollinate with just about anything. It pays sometimes to intervene before plants set seed, just to sway the odds a bit – for example, some forms such as mauve poppies and common purple foxgloves will predominate, but if you cull these before they set seed you'll raise the chances of getting something special.

BULBS

Planting Madonna lilies

It might seem a strange time to be planting lilies, but the lovely Madonna lily (*Lilium candidum*) is dormant just about now. Next month the bulbs start producing basal leaves which will stay there all winter, so now's the best moment to get them in. You'll probably have to buy bulbs by mail order from a specialist, but they're worth the effort. The lilies have been favourites ever since the days of ancient Crete and in medieval times were popularly associated with the Virgin Mary, hence their name.

The bulbs like a warm sunny position in well-drained soil, and always did well in cottage gardens where they were sheltered at the base by other plants. Unlike other lilies, it's important to plant them shallowly, just below the surface with a covering of no more than 2.5–5cm (1–2in) of soil. Give them a good dressing of compost and a handful of general fertiliser after

flowering, and they'll keep on stunning you every summer with their pure white, heavily scented flowers on stems that are 1.2m (4ft) high or more.

Planting autumn-flowering bulbs

I like to plant autumn-flowering bulbs in late August or early September, but finding them in the shops is the difficult part of the job. The answer is mail order, and if you send for them early this month you'll still have time to get them in for flowering this year.

The well-known 'autumn crocus' is popular, although it isn't a crocus at all but a *Colchicum*; it's also known as 'meadow saffron', though it isn't saffron coloured either but rather pale lilac (in my view, this kind of muddle is one of the best arguments for sticking to Latin names). Whatever you call it, it's an eye-catching bulb, but it can look a bit naked without leaves and it also tends to flop in wet weather. Avoid both problems by planting it in grass or where it can show through other low-growing plants for support and modesty.

There are proper crocuses that flower in autumn. The most popular are the purple or white *C. speciosus* and the true saffron crocus (*C. sativus*). This has lilac flowers with darker veins and a purple eye, and vivid red stamens from which saffron spice is derived. *C. speciosus* will tolerate some shade, but the saffron crocus needs full sun. Plant all these kinds under a 10cm (4in) covering of soil.

Nerines are beautiful flowers from South Africa, and a good clump will make you the envy of your gardening friends. The flowers are produced before the leaves, like

123

the autumn crocuses, the spikes bearing anything up to eight or nine blooms, with pink curling petals revealing purple stamens. You'll certainly need patience with these, because they're not too fond of cold weather. The only one that's frost-hardy is *Nerine bowdenii*, and even with this I would suggest that northern gardeners grow it in a large pot, and bring it in to a cold greenhouse or conservatory for the winter. Elsewhere you can plant the bulbs at the foot of a south-facing wall or fence in full sunlight. They need a real baking in summer if they're to flower well, so plant them with the top of the bulb level with the soil surface.

BELOW Humidity is important under glass, and most plants appreciate misting over at this time of year.

CONTAINER PLANTS

Sowing for late colour

If you've got opened packets of half-hardy annuals with some seeds left over from spring sowing, try using them up this month to provide a late batch of plants to flower in autumn and winter in containers. The naturally high temperatures and long day-length will bring them through in no time and they'll still be able to make small bushy plants for tucking into containers outdoors in sheltered sunny spots.

Alternatively you could also take some soft cuttings of ageratum, the dwarf *Begonia semperflorens*, busy lizzies, petunias and even lobelia, and insert several in a small pot to grow on unthinned and to flower late as excellent pot plants.

SHRUBS, TREES & CLIMBERS

Summer-pruning vigorous shrubs and climbers

Gardening advice is not always as realistic as it could be. I'm just as guilty as any 'expert' because we all preach perfection, even though many gardeners don't have the time to follow our advice to the letter.

For example, it is recommended that wisteria should be pruned every August by reducing sideshoots to 3–5 leaves. That's all right on small plants, but if yours covers the whole house it'll take for ever. And then you're exhorted to go back and do it again in February. Personally I'd prune large plants back wherever they're not wanted, and leave it at that. This is the time of year that one is in the garden and notices these things, and it's better to prune now than not at all. I honestly don't think that exact pruning makes that much difference to flowering, and if your wisteria doesn't flower it's more likely that it's facing the wrong way, or it may be too young.

Rambler roses are another sore point. They get very tangled and are much more difficult to prune than many books imply. So if you're growing something vigorous like an 'Albertine', you'll have to modify the instructions. Give the plant its head for the first few years, tying in the shoots to cover as much space as possible. Start pruning in the third year, remembering that the rose flowers on the previous year's wood. Try to prune those sideshoots that have flowered back to within a couple of inches of the stem. Then tie in the new shoots for flowering next year.

RIGHT While still relatively small, pampas grass (*Cortaderia*) is an excellent choice for providing clumps of evergreen foliage in a warm sunny border, where blue agapanthus is also very much at home.

In fact there's more latitude with pruning than many of us suspect. For example, I once bought a *Eucalyptus pauciflora* 'Nana', which I naturally expected to be dwarf with a name like that. But it actually grew to about 15m (50ft). Fed up with this spindly giant I took the saw to it one August, but only after noticing a fine crop of healthy shoots growing from the base of the trunk. Now I grow it as a shrub and prune it back every year – February is the time for this according to the books but, like a lot of pruning, it's sometimes best carried out when you see the plant really needs it, and have the time and inclination to do it.

Taking semi-ripe cuttings

This is a wonderful time of year for visiting friends and relatives – not for social reasons, but for pure selfish gain. Their shrubs will be fine and bushy by now, and they won't miss a cutting or two. Before you go plundering it's a good idea to be prepared, as the cuttings will need instant attention when you get home. The best way is to make a cuttings frame, as explained in May (see page 81), and then just grab a few plastic bags and you're ready.

Many of the shrubs that I've found difficult to propagate from soft cuttings in early summer – box, hebe, santolina, and so on – seem to root quite freely at this time of year, but it's semi-ripe material that you use now. Look for cuttings that are about 8cm (3in) long and just going woody at the base.

There's no need at this time of year to keep the pots in the greenhouse or propagator, and they're in fact much better outdoors as long as you protect them from drying out. They'll be perfectly safe in a shaded frame, but you could strike the cuttings direct into a bed prepared with plenty of sharp sand and then covered with a large glass or polythene cloche – shade it with diluted white emulsion and they'll root in no time.

ROSES

Deadheading

The sole object of any flowering plant is to produce seed. But if you prevent it from doing so, it'll go on trying until the frosts come along and curtail its efforts.

So the quicker you remove faded flowers from annuals, tender perennials and roses, the more they'll produce. It can be backbreaking and perhaps fiddly but, like weeding, it has the

125

advantage of getting your nose right down there among the plants. Find out first, though, whether your roses produce attractive hips before you deadhead them, because if they do, you must obviously leave the dying flowers on.

Rugosa roses, for example, are noted for their huge hips like crab apples, while many *Rosa moyesii* hybrids, such as 'Geranium', 'Highdownensis' and 'Sealing Wax', have vivid red flagon-shaped hips. It would be pointless deadheading these, but most other roses will benefit, especially floribundas: they look tidier and will usually flower for longer. It's also a chance to do a bit of light pruning, so take your secateurs too, and cut each spent head back down at least to the first good leaf bud you come to – you can reduce the stem further if it looks rather long, always cutting just above an outward-facing bud or strong sideshoot. This will help shape up the plants as well as promote more growth.

BELOW The species rose, *R. moyesii,* is noted for its conspicuous red hips: 'Sealing Wax' has some of the largest and brightest.

LAWNS & HEDGES

Preparing to sow or turf a lawn

The two great talents you need for creating a wonderful lawn are a good eye and big feet – policemen should have the best lawns going. Whether you start with seed or turf, the preparation is really the secret of success and needs doing at least a month before you sow or turf, which is why I'm telling you about it now.

Start by digging over the whole area one spade deep, at the same time removing every perennial weed – docks, dandelions, daisies, buttercups and so on – together with all their root fragments. If there's a real mass of tangled weeds such as couch grass or ground elder, it could be worth spraying with glyphosate herbicide just this once. If you find the soil is really heavy and wet, make sure you don't have a 'hard pan' underneath – a solid layer caused by compaction – which you will have to break through.

Then simply dig in about a barrow-load of coarse grit per square metre to improve drainage, and as much manure or spent mushroom compost as you can spare. After that, leave the soil for a few weeks to allow annual seeds to germinate and for the soil to settle. When the weeds show themselves, hoe them off and you're ready to start levelling. And this is where your eye and feet come in.

Level with the back of a fork first and then go back over every square centimetre of soil, treading it down hard – provided the surface is dry it doesn't matter how firmly you tread, the grass will love it. It's a much more effective method than using a roller, which can ride over low patches leaving them soft. Then rake the soil level, stepping back from time to time to crouch down and squint across the surface: that way, the high and low spots are easy to see. When you're really satisfied, you can start sowing or turfing, either in September or in April, although spring sowing may involve more watering later.

Sowing the lawn

Don't be over-optimistic in your choice of grass seed. The finest mixtures look good on the packet, but need very regular attention: mowing twice a week, feeding, top-dressing, spiking and raking are all necessary to keep it in tip-top condition. If your children want to play football on it, forget the bowling green look and go for a tough rye-grass mixture – life is far too short to be forever nagging about the lawn.

Allow for 50g/sq.m (1½oz/sq.yd), although you can use less – it just takes longer to establish. Spread the seed thinly over the area, and go over it again with whatever's left until you've used all the seed. I find a good way is to put two 23cm (9in) plastic pots one inside the other, with the holes in the bottom misaligned; then you simply fill the top pot with grass seed and shake them over the soil surface. Rake the seed in using a spring-tine lawn rake, aiming to cover up at least half the seeds, and then stand back and wait for germination, which

RIGHT A well-tended lawn can be like a cool calm oasis when enclosed by meandering borders packed to the edges with vigorous flowering plants.

should take about a couple of weeks. If shortage of water might be a problem, have a hose and sprinkler to hand just to wet the surface from time to time.

If you feel all this is too much trouble and would prefer a faster result, see page 168 where I pass on the secret of laying turf successfully.

Trimming hedges

Because we all crave privacy and shelter from wind in our gardens, speed of growth is the name of the game when it comes to hedges. But by their very nature, most fast-growing plants that are suitable for the purpose just keep on going. So you need to keep an eagle eye on them while they're young and restrain them when necessary.

With most hedging plants, you simply let them go until they reach a little higher than the required height before cutting them back.

TRIMMING HEDGES

Fix a brightly coloured string to a couple of posts positioned at either end of the required cut, and trim by hand about 8–10cm (3–4in) in from the edge all along the line, using the string as a guide. Once you've established this finished level, take down the string and posts and finish the rest by eye with shears or a hedge trimmer.

Conifers can be allowed to grow 90cm (3ft) taller than needed, before pruning them back to 15cm (6in) below that height to develop a bushy top (see page 114). Beech and hornbeam are treated in the same way, but let them grow only 30cm (12in) taller than you want. Quickthorn and privet are best cut back hard after planting to force them to bush out right from the base. Privet is then trimmed two or three times in the summer, as shown on the left, while quickthorn is trimmed now if you want to have the pleasure of the flowers, or in spring if you want to keep it neater.

Formal hedges of box, yew or other evergreens will need attention even though you trimmed them to an immaculate finish in spring. Growth will be slowing down soon, so if you clip them now they should keep their strict outlines through the coming autumn and winter.

Whether you've got a new hedge or an established one, now is an ideal time for trimming. I like to cut my hedge by eye, stepping back every now and then just to make sure it's going right. After all these years I jolly well ought to be able to get the tops straight. But it's not easy, especially if you're using a power hedge trimmer.

I reckon cutting hedges with shears is by far the most accurate and satisfying way, but for a big expanse it's unrealistic. I use a petrol-engined machine, but there are many excellent mains electric models too; make sure you fit a circuit breaker to the socket before you use one, though – it could save your life. There are also battery machines which will do a good job for anything up to an hour or more before they need recharging.

VEGETABLES & HERBS

Protecting young seedlings

This is really the last chance to sow salads and a few other quick-maturing crops for harvesting later this year; but with temperatures normally so high this month, the sowings and seedlings need some shade to keep them comfortably cool. I provide the shade by draping a bit of 1.2m (6ft) wide windbreak material over the framework of my cloches. These consist of lengths of alkathene water pipe pushed into the ground to make large hoops spanning my 1.2m (4ft) wide beds (see page 35). In winter these are covered with polythene, but at this time of year I cover them instead with shading material which stays on until the weather turns cooler.

LATE SALAD CROPS TO SOW THIS MONTH

Restrict lettuces now to fast growing varieties such as 'Tom Thumb' or 'Little Gem', which should mature in about ten weeks. Try sowing some corn salad, which will carry on cropping through the winter, as will land cress. The endive 'Sally' is a great success if sown this month – the crisp self-blanching hearts staying in good condition until Christmas. Radishes are worth sowing too, both summer kinds such as 'French Breakfast' and 'Sparkler', and also cold-tolerant varieties like 'Robino' or 'Ribella', and winter 'China Rose' or 'Black Spanish'. And you may also try a hardy spring onion like 'Winter White Bunching'.

ABOVE Sheltered by a sunflower screen, rows of 'Primo' cabbages and 'Atlantic Giant' pumpkins almost fill the bed.

Then, if some of the crops fail to mature before cold weather sets in, I put clear polythene over the hoops for a more or less guaranteed harvest at the end of the year.

Before sowing try to rake some compost into the top 5cm (2in) of soil to assist water retention. I also use a sprinkle of pelleted chicken manure to feed the plants. Make sure the seeds have enough moisture to get them through the soil by taking out a shallow drill for sowing and watering it first. Allow the water to drain away, then sow the seeds and cover them with dry soil – then try not to water until the seedlings are showing through.

Growing Chinese vegetables

Many oriental leaf vegetables are used to cool summers and mild winters. It's easy to protect the sensitive varieties from the frost, but our hot summers often cause a lot of them to bolt to flower, which is why they're recommended for sowing after the longest day.

They're particularly useful because they'll grow right through the autumn, only stopping when it gets really cold, and even then a cloche or two will keep them going.

I suggest you start with the familiar Chinese cabbage, essential for autumn salads and stir-fries. The newer F_1 hybrids 'Green Rocket' and 'Tip Top' make tall cylindrical heads packed with crisp leaves. Grow plants about 38cm (15in) apart each way, and make sure they never go short of water.

Chinese kale, also called Chinese broccoli, can be harvested about 10–12 weeks from sowing. You can space plants of a variety like 'Green Lance' as close as 25cm (10in) apart and you'll soon be cutting fat heads of flower buds a bit like calabrese – smaller sideshoots follow, but you can also eat the stems if you peel off the tough skin.

I wouldn't be without the spicy leaves of mustard greens or Chinese mustard, which are grown in the same way as Chinese kale. For a milder flavour, harvest them young by snipping leaves off with scissors; but if you prefer something a bit hotter, leave them longer and they'll really add some spice to your cuisine.

FRUIT

Planting strawberries

If you don't already have strawberries, now is the time to buy some – either as bare-rooted plants or you can pay a bit more and get pot-grown ones which get away much faster.

Once you have bought your plants, you'll need to make a bed to plant them in. Raised beds are now all the rage commercially, but have

STRAWBERRIES THROUGH THE SEASON

I reckon it's possible to start eating strawberries in May and continue until the first frosts. The basic sequence starts with 'Honeyoye' – buy twice as many of these as of later varieties, so you can cover half of them with cloches in February to get an even earlier crop. Follow these with the maincrop 'Tenira', not as heavy-yielding as the standard 'Elsanta' but much tastier. After this the perpetual variety 'Aromel' will keep supplies going until beyond late summer.

I also grow the French variety 'Mara des Bois', which is as large as ordinary cultivated kinds but has the distinct flavour of wild strawberries – and what's more, it produces one crop in the spring and another in the autumn. Finally, I wouldn't be without 'Cambridge Late Pine', which is an old strawberry raised just after the last war, and well worth keeping going: its flavour is unique, very sweet and aromatic.

129

PROPAGATING AND FORCING STRAWBERRIES

Use a wire 'hairpin' to peg plantlets down, either direct in the ground or in 8cm (3in) pots of compost. Once rooted, the plantlets can be detached from their parents.

been used in gardens for years and are still reckoned the best method. Make the beds about 1.2m (4ft) wide, dig them over thoroughly and incorporate lots of well-rotted manure or compost. This should raise the surface about 8–15cm (3–6in) above the paths, and you can either keep this in place with edging boards or simply mound up sloping sides with a rake.

Cover the beds with black polythene, buried at the edges, and plant through cross-slits cut in the plastic at 60cm (2ft) intervals. That way there'll be no weeding to do, no need to mulch with straw later on, and very little watering either, especially if you install buried irrigation. For this you need a 'leaky pipe', which oozes droplets of water along its length once it is connected to a hose. Run a pipe down each side of the bed, about 30cm (12in) in from the edge, before you set the black plastic in place.

Tidying and propagating strawberries

By this time of year your plants will have finished fruiting, and many young runners will have started rooting into the soil between the parent plants. If you don't want to grow more plants, you can use a rotary mower to cut down the main plant so that only the bare crown is left in the centre. If you do want to propagate more plants, use a pair of shears to cut down the parent plant to ensure you don't disturb the runners. Then select the best plantlets and pin them down as shown on the left.

Forcing strawberries

If you want to have the earliest possible fruit, transfer a few rooted plantlets to 13cm (5in) pots. Leave these outside where you'll notice them and remember to water if necessary. In December, turn them on their sides: they'll have stopped growing by then, and should not be allowed to get waterlogged or they'll rot off. After a good cold rest they'll be bursting to grow, so in February bring them indoors – into the greenhouse or on to a sunny windowsill. Remember you'll need to fertilise the open flowers by dabbing each one with a soft paintbrush, because there'll be few insects around that early. Even without any heat you'll still be picking fruit weeks ahead of outdoor crops, but a little warmth will bring them on even earlier.

Summer-pruning tree fruit

In Victorian times head gardeners were a feared and respected race, but I reckon they actually made the art of pruning seem more difficult than it really is in order to preserve their superior place. But nature gives you a helping hand along the way, so it's not nearly as difficult as some would make out – in fact, pruning apples, pears and soft fruit like gooseberries and red currants can be as complicated or as simple as you want to make it.

Trained forms – cordons, fans, espaliers and so on (see page 68) – are pruned now rather than in winter. Since cordons are the easiest

PRUNING FRUIT TREES

| 3 years old | 2 years old | | 1 year old | this year |

Each year the new growth of the main sideshoots can be pruned back to about 8cm (3in), cutting just above a bud to form new fruiting spurs.

Also shorten any new shoots growing from established spurs to 2.5cm (1in) long, again cutting just above a bud.

LEFT Many vegetables make decorative foliage plants, and few can rival the lush extravagance of courgettes or the towering magnificence of runner beans.

form to explain, let's start with these. They consist of one or more stems, on which you build up collections of short twiggy sideshoots called 'spurs', and it's on these that the fruit is borne. The main leading shoot will be needed to increase the length of the stem, so leave that alone until it reaches full height, then cut off the tip and turn it into a spur.

Espaliers and fans are no more complicated: each is a series of branches, and all you do is treat each branch as if it were a cordon. So once you've spent about 10 minutes on each tree, you can happily pass the rest of the day making apple pie – or eating it.

Dealing with raspberries

Once summer raspberries have been harvested, cut out the old canes and tie in the strong new ones 10cm (4in) apart.

MISCELLANEOUS

Discouraging slugs

One of the biggest threats to plants in any garden is slugs, which seem to be on the rampage for most of the year. Soft young leaf growth is the gourmet slug's version of a Waldorf salad, and as yet there's no final answer to the problem. But there's a lot we can do to give our plants a helping hand.

First, get nature on your side. If slugs are hungry, birds and black beetles and frogs are even hungrier, and these will eat both the slugs and their eggs. The eggs, and later on the baby slugs, are often just below the soil surface and regular hoeing will turn them up for the birds or carabid beetles. To catch the night-feeding adult slugs, put out a few boards or bits of tile or slate for them to hide under at daybreak;

then simply turn them over to expose them to their enemies.

Cut-down plastic bottles are effective barriers – select vulnerable plants like young hostas, lupins and delphiniums, and all brassicas, and surround them with a plastic screen pressed a little way into the soil. I'm doubtful about the effectiveness of rough materials like toasted eggshells and gritty ash. A collar of lime works for brassicas, but for other plants it may change the acidity of the soil too much. Soot is an effective barrier and does nothing but good to the soil provided it is weathered for a few months. If you can bear to do it, picking up slugs and snails, or trapping them and then disposing of them can help a bit, but alas, there will be thousands, so you can never hope to win. Hunt them down at night with a torch – and don't give in to the temptation to throw them next door, because they have the homing instinct of pigeons.

I haven't mentioned pellets because I worry about the risk they pose to wildlife, although evidence of this is fairly rare. They are certainly the most effective control, but I never use them myself. If the problem gets really out of hand and slugs become a serious plague, you might have to admit defeat and not grow susceptible plants like hostas. Remember though, a cold winter may not thin the slug population much, but it does kill a lot of their eggs, which is something to be said in favour of hard frost.

PLANTS FOR
august

1 Commonly known as bergamot, bee balm or Oswego tea, hardy perennial *Monarda didyma* develops into a neat clump of 90cm (3ft) herbaceous flowering stems, in a number of warm colours.

2 The large hollyhock-like blooms of *Lavatera* 'Barnsley' open in profusion all summer and cover the 1.8m (6ft) hardy shrubs with masses of conspicuous 5cm (2in) flowers. These are pure white with a red eye, fading to a soft pink.

3 *Bracteantha* (formerly *Helichrysum*) *bracteata* 'Drakkar Mixed' is the familiar straw flower, with brightly coloured papery petals. Often used for dried indoor arrangements, it is sown under glass as a half-hardy annual and grows up to 90cm (3ft) high.

1

2

3

4 The late-flowering clematis 'Madame Julia Correvon' is a viticella hybrid. Very hardy, it grows to 4m (13ft) eventually; both foliage and blooms are larger than others of its type, and the flower display is long and generous.

5 *H. paniculata* 'Grandiflora' is one of the showiest hydrangeas. Very hardy and shade-tolerant, it is 3m (10ft) or more tall and wide, with vigorous open woody stems. Annual pruning and mulching promotes large blooms.

4

5

*E*arly autumn was the time for new plants to go into the borders. Before they were planted, Geoff would read up everything he could about them. He was very particular about naming them correctly, as well as about giving them the best possible conditions. He might talk about plants using their common names, but he always knew the botanical ones. He once said that although a little learning can be a dangerous thing, a little Latin could be very helpful. If, for example, you knew that 'flore pleno' simply meant a double version of a flower you were half way to visualizing it. The only trouble with having studied Latin myself was that his botanical Latin sometimes clashed with my classical Latin – in the pronunciation of such names as 'Senecio', for example. However, as I adjusted to his over the years, I found my Latin vocabulary broadening – for instance, I hadn't realised that 'flavus' meant yellow.

Ornamental grasses make forceful statements in a large border, where dwarf pampas grass, *Cortaderia pumila*, flowers behind the sword-like leaves of phormium and the arching heads of *Pennisetum alopecurioides*.

september

key tasks for september

ANNUALS & BEDDING PLANTS
○ Take cuttings of bedding plant, before the first frosts, page 136
○ Prepare tender perennials, including dahlias and fuchsias, for over-wintering, page 137

BORDER PERENNIALS
○ Overhaul borders, planting and dividing hardy perennials, page 138
○ Collect and sow ripe seeds, page 139

ROSES
○ Take cuttings of roses, page 139
○ Save and sow seeds from rose hips, page 139

BULBS
○ Plant bulbs outdoors for next spring and summer, page 140
○ Force hyacinths for Christmas, page 141

LAWNS
○ Give lawns a little early autumn care, taking out weeds and 'thatch', page 142

VEGETABLES & HERBS
○ Store squashes for winter, page 142
○ Prepare onions for lifting, and plant new sets, page 142
○ Plant and sow spring cabbages, page 142

FRUIT
○ Protect, pick and store tree fruits, page 144

MISCELLANEOUS
○ Consider buying a greenhouse before winter sets in, page 144

ANNUALS & BEDDING PLANTS

Taking cuttings of bedding plants
Tender perennial bedding plants, usually grown as summer annuals, are all likely to be hit by the frosts quite soon. Pelargoniums, petunias, marguerites, fuchsias, abutilons, diascias and those wonderful South African osteospermums are all at risk, but there are ways to ensure their survival unscathed over winter. If you haven't room to keep the old plants safe under glass until next spring, try taking cuttings, which is very easy to do at this time of year.

Choose a strong healthy young shoot about 8cm (3in) long, and trim it just below a leaf joint with a sharp knife. Remove the bottom leaves, leaving two or perhaps three at the top, and cut off pelargonium stipules, those small green 'leaves' underneath each leaf stalk. Pelargonium cuttings can be dibbled into compost straight away, but other kinds are best plunged into a fungicide solution, and their cut ends then dipped in hormone rooting powder.

Insert the cuttings to half their depth in cuttings compost, or you can make your own from equal parts of peat-free compost and vermiculite. Arrange the cuttings around the edge of 10cm (4in) pots or, if you have a lot, use modules – these are like large seed trays divided into separate cells, and you just put one cutting in each cell.

Place in a shaded frame for a few weeks until rooted, and then pot them up individually into 8cm (3in) pots. As soon as frost threatens, bring them inside, into a conservatory or spare room kept at least frost-free and ideally at 7°C (45°F). Don't put the pots on a windowsill, because it will be too cold: instead, arrange a table near the window and draw the curtains at night for protection.

Keep the cuttings fairly dry during winter and don't feed at all. They'll tick over until the end of February, when you can bring them into the kitchen or sitting room where it's warmer. Start to feed with liquid fertiliser, and they'll grow into fine young plants for putting out in late May or early June.

Over-wintering tender perennials
All those glorious perennials need last-minute care to make sure they are safe all winter until you coax them back into growth next spring.

Dahlias should really be left outdoors until the frost blackens their foliage before you dig them up for storing in a frost-free place. Lift the tubers, shake off as much soil as you can, and then trim off all the old stems. Tip the tubers upside down to drain for a week, then pack them, right way up, in cardboard boxes, and store them in a cool greenhouse or a spare room.

Perennial salvias such as *S. patens* can be lifted after the frost has finished off their tops, and will keep safely in a little moist compost under the greenhouse staging. The more familiar scarlet salvias will also keep from one year to the next if you pot them up and keep them just moist in good light.

The dusky maroon *Cosmos atrosanguineus* can be treated like a dahlia, or in milder counties you could risk it outdoors under a thick mulch of bark. Marguerites (argyranthemums) can be potted up like houseplants and will often

flower into the winter, or you can store them like pelargoniums, only not quite so dry.

Potting up fuchsias
Tender fuchsias that have been bedded out or used for hanging baskets can be treated in two ways. Either fork them up and pot them in fairly small pots, and then bring them into a heated greenhouse or a cool well-lit room to carry on growing. Otherwise cut the tops back by half, pot them up and leave

ABOVE A small border can support an amazing variety of plants, with productive kinds such as artichokes and perennial onions tucked among summer flowers, provided the soil is regularly fortified with compost or well-rotted manure.

them in a cold but frost-free place. Don't let them dry out, but avoid over-watering. In the spring trim them back further to leave about 2.5–5cm (1–2in) of last year's shoots (see page 41).

137

BORDER PERENNIALS

This is a good time to start overhauling borders, because you will still be able to see where everything is and how much space it takes up. Start with the herbaceous perennials this month, move on to evergreen shrubs next and get on to the deciduous shrubs after their leaves have fallen.

Planting new perennials

Garden centres often stock a good range of perennials in 10cm (4in) pots at this time of year. If they're reasonably priced you can buy four or five to plant in groups to join up quickly and make large clumps.

Revive as large an area of soil as you can: work in well-rotted manure, garden compost or spent mushroom compost for all but acid borders. New plants will also benefit from a little general organic fertiliser or pelleted chicken manure. Prepare the whole area, not just planting holes because these can act as sumps and drown the plants.

When you knock the plants out of their pots, check to see if the roots are running round the bottom in a tight coil. If they are, ease them out a little so that they start to grow out and search for water and food. After planting, even if the soil is quite wet, water the plants in. This gives them a good start and also helps to settle the soil around the roots – they shouldn't need any more water until the spring.

Dividing old perennials

Most herbaceous plants thrive on being lifted, split up and replanted every 3–5 years. But it's worth looking them up in a book, because some, including the ice plant (*Sedum*) and yarrow (*Achillea*) like this treatment every year, and a few, particularly gypsophila and peonies, prefer to stay put. Others, such as alstroemerias and Japanese anemones, take a season or two to settle down after being disturbed.

Some perennials might have outgrown their allotted space, while others will have an ugly bald patch in the centre of the clump with all the young growth on the outside. These should all be lifted with a fork and put on to a large piece of polythene. You can often break or cut off a few juicy young bits from the outside of the clump with a spade. These are then transplanted into soil revitalised with plenty of good compost, while the tired old centres are thrown away. Or you can split clumps with two digging forks inserted back to back to divide them into smaller pieces.

LEFT Against background hints of early autumn mists, the Rugosa rose 'Roseraie de l'Hay' draws to the end of its long flowering season, while *Cosmos* 'Sensation', always at its best in autumn, blooms profusely.

Collecting seeds

Collecting seeds is the cheapest way to produce hundreds of extra plants, and it's great fun to do. Choose a dry day and look for flower heads containing brown dry seedpods. Cut the whole head and put it into a paper bag – don't forget to label it clearly. If the seedheads are even the slightest bit damp though, lay them on newspaper to dry.

After a week or so, tip the contents onto a sheet of paper. Often the seeds will have fallen out, but if not, break open the pods and shake them out. However careful you are, you can't avoid a mixture of seeds and chaff, which must be separated because it's the chaff that harbours diseases. Use a flour sieve or the point of a knife, or simply blow the chaff away gently.

Most hardy perennial seeds can be sown straight away on top of moist compost and covered with a shallow layer of coarse grit. Put them in a cold frame and they'll either germinate in a few weeks' time or next spring. Half-hardy seeds should be stored in labelled envelopes in a cool dry place for sowing next spring in gentle heat.

SELF-SET SEEDLINGS

Many plants shed seeds naturally to produce seedlings for the following year, and it's a pity to waste them. Some, like opium poppies for example, can be left where they grow to flower in natural groups. Others such as hellebores are best lifted and transplanted at the seedling stage, or they'll create too much competition for their parents.

ROSES

If you're particularly fond of one or two roses in the garden, why not try and propagate a few more from cuttings or seeds? They may not come true, and some varieties are reluctant to form roots, but if you're prepared for the occasional loss, it's worth having a go.

Taking rose cuttings

You can take cuttings any time from now until about Christmas but, like all hardwood cuttings, you'll be more successful while the soil still has some summer warmth left in it. Look for strong healthy stems about pencil-thick, and cut them low down on the bush. Deal with them as shown on the right.

You can avoid the need for weeding by preparing an area as big as you'll need in advance, digging it a spade deep and working in a little sharp sand and good garden compost on heavy soil. Once you've buried the cuttings, cover the area with woven plastic mulching sheet, making slits to let the rose cuttings poke through to the light. Bury the edges of the sheet in the soil to secure it. After that there's nothing to worry about until transplanting time, about a year later.

Roses from seed

Most species of rose come true to type from seed. Just gather a hip or two, split them open and remove the seeds. Sow these straight away in a pot or tray of well-drained seed compost, and cover with a layer of grit. Put a piece of wire netting over the pot to deter mice, and place in a cold frame. Seedlings may appear this coming spring, or next.

TAKING ROSE CUTTINGS

I Cut stems of at least the thickness of a pencil, preferably just above a new shoot.

2 Trim the bottom to just below a bud, and the top to just above one, leaving the cuttings about 20–23cm (8–9in) long. Dip the bottoms in hormone rooting powder.

3 Cover the bottom of a slit trench with coarse sand, then bury the cuttings, leaving about 8cm (3in) above soil level.

BULBS

Planting spring bulbs

There's a whole range of bulbs on offer about now that are almost guaranteed to provide a bright and cheering show for you next spring. The ones to start off with are daffodils: if they have the chance to make a really good root system before the worst of winter, they'll reward you with better and earlier flowers. The flowering season is said to last for a hundred days, starting with the earliest, the small cyclamineus varieties which appear in February, and ending with Pheasant's Eye kinds such as 'Actaea', which are usually still flowering in May.

As with all bulbs, it's essential to plant them at the right depth because shallow planting is one reason why they can go blind after the first year. As a general rule, get all bulbs in so they are covered with 2–3 times their own depth in soil.

Tulips are best left until last – planting them in early November (see page 166) helps protect them against slug damage and the fungus disease tulip fire.

Crocuses are popular favourites that go in now, as soon as possible, and there's a huge selection to choose from, either as single colours or (more cheaply) as mixtures; one of the earliest is *C. tommasinianus*. All are best planted in large informal groups in the sun; cover them with about 5cm (2in) of soil.

There are several ornamental onions (*Allium*) which make a bold display, generally with rounded flower heads. Short-stemmed *A. moly* and *A. ostrowskianum* are for the front of the border, but there are other later-flowering kinds that are much taller. For example, *A. giganteum*, *A. rosenbachianum* and *A.* 'Gladiator' can reach 1.2–1.5m (4–5ft) and look splendid in the middle or back of the border. Leave them undisturbed and they will form quite large clumps.

Anemone blanda is one of the best and most reliable of the small spring-flowering bulbs, and ideal for a shady spot under deciduous shrubs. It makes large clumps of brightly coloured daisies in shades of blue, and there's a pure white form too. The crown imperial fritillaries (*Fritillaria imperialis*) have been grown in cottage gardens for centuries and are not to be missed. They produce large yellow or orange flowers on tall stout stems, but cover them with at least 10cm (4in) of soil or they may not flower in future years. Smaller fritillaries such as our native snake's head (*F. meleagris*) are superb in retentive soil in sun or part shade.

Work in a bit of garden compost and a light dressing of organic fertiliser before planting in the ground or in containers. The answer to the problem of untidy bulb foliage after flowering is to tuck the bulbs among herbaceous plants such as hostas, rodgersias and brunneras. When the bulbs are

NATURALISING SPRING BULBS

1 Instead of arranging bulbs formally in neat groups, scatter them in natural drifts on the surface of the grass and plant them exactly where they have fallen.

2 Lift large turves with a spade and plant several bulbs underneath each one, or use a cylindrical bulb planter to excavate a plug of soil. Plant the bulb and replace the plug.

PLANTING DEPTHS FOR BULBS

As a rule of thumb, the ideal planting depth for any bulb is roughly three times its own size from tip to base, although a little more or less isn't critical.

in flower the herbaceous plants have lost their leaves, but once the bulbs have finished, up come the hostas etc., unfurling their leaves and covering untidy foliage.

Alternatively, sow some of the hardier annuals over the bulbs: calendula, convolvulus, echium, eschscholzia, godetia, iberis and nigella are ideal. These will take over in late spring and flower until about July or August, often seeding themselves afterwards.

Starting bulbs in pots

I'm hopeless at remembering where I planted my last lot of daffodils so, instead of putting my new ones straight into the borders, I pot them up during the first part of this month, and plunge the pots in compost outdoors until the spring, as shown below.

They can stay in the plunge bed until the tips poke through in the spring. By that time, those in the borders will also be showing, so you'll know exactly where to plant the new ones. When you do, plant them deeply so that you bury the white blanched part of the stems that was covered with compost.

Planting summer bulbs

Although attention is concentrated on bulbs for spring right now, don't forget the summer-flowering ones, including galtonias and camassias, that should also go in now. Summer hyacinths (*Galtonia*) produce 90cm (3ft) tall white spires that make a fine sight in the borders, while camassias make clumps of grassy foliage, from which arise 75cm (30in) tall spires of starry flowers in shades of blue and also white. They both like rich retentive soils, bulk up quite fast, and can be split and replanted every few years.

Forcing hyacinths indoors

If you're after hyacinths for Christmas, make sure you buy specially prepared bulbs. Plant them early, certainly by the middle of this month, in separate pots or

ABOVE An inspired partnership between autumn-flowering bulbs, *Nerine bowdenii* and *Colchicum speciosum*: both are stars of the warm sunny border at this time of year.

PLUNGING BULBS

Once potted up, hardy bulbs are best kept in a corner where it is cool but frost-free. Covering them with a thick mulch stops them freezing, and also ensures complete darkness to coax them into growth. I make a plunge bed of old compost, and cover the pots so that the bulbs are buried at the same depth as if planted outdoors.

together in boxes, and put them into a shady corner covered with a good depth of moist garden compost; alternatively a cool but frost-free garage will do. The idea is to try to encourage plenty of root growth before the shoots appear.

Bring them inside into a cool room after about twelve weeks, or when the buds can be seen. When they begin to colour up transfer them to bowls, using three or five bulbs per bowl. If you do it that way, you can make sure that all the flowers are at the same stage of development for a balanced show that will perfume the whole house by Christmas week.

LAWNS

Early autumn care

At this time of year, especially after a dry summer, lawns may need a spot of intensive care. Start by taking out deep-rooted weeds such as dandelions. Tackle them with a daisy grubber, one of those new tools that twist them out, root and all, or cut them out with a knife, getting down as deep as you can, but don't use a weedkiller. For weeds in large patches, use a large pruning knife or one with a curved end. If this leaves a bald patch, you can re-seed straight away by adding grass seed to a mixture of soil, garden compost and sharp sand.

Dead growth or 'thatch' may have accumulated at soil level, and where this has happened it should be scratched out with a rake.

BELOW Dead 'thatch' builds up around grass roots after a summer of mowing, and needs to be raked out vigorously.

VEGETABLES & HERBS

Storing squashes

Marrows, pumpkins and all the other winter squashes need proper seasoning before they can be stored indoors. Cut them when they are full size and a good colour, and then lay them out in the sunshine to harden for a fortnight, or in the greenhouse or a sunny window if it's wet. After this treatment they will keep in good condition in a frost-free place well into winter.

Courgettes can be stored until Christmas or so if you leave a few fruits to grow as large as small marrows. Raise them up off the ground on bricks or a piece of wood to get a sun-tan, turning them from time to time between now and the end of October. When the skins are hardened they will keep just like proper marrows and, what's more, the flavour improves with every week in store.

Preparing onions for lifting

Maincrop onions that are starting to turn yellow at the tips should be prepared for lifting now. Insert a digging fork under the bulbs and lift them slightly to loosen the roots without breaking them. This will hasten ripening, but don't bend the tops over as this can invite disease.

Planting autumn onion sets

At the same time you can plan for the next crop by planting autumn onion sets. Varieties such as 'Radar', 'Swift' and 'Unwin's First Early' mature in late June or July, so they are way ahead of the main crop, and you can even use them sooner direct from the ground. Plant them between now and early November, 8cm (3in) apart in drills just deep enough to cover the top of the set. Use about half the fertiliser application normal for summer-grown crops, and then give them a boost next March with a dressing of high nitrogen feed.

Planting spring cabbages

Spring cabbage plants sown in a seedbed last month can be planted out now, especially if you have cleared maincrop onions for storing. Simply clean and weed the bed, rake in a half-dressing of general fertiliser, then level it off and it will be ready for the young plants, spaced 15cm (6in) apart in rows 30cm (12in) apart.

Next spring you can use every other plant for spring greens, and then give the rest a feed to encourage them to heart up for later. There's still time to sow another batch of a fast variety like 'Duncan' or 'Pixie' for continuity, either in a seedbed for transplanting next month or where they are to grow, thinning the seedlings to the right spacing.

Flea beetles often attack these young cabbages, drilling tiny holes in their leaves, but here's a way to get rid of them without killing all the beneficial insects too. Take a 10 x 15cm (4 x 6in) board and coat one side with petroleum jelly or fruit tree grease. If you pass the board over the affected plants, the beetles will jump up and stick to the grease – hence the 'flea' in their name.

RIGHT The allotment garden at Barnsdale shows how much can be packed into a small space without compromising good looks: sweetcorn, tomatoes, beans and onions make maximum use of a narrow bed.

FRUIT

Protecting tree fruits

It's not a bad idea to take steps this month to protect your ripening apples, pears and other tree fruits from hungry birds. Just one peck is enough to start them rotting or to attract wasps, who promptly set upon the fruit to complete the job. In the banana plantations of Central America the trees are almost constantly festooned with polythene bags, and that's one safe bet for controlling birds. If you have the time, put a perforated clear polythene bag over the top of each ripening fruit, secure it with a twist tie, and you will be guaranteed to get there first. If you grow trained trees, it's not too difficult to cover the whole tree with netting, while on larger trees you could try hanging a few strips of brightly coloured polythene in the branches as a deterrent.

Picking and storing tree fruits

Early apples such as 'Discovery' and 'Katy' should be eaten straight from the tree, of course, because they don't store very well. But sometimes that's easier said than done, especially if birds and wasps are going for them. To foil this, I pick my apples when they're ready to eat and store them in the same way as later varieties. You can keep them in the traditional way, by wrapping them individually in paper and then laying them out in single layers in open trays in a cool shed or garage.

Another way is to put about 1kg (2lb) of undamaged apples into a polythene bag and close the top. There will be a build-up of carbon dioxide – the gas used by fruit farmers to prolong the life of fruit in cold stores – in the bag. But you don't want too much of it, so make two pinpricks in the bag and then store in as cold a place as possible (but not freezing), where the fruit should last for a couple of months.

Harvesting and storing perfect pears is a work of art. William Robinson, the great Victorian gardener, reckoned there was just one day in the year when pears would be perfect for picking. That's perhaps a bit extreme, but they're certainly difficult to time. If you like them on the hard side, it's no problem; but if you prefer them soft and juicy, you need to pick them just before they are fully ripe andthen store them on their ends in open boxes in a cool place. Bring a few at a time indoors to finish ripening for two days, to eat at their succulent best. And how do you know that perfect day when they are ready to pick? Experience – so keep experimenting!

LEFT Even early apple varieties will keep for several weeks in the cool darkness of a polythene-lined underground store.

MISCELLANEOUS

The benefits of a greenhouse

I wouldn't be able to achieve half what I do in the garden without my greenhouse. I raise all my own bedding and vegetable plants there. I overwinter tender perennials, and in summer I raise crops such as tomatoes, aubergines, cucumbers, peppers and melons, as well as flowering pot plants.

A greenhouse will pay for itself in about two years – but if you include entertainment and enjoyment, it won't owe you anything after the first month. But don't wait until the spring before getting one. Wise gardeners get one jump ahead and you could make a start straight away with protection for chrysanthemums, dahlias and

EARLY BLOOMS UNDER GLASS

As soon as you have your greenhouse, raid the perennial border for astilbes, hostas, dicentras, pulmonarias and hellebores. Young divisions of these can be potted up in containers as small as will take them comfortably. Stand them in an unheated greenhouse, or in a cold frame for bringing indoors in late February, and they'll give you a really early spring display long before outside plants have woken up. If you also buy a couple of patio roses and pot these up in the same way, they'll make an extra-early show. But don't keep the plants in the warm too long after flowering; they'll be better off planted outside once more.

ABOVE Although essentially practical, some greenhouses are attractive structures, and this octagonal cedar-wood design will double as a small decorative summerhouse.

fuchsias, and a sowing of winter vegetables such as hardy varieties of lettuces and carrots.

Choosing a greenhouse

Choice depends on your budget. Buy as big as you can afford, but remember you do get what you pay for. Small polythene ones cost a fraction of a smart aluminium house, while the permanence of glass is comforting and presents fewer problems to growing plants than plastic. Make sure there's enough ventilation: at least one roof vent per 1.2m (4ft) run is necessary, preferably side vents too, so a 2.4 x 1.8m (8 x 6ft) house should have at least two vents in the top and two in the sides. I would also recommend the built-in base most manufacturers offer – this gives a good professional finish and makes erection easier.

145

PLANTS FOR
september

1 The dwarf guelder rose, *Viburnum opulus* 'Compactum', forms a dense 1.5m (5ft) deciduous shrub, with showy flattened heads of white lacecap flowers in June, and red berries and leaf tints in autumn.

2 *Imperata cylindrica* 'Rubra' or Japanese blood grass, here seen with *Sedum* 'Vera Jameson', is a deciduous 45cm (18in) grass for good soils. Noted for its bright red autumn leaf tips, it is not quite hardy and benefits from winter protection.

3 The sea holly hybrid, *Eryngium* x *tripartitum*, is a branching and colourful hardy herbaceous perennial. Its 75cm (30in) stems grow from a basal rosette and are crowned with steely-blue rounded flower heads.

4 Like all its *Allium* relatives, the leek (*A. porrum*) has dramatic ornamental flower heads if plants are left for a second season.

5 *Caryopteris clandonensis*, a hardy perennial shrub, grows up to 1.2m (4ft) tall. It flowers well on most soils, especially light sandy ones, and needs hard pruning every spring.

OVERLEAF Maples are supreme trees and shrubs for autumn tints: here the rich incendiary red of *Acer palmatum* 'Osakazuki' is all the more vivid against the buttery yellow foliage of the snakebark maple, *A.* 'Silver Vein'.

1

2

3

4

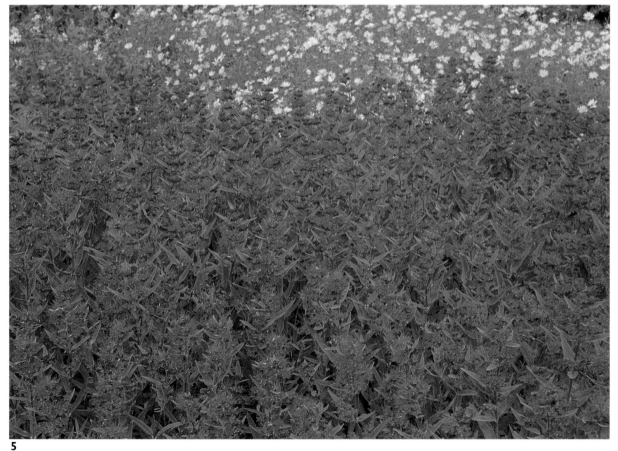

5

Recording had finished by the beginning of October, leaving Geoff the time for major appraisals in the garden. Throughout the year he kept copious notes which he used as the basis of his articles and books, but also as a fount of ideas for new projects. We would walk round the garden while Geoff bounced his ideas off me, describing in detail what he could see in his mind's eye: he really was able to visualise the completed plan perfectly in 3-D.

Much as Geoff enjoyed the daily demands of the garden, especially the propagating, what excited him more than anything was the start of a big new undertaking. He'd make plans in great detail so that when they went into action, everything seemed to fall seamlessly in place. Coming home one day from the school where I taught, I found that what had been the cottage garden had disappeared from outside the kitchen window. Inspired by Beth Chatto's garden in Essex, he had decided to make a Mediterranean garden. Within a month it had taken shape and been planted. Within a couple of years it looked as though it had always been there.

Dramatic colour compositions and contrasts are typical of October: bright michaelmas daisies and the opulent foliage of purple sage blend with the changing tints of background shrubs and trees.

october

key tasks for october

CONTAINER PLANTS
○ Plant up outdoor containers for winter and spring, page 152

SHRUBS, TREES & CLIMBERS
○ Plant new trees and shrubs now to minimise the stress to the plants, page 153
○ Take hardwood cuttings while the soil is still warm, page 156
○ Move large shrubs, page 156

LAWNS & HEDGES
○ Plan space for hedges, page 157
○ Choose deciduous or conifer hedges, page 157
○ Plant hedges of all kinds, page 158

VEGETABLES & HERBS
○ Harvest root crops for storing, page 159
○ Plant garlic before the weather turns cold, page 159
○ Protect late vegetables against frost, page 160

FRUIT
○ Harvest maincrop apples, page 160
○ Protect apple and pear trees against winter moth, page 160
○ Prune blackcurrants, page 160
○ Invest in a fruit cage to protect next year's crops, page 160

MISCELLANEOUS
○ Start digging, but take it gently, page 161
○ Encourage earthworms, page 161

CONTAINER PLANTS

Containers for winter plantings

I've seen summer displays in plastic buckets, china chamber pots, and discarded boots or shoes. But for winter use, choose containers made of clay, stone or wood, which offer more protection. Make sure that they're frost-proof and, even if they are, give them the best chance of survival by avoiding waterlogging: if water freezes in a pot, it could expand and crack it. And even the hardiest plant can be vulnerable if the roots get frozen. This could seriously injure plants, especially evergreens which do not go dormant in winter and can suffer badly from dehydration if the contents of the pot are frozen solid. So before the hard frosts arrive, wrap containers all round with a few layers of bubble polythene or sacking, tied in place with string. Wet soil won't do the plants any good either, so check that there are plenty of drainage holes, and stand the containers on a few pieces of slate or tile to keep the holes clear of the ground.

Planting up pots for winter and spring

Start by putting a good layer of pebbles or broken clay pots in the bottom before filling with compost. I like to use a very free-draining mixture, which is very important for anything that's going to stand outdoors all winter – soil-based John Innes No. 1 or 2 composts are ideal. If you're replanting a pot already filled with a JI mixture, just stir in some garden or mushroom compost, plus a handful of general fertiliser. For new pots, start with

SHRUBS, TREES & CLIMBERS

The best time for planting

Up to the early 1960s, nurserymen (there were no garden centres in those days) grew their plants in the field and lifted and sold them to us through the autumn and winter. Then came plants in containers, and we began to buy most of our plants in the spring when the weather warmed up a bit. But in fact the traditional autumn planting of trees and shrubs is still best, and essential for bare-rooted ones. Planting is a cause of stress for plants: they are seriously disturbed and have to get used to new conditions above and below ground.

So it's sensible to plant deciduous trees and shrubs at a time of least stress, between now and early spring. Growth of shoots comes to a standstill, and there's little or no water loss – lack of water is the biggest cause of failure at other times of year. The plants can put all their energies into making new roots while the soil still has much of its summer warmth. What's more, after losing their leaves, deciduous trees and shrubs actually have a natural surge of root growth.

Evergreens are slightly different. Instead of shedding their leaves all in one go, they drop them continuously, a few at a time, so growth never stops. So even in winter there'll be some water loss from the leaves, though with lower temperatures it'll certainly be less than in summer. This means that for evergreens, as well as deciduous plants, the best time to plant is now, when the soil's still warm, shoot growth is at its slowest, and there's little likelihood of drought.

the drainage layer and then cover this with fresh potting compost, at least 15cm (6in) deep and about 23cm (9in) from the top.

Bulbs are obvious winners for early colour. Plant daffs 5–8cm (2–3in) apart, and then cover them with an 8cm (3in) depth of compost. On this set a tier of tulip bulbs, about the same distance apart – even if you inadvertently plant one right on top of a daff, the lower bulb will soon find a way through. Cover these, and then plant some bedding.

To add a bit of height, I like to use a bushy evergreen in the centre, something like a small *Viburnum tinus* or a variegated elaeagnus, such as *E. pungens* 'Maculata' or *E. × ebbingei* 'Limelight' which can be planted out in the garden in late

ABOVE The varied succulent stonecrops such as *Sedum telephium* 'Autumn Joy' are important flowers both for late colour in borders and containers, and as a food source for the last butterflies.

spring when you change the planting scheme. Around this centrepiece you could plant wallflowers, forget-me-nots, winter pansies and bellis daisies: bear in mind there won't be a lot of growth between now and spring flowering time, so choose good bushy plants and set them in the container so that they're almost touching.

Finally push in a few small bulbs like crocus and muscari, and you'll have all the ingredients for a stunning show from early winter through to mid-spring.

There are exceptions to the general rule that autumn is the best time for planting trees and shrubs. The plants which are best left until spring are those that don't like wet conditions – most of the grey-leafed species, such as santolina, and certainly any with woolly leaves, such as stachys; any species of borderline hardiness, such as French lavender; and those that move reluctantly, such as silver birch.

Planting deciduous trees and shrubs

If you observe a few basic rules, you shouldn't go far wrong. Always prepare as wide an area as possible to avoid the possibility of isolated holes filling with water and drowning plants. Dig thoroughly, adding plenty of organic matter such as compost, manure or one of the bagged planting mixtures, and add some bonemeal. Plant at the same level as the tree or shrub grew before, firm gently afterwards. Stake trees securely with supports that come about a third of the way up the stem and attach them with adjustable tree ties.

Use a general fertiliser in spring, keep an eye on watering during the first summer, and control the weeds because competition from these can really set back growth. The best way to do this is to surround the base of the tree or shrub with a square of woven planting fabric.

LEFT Bold planting on a grand scale emphasises the passage of seasonal colour at Barnsdale. Massed groups of michaelmas daisies flower early in autumn, followed by the bright-tinted foliage of acer and sumach, with the vivid red stems of dogwood continuing the sequence.

PLANTING A BARE-ROOTED TREE

Prepare the hole and hammer in a short support stake (about one-third of the tree's height) then place the bare-rooted tree in the hole. Use a cane to check that the old soil mark on the stem of the tree will correspond with the new soil level when the hole is filled in. Fix the tree to the stake with a proper plastic tree tie and attach the tie to the stake with a short nail. The tie can be adjusted as the tree grows, and removed altogether after three years.

PLANTING A CLEMATIS

Plant clematis so that the top of the compost that surrounds the rootball is about 15cm (6in) below soil level, in case it is attacked by clematis wilt. Lean the plant towards its support or host and, until it is established, leave in a cane to support its leading stem.

TREES FOR SMALL GARDENS

I firmly believe an important choice like this should be left to you, but for what it's worth, here are my top four small trees.

Acer griseum is perhaps the best specimen maple for small gardens. It has amazing bark which becomes bright cinnamon in colour and peels in a most attractive way.

Amelanchier lamarckii begins with young bronze foliage as a background to delicate sprays of white flowers in spring; then, in autumn, the leaves turn red in sunshine and yellow in the shade, so you often get both colours together. It's truly an inspiring sight.

Cercidiphyllum japonicum, the katzura tree, has no flowers but the foliage is nothing short of superb. In spring it starts out bronze and then turns to delicate shades of green and pink; in the autumn the leaves go red, orange and yellow, filling the garden with an enticing smell of burnt toffee just before they fall.

If you want fruit as well as blossom and colourful leaves, don't forget the crab apple (*Malus*). One of my favourites is 'Evereste', with green leaves and masses of tight red buds in spring, opening to white flowers that are followed by a multitude of orange fruits in autumn. 'Golden Hornet' is popular, with white flowers and yellow fruits. The best of all reds is surely 'Profusion', which is wreathed in wine-red flowers, dark red fruit and crimson foliage; the best for making jelly is 'John Downie'.

Planting evergreens

On the whole evergreens are planted in the same way as deciduous trees and shrubs, but because they never really go dormant, it's particularly important that you don't damage their system of fibrous roots, and you should always remove any hessian wrapping. This will rot away naturally, but it's best to give the roots free rein right from the start. Unlike deciduous plants, evergreens benefit from the addition of a general fertiliser to the soil when planting, and a further handful sprinkled around the plant afterwards. It's unlikely at this time of year that the roots will dry out, but you might need to water in a very dry autumn. An occasional spray over with water in a mild dry winter is helpful, as is a screen of windbreak material arranged on one side to protect the plants from cold drying winds.

Taking hardwood cuttings

Cuttings from many shrubs root easily at this time of year while the soil is warm enough to encourage rapid rooting, and this is certainly the cheapest way to fill your garden with trees and shrubs. The shoots you need are those which have grown this year and are near enough pencil-thickness or more. Take them as low down on the plant as possible, because the hormones that aid rooting tend to sink to the bottom of the plant this late in the season. The basic procedure is the same as I showed you for rose cuttings on page 139. Trim the shoots, leaving a cutting 15–45cm (6–18in) long depending on the size of the parent plant and the distance between leaf joints; dip the bottoms in rooting hormone; and bury all but the top 5–8cm (2–3in) in a slit trench.

This time next year you'll be able to transplant them. Remember to be fairly ruthless about cutting the young plants back to leave about 10–15cm (4–6in) of growth: this will encourage them to bush out. In

HARDWOOD CUTTINGS

Leave all the buds on a hardwood cuttings if you want stems to develop from below ground. Gooseberries and other soft fruit that are to be grown on a 'leg' or clean stem should have all but the top few buds removed before the cuttings are planted.

SHRUBS TO GROW FROM HARDWOOD CUTTINGS

Berberis, buddleia, cornus, cotoneaster, elderberry, escallonia, forsythia, garrya, jasmine, kerria, laurel, leycesteria, olearia, philadelphus, roses, spiraea, tamarix, weigela and willow. Also take large quantities of privet and box cuttings for hedging.

And don't forget fruit such as gooseberries, blackcurrants and red or white currants, as well as quinces, figs and grapes.

---

cold gardens, you can do exactly the same inside a cold frame to give that extra bit of protection and rather more success.

Moving a large shrub

After several years' growth shrubs and trees will usually have developed big root systems, so moving them can be risky unless you take great care. It often helps to prepare them a season in advance by trimming the roots (see page 47).

This month you can really get down to the job. Evergreens are best moved now, while deciduous plants can be moved successfully any time between now and early March. Start by digging a trench all round the plant, slightly beyond the one cut earlier if you've already trimmed the roots. Dig right to the subsoil, and then cut underneath to form as large a rootball as you can manage to handle.

Once you're half-way under the plant, you should be able to tilt it enough to work a piece of sacking or polythene underneath. Then dig under the plant from the other side until you meet the sacking, which you can pull right under by tilting the plant again. Tie the sacking so the rootball's completely contained.

Now all you have to do is lift it out, which is easier said than done. If you tie a stout post firmly to the sacking, two strong people should be able to manage it without too much grunting.

Remember to dig the hole in the new spot first. Then plant as I describe on page 155, setting the shrub in position and securing it, if necessary, with ropes, which can stay in place for at least a year to prevent rocking and breakage of the young roots.

MOVING A LARGE SHRUB

1 Cut all round the shrub, digging out a trench and trimming roots as you go. Then excavate from one side until the shrub can be tilted away from you.

2 Tuck a piece of strong sacking under the rootball. Dig under the other side and pull the sacking through so that the shrub sits in the centre.

3 Knot the ends of the sacking round the stem and, for large shrubs, slide a pole under the knots to make lifting easier when you transfer the shrub to its new home.

LAWNS & HEDGES

Planning for hedges

However friendly your neighbours might be, you probably don't want them breathing down your neck all the time. So why not plant a boundary hedge, and let your privacy creep up on them? It will provide a soft leafy barrier and make a perfect home for wildlife.

And if you live in a windy spot, there's no doubt a hedge makes a far better windbreak than a fence or wall. When the wind is filtered through the foliage, it is slowed down to an acceptable speed; when it meets the solidity of a fence, however, it whips over the top and eddies down the other side, sometimes actually increasing in speed and turbulence.

The big problem for small gardens is that a hedge will take up more room than a fence. You need to allow 60–90cm (2–3ft) width at the least, and an informal hedge would take more. But there's no reason why it should not act as a support for a variety of climbing plants, making a fine background for a border.

Choosing deciduous hedges

A formal hedge is clipped closely and can be confined to quite a small strip, whereas an informal one is left to grow naturally and so takes up much more room. Your hedge can be just one plant, such as quickthorn, berberis, escallonia or viburnum, or you can simply plant a mixture of shrubs in a row. If you have the room and want to attract wildlife, you can't do better than a mixed hedge of native species such as quickthorn, hazel, blackthorn and ash – grow native roses through it, together with blackberries and clematis, and you will create a breath of fresh country air.

Most informal plants can also be clipped neatly. Quickthorn, also known as hawthorn (*Crataegus monogyna*), for example, can be cut back to make a hedge no more than 45cm (18in) wide, and this will encourage close bushy growth that attracts nesting birds. One of my own favourites is beech, which makes a fine green formal hedge in summer and retains its russet-coloured leaves all winter; the old leaves are pushed off by the new ones in spring. If your soil is the least bit waterlogged though, grow hornbeam instead.

Choosing coniferous hedges

In a formal garden you might prefer a conifer. Yew (*Taxus baccata*) is undoubtedly the aristocrat – it will grow only 23cm (9in) or so a year while young, but it has the great advantage of being able to regrow from old wood. As well as the dark green yew, there are also golden forms. *Thuja plicata* (western red cedar) shoots up about twice as fast and also regrows from old wood: I particularly like 'Atrovirens', the brightest green variety.

Leyland cypress is the fastest growing of all, and worth considering for a boundary hedge or windbreak. But beware, there are several clones or varieties and it's vital to choose a drought-resistant one that will not turn brown in dry summers, which could be a disaster because new growth won't regenerate from the old wood. I would go for the slightly greyish 'Haggerston Grey' or the slower growing 'Castlewellan Gold'.

Planting hedges

If you prepare the soil well with plenty of organic matter, you shouldn't have problems with drought damage. Cultivate a strip 90cm (3ft) wide, preferably 1.5m (5ft) for large boundary hedges, and continue all along the planting line, working in a barrowload of compost or rotted manure per metre (yard) run. Rake in a couple of handfuls of bonemeal per square metre, level the ground and then peg out the centre line of the hedge, positioning the string just to one side to leave room for the plants themselves.

Deciduous hedging species may be bare-rooted and quite small, but they transplant well at this stage. With conifers, buy pot-grown plants about 30cm (12in) high – smaller, cheaper plants are often no more than rooted cuttings and take a good deal of nurturing in the early

stages. Buy 10 per cent more than you need, and grow the extras in pots so that you have replacements just in case. And buy all the conifers at the same time if you want consistent colour.

If you live on an exposed site, protect young conifers from wind damage with a screen of plastic mesh on strong posts for at least the

ABOVE Brilliantly tinted autumn leaves temporarily decorate a trim formal hedge. With growth slowing down, mowing and hedging are almost over by now.

first year. Make sure all new hedges get regular watering next season, and feed them just once with a general or rose fertiliser in March.

BELOW Young bare-rooted deciduous species such as beech can be planted now in well-dug soil to create a new boundary hedge.

PLANTING A HEDGE

After trenching the site, replace and level the soil. Stand the plants along the centre line, deciduous species about 45cm (18in) and conifers 90cm (3ft) apart. Plant them firmly at the depth at which they previously grew, and water in with dilute liquid feed.

VEGETABLES & HERBS

Lifting and storing root crops

I leave a few vegetables in the ground to survive the rigours of winter. Parsnips, scorzonera, salsify and celeriac, for example, are much tastier after a nip of frost, although it's worth checking now and again to make sure there's no damage. And if hard frost threatens, make life easy by digging up a few of each kind and keeping them under cover.

Carrots, beetroot and turnips, however, should all be lifted and stored as soon as you can. Fork them up carefully to avoid damaging them, set any spoilt samples to one side for immediate use, and then store the perfect roots in boxes of just-moist sand or garden compost. If you don't have either, ordinary garden soil or bark chippings will do. Put them in as cold a place as possible, but make sure it's frost-free, and raise the boxes off the ground to ensure good ventilation.

Potatoes should be forked up carefully, left on the surface to dry for an hour or two, and then put into paper bags: again, only store the perfect tubers. Take care to lift all of them, even the smallest, because if you don't they'll regrow next year like weeds just where you want to grow something else. However, if any do grow again, leave them until they're worth digging up as first earlies – you'll find they nearly always come before any that you've planted.

Planting garlic

Even though you might associate garlic with warmer countries than ours, the crop produces much better

ABOVE Each fat garlic bulb can be split into a dozen or so cloves for planting individually this month, outdoors or in a frame.

yields if it is exposed to a couple of months of really cold weather early in its life. That's why it's always best to plant the cloves now, rather than in the spring. If your soil's unworkable at this time of year, start the cloves in small pots or modules, and keep them growing in the cold frame until you can plant out the young plants in the spring.

Buy seed bulbs if you can. The garlic you buy at the greengrocer will almost certainly grow, but it may be infected with virus, which will reduce yields. Gently break whole bulbs into the separate cloves, and keep the fatter ones for planting – the long thin central cloves are better used in the kitchen. Prepare a sunny spot in the same way as for shallots (see page 32), and then take out shallow drills 15cm (6in) apart. Space the cloves (pointed ends uppermost) 5–8cm (2–3in) apart in the drills, and then cover so the tips just show; on light dry soils you can bury the cloves up to 5cm (2in) deep. And then just leave them alone – each clove will develop into a fat bulb next summer.

PLANTING GARLIC

If you can't work outside, start garlic cloves in modules, planting a clove in each cell with its point just above the surface. Don't be tempted to keep them warm: the cloves need cold exposure and are best stored over winter in a cold frame.

Protecting late crops

Now's the time to dust down all the cloches you can muster, and put them over the last of the summer vegetables. French beans, tomatoes and courgettes can all be encouraged to run on a bit and ripen those last few fruits, while protecting lettuce, spinach and other leaf crops improves their quality just that little bit. If you haven't any ready-made cloches and there's a threat of frost, cover the rows with one or two thicknesses of fleece or 3–4 pages of newspaper, which will keep out about 2°C (4°F) of frost. And hold down the edges with a few bricks or stones in case the wind gets up. If you have some clear polythene, you can improvise cloches with old wire coat-hangers, opened out and bent into hoops to place over the rows every 90cm (3ft): lay polythene over these and you have a very effective tunnel cloche that could save the crop.

If you have cloches in position, you can sow pea 'Douce Provence' and broad bean 'Aquadulce Claudia' for early harvesting next year.

BELOW Maincrop apples such as 'Spartan' should be ready for picking and storing.

FRUIT

Harvesting apples

Maincrop varieties such as 'Spartan', 'Sunset' and most of the russets and cookers will be ready to harvest about now. Picked when they are ripe and sound, they will keep well for two or three months if they are stored in the same way as earlier types (see page 144).

Guarding apples and pears against winter moth

To protect next year's crop, put grease bands around apple and pear tree trunks (and their stakes) to trap the grubs as they head down to their winter quarters underground.

Pruning blackcurrants

It used to be recommended that blackcurrants should be pruned at the same time as you harvest the fruit, to save coming back to do another chore. But recent research has shown that pruning so early in the season removes part of the plant's food factory and can reduce subsequent crops.

So prune now, once the leaves have turned colour, by removing a proportion of older stems right down to the ground, or low down on the bush at a joint where a strong sideshoot is emerging. The cut shoots can be used as hardwood cuttings by trimming them to about 23cm (9in) long and just pushing them into the ground. But don't do this if you've seen big-bud disease on the bushes or suspect they may have reversion disease (the leaves will be narrow and look like stinging nettles).

Alternatively, you can grow blackcurrants as biennial croppers by cutting all the stems down to the ground every other year. This is an ideal method if you're short of time or have problems bending and finding which shoots to remove. With liberal feeding, this method can produce very heavy crops, but obviously you would need twice the number of plants to provide a crop every year.

Caging soft fruit

I have something of a love-hate relationship with the birds in my garden. While they're singing sweetly or demolishing snails and greenfly, they can do no wrong. But when they turn to my fruit bushes, I have been known to curse.

I invested in a fruit cage, and then planted it up with all those soft fruits that are prone to attack and difficult to protect in other ways – strawberries, for example, are vulnerable but can stay outside because they're easy to cover with netting at the appropriate time. And talking of time, now is the right moment to install a cage: fruit might be a little scarce, but in a few weeks finches could start attacking the buds on gooseberries and other bushes, which will certainly reduce their crops later on.

The type of cage you buy depends on what you can afford and how much fruit you have. The least obtrusive and longest lasting are made of tubular steel with a permanent side net, and a separate roof net that should be taken off soon in case snow should build up and bring the whole lot down. But the net goes back in early spring to protect those fattening fruit buds. A self-closing door is useful to prevent birds slipping inside and getting trapped while your back's turned.

MISCELLANEOUS

The art of digging

The soil is moist but not sodden at this time of year, and the weather is cool but not icy – perfect conditions for the major task of digging, but don't rush it. Just as soon as bare soil's available, I like to start winter cultivation: that way I can take my time, and avoid overdoing it.

Existing borders need little deep cultivation, and it's new beds, any areas that are to be replanted and, above all, the vegetable plot that will need more thorough digging. The first job, I reckon, is to cover the vacant soil with clear polythene sheeting. Any day now, we can expect the winter wet to set in and that can hold up work for weeks, but if you keep the soil covered you'll be able to dig exactly when you want to.

There's no point trying to be macho about the job. Use a spade that's the right weight for you and see if you can run to stainless steel, which is so much easier to use. If you can't manage a spade, use a fork. Then every few minutes, stop for a breather and clean off any soil sticking to the blade. It's a good excuse to straighten your back, and makes life much more pleasant.

Double- and single-digging

Double-digging two-spades deep is usually only for masochists or gardeners with a new plot, but if you're making a deep bed, or you find that the builders have compacted the surface before bulldozing a hundred tons of topsoil over it, I'm afraid you'll have some hard work ahead – but only once. After that, normal single-digging is usually enough. Dig to the full depth of the spade and throw the soil forwards as you go. This leaves a shallow trench in front of you, and a freshly dug sloping mound ahead of that. This is the moment to add manure – well-rotted horse or farmyard manure if you can get it – and compost: garden compost, spent mushroom compost or composted straw. Place these on the slope, rather than in the bottom of the trench – that way, they'll spread through all levels of the dug soil.

Above all, try to work up a rhythm that is smooth and gentle. And stop just as soon as you feel your back has had enough – there's all winter to get the job done, so there's no point risking injury.

Keeping worms working

Whereas slugs are to be firmly discouraged, earthworms need positive discrimination to keep them happy and working hard on our behalf. Every year worms bring

ABOVE Fresh ground is best double-dug to provide the perfect conditions for success in the seasons to come. Brussels sprouts are protected from birds and frost with fleece.

tons of soil to the surface, improving aeration and drainage, and we all know that wormcasts are wonderful stuff – when worms digest soil they grind it down and form it into pellets that are coated with mucous which actually contains plant growth hormones. Their other major act of charity is to drag organic matter into the soil where they grind it down; bacteria then breaks it down further, and plant foods are released.

It's obvious we need to encourage them, and that's done by providing plenty of organic material. Garden compost and rotted manure are ideal. My advice is to dig these into the vegetable plot, but just leave them as a mulch on the soil in the borders to give the worms something to do in the long nights.

161

PLANTS FOR
october

1 With its prettily mottled leaves which die down during the summer, hardy *Cyclamen hederifolium* (*C. neapolitanum*) is perfect for naturalising beneath trees and shrub. Its pink or white 10–15cm (4–6in) blooms appear any time from August to December.

2 Angel's trumpets (*Brugmansia*, formerly *Datura*) are tender vigorous semi-evergreen shrubs 3m (10ft) high and wide, with 15cm (6in) long flowers. They are best grown in large containers for summer display outdoors, and brought under cover this month.

1

2

3

4

3 The Japanese anemone, *A. x hybrida,* is a hardy 1.5m (5ft) late-flowering herbaceous perennial with an outstanding white form 'Honorine Jobert'.

4 *Sorbus aucuparia* 'Fructo Luteo',one of the rowans, is a fine hardy deciduous tree up to 6m (20ft) high, with vividly coloured spring and autumn foliage and creamy-yellow berries.

5 The rich autumn tints of Boston ivy, *Parthenocissus (Ampelopsis) tricuspidata,* commend this hardy deciduous 15m (50ft) climber for all walls, even north-facing ones.

5

163

*W*hat Geoff called our plant-hunting trips took place towards the beginning of the month, during the half-term break of the school where I taught. Geoff had specially equipped our Land Rover with shelves that fitted across the windows, the right size to take two decks of plants. We would pick an area of the country, arm ourselves with a copy of *The Plant Finder* (published annually under the auspices of the Royal Horticultural Society), and set off, navigating our way from nursery to nursery, and staying at B & Bs on the way.

Geoff would talk to the owners of specialist nurseries, and buy plants that they recommended. He loved to experiment, to try growing plants that were new to him, to learn more about them. By the time we came home we could hardly see out, and there was scarcely enough room in the car for the one small suitcase that I had been allowed to take with me.

A cold November morning reveals the formal outlines of this potager, where dwarf hedges, simple box topiary and standard roses provide a permanent framework for the ever-changing crops.

key tasks for november

BULBS
○ Plant tulips early in the month, page 166
○ Plant lilies between now and April, page 167

ROSES
○ Plant roses after their leaves have fallen, page 168

LAWNS
○ Lay turf on prepared soil, page 168

VEGETABLES & HERBS
○ Force Belgian chicory for eating at Christmas, page 170
○ Lift and heel in winter leeks before the ground is frozen solid, page 170

FRUIT
○ Plant new apple and pear trees, page 170
○ Carry out winter-pruning, page 171

MISCELLANEOUS
○ Collect autumn leaves and stack them to make leafmould, page 172
○ Protect plants against frost and alpines from the rain, page 173
○ Insulate the greenhouse ready for winter, page 173

BULBS

Planting tulips

Save planting tulips until all the other spring bulbs are safely in, and you'll stand a better chance of escaping the fungal disease tulip fire. But don't wait too long: the first half of the month is the best time; and make sure you choose sites where the tulips will be happy.

Find the sunniest spots you can, and if your soil is heavy lighten it by adding coarse grit, and plant the bulbs on a layer of grit to protect the base plate from sitting in water. Then, if you want your tulips to be a permanent feature, you'll need to arrange for plenty of sunshine to bake the bulbs. In mixed borders that can be a problem because the foliage of other plants is certain to shade them, and most eventually die out in these positions.

A traditional way round this is to grow tulips as part of the spring bedding scheme and, mixed with wallflowers and forget-me-nots, they take some beating. After flowering the bulbs can be lifted, packed close together in a corner to dry off and stored until they are replanted next autumn. Another way is to plant them among sparse-leafed plants that will not cast too much shade – flag irises, for example, enjoy similar conditions and will cause few problems. The bulbs can then stay there for years.

You can also grow them in pots. Either use the plunge bed system (see page 141) or plant in groups of six or seven in 20cm (8in) pots, and keep them over winter in a cool shady part of the garden. You can then plant them, pot and all, where you need a splash of colour or wait

RIGHT From late summer until mid-spring naturalised species of hardy cyclamen revel in well-drained leafy soil.

until they flower and stand them in groups on a path or patio. After flowering, move the pots out of sight and allow the foliage to die down naturally before drying and storing the bulbs.

Planting lilies

From now until the end of April, whenever the ground is workable, lilies can be planted outdoors, 15cm (6in) deep in groups. On heavy soil, plant the bulbs on their sides on a layer of sharp sand and pack a little more sand around them to improve drainage. (See also page 180.)

LONG-LASTING TULIPS

Both Darwin and Cottage varieties, often lumped together in catalogues as 'May-flowering', are robust, and available in a wide selection of colours. Plant them in large informal drifts rather than in rows like soldiers. If you want some of the earliest to flower, look for species such as the bright yellow *Tulipa tarda*, or *T. turkestanica* with its cream star-shaped flowers.

One of the oldest varieties still in cultivation is the tall, bright red *T. praestans* 'Fusilier', which flowers in late April and has been grown since the 1600s. And don't miss out on early 'Keizerskroon' with yellow-edged red petals, which has been here since 1750, or 'Couleur Cardinal' with red and purple flowers, which dates from 1845.

ROSES

Planting roses

You can buy bare-rooted roses now. They'll be a bit cheaper than container-grown plants and have a much better chance of establishing well. And there's no better time to plant than now, when they have lost their leaves. They're glorious plants and I wouldn't be without them, but they can be an awful lot of trouble. To ensure they live for a long time and really give their all, you must start right, taking extra care when planting, and then continue on the straight and narrow.

First, prepare the ground thoroughly. Roses need to be well fed because they flower more or less throughout the summer, and you're going to hack them back each year. So cultivate as large an area as you can, make each hole big enough to take the full spread of the roots without vicious bending, and work in rotted manure, garden compost or one of the tree and shrub planting mixtures that you can buy. No fertiliser is necessary at this stage, but remember to give the plants a feed in spring – use a special rose fertilizer that has all the nutrients in the right proportions.

Many roses you buy now will be pruned back to leave shoots about 15–20cm (6–8in) long, and they can be left like that until the spring pruning. If they haven't already been cut back, do it before you plant because you'll find it's easier while you're standing up. Chop each stem back quite hard, reducing shoots thicker than a pencil to about 8cm (3in) long and thinner ones to 2.5–5cm (1–2in). Always cut back to just above a bud and

PLANTING ROSES

Plant the rose deep enough for the joint between the stems and the rootstock to be about 5cm (2in) below the surface when you refill the hole with soil. If you can't quite tell this point, go by the old soil mark on the stem, and make sure this is buried out of sight. Firm the soil gently with your foot after refilling, and mulch the surface with compost, rotted manure or bark.

remember that it will grow in the direction it's facing, so the usual advice is to make a sloping cut above an outward-facing bud.

Rose replant disease

If you're thinking of removing old roses and planting new ones in the same bed, you may have problems because the new roses are likely to sulk and eventually die from a disorder known as rose replant disease, about which very little is yet known. If you must plant in the same place, dig out as much soil as possible and exchange it with fresh from another part of the garden. For just one or two plants, you might then get away with it if you use plenty of manure or garden compost, but planting in another spot is much the best bet.

LAWNS & HEDGES

Laying turf

Lawns made with turf are more expensive than those grown from seed, but more or less instant. Buy the best turves you can: cultivated ones that are guaranteed weed-free will cost about twice as much as coarse weedy 'parkland' turf from cow pastures, but will save hours of heartache and remedial work later.

In most parts of the country this is about the best time of year for laying turf, since the soil's still warm and it's most unlikely the turf will dry out after laying – only delay if the ground is frozen or too wet to walk on. If you've prepared the ground as I suggested in August (see page 126), all you need do now is hoe off any weeds and rake the surface level again, adding a little general fertiliser as you go.

Start by laying out the edging turves all round. Use a full turf at each corner, standing outside the area you've just levelled and tamp the turves down with the back of a rake. Then rest a wide plank such as a scaffolding board on the longest straight row of turves and stand on this while you continue laying across the ground. When you get to the end of a row, place the last turf over the edging turf and trim the excess with a knife so that it fits snugly.

You should only need to water if it's exceptionally dry: sprinkle the grass little and often to keep it fresh and moist until it's established.

RIGHT Autumn leaves are a precious free resource; to protect the turf, don't leave them for too long before gathering them.

VEGETABLES & HERBS

Forcing chicory

If you sowed Belgian or Witloof chicory seeds in June (see page 97), the roots should be ready for digging up and forcing, as shown on the right, by now. Each root will produce a fat white shoot or 'chicon' after five weeks or so, three weeks if you keep them at about 13°C (55°F). The chicon is the bit you cut off to eat, while the root is then thrown away.

Winter leeks

Winter leeks, such as 'Musselburgh' and 'Giant Winter', have dark strong leaves and improve in flavour after a good frost. They should be the right size by now, and I like to lift a couple of dozen or so at a time and either heel them in in a trench of compost near the back door, or keep them in a bucket of

BELOW Lift and heel in a supply of leeks where they will not freeze in the ground in hard weather.

FORCING CHICORY

1 Start by carefully digging up the roots, which are shaped rather like a parsnip. Trim them by cutting off the dead foliage and shortening the other end to leave each root about 15–20cm (6–8in) long. Store the roots in a box of moist sand or old potting compost until needed.

2 Every few weeks you can take out a batch of roots for forcing. Place them upright in a deep box or pot – five will just about fit into a 20cm (8in) pot. Pack moist sand, soil or compost around them, and stand the container somewhere warm and dark.

compost in the shed. Here they will happily last for months and are conveniently to hand when the ground is frozen. I also transplant a few groups to the back of the borders, where they will soon root again and produce superb round seedheads next summer.

FRUIT

Choosing apple and pear trees

Both apples and pears are best planted in late autumn or early winter, especially if they are bare-rooted. Container-grown trees can, in theory, be planted any time but they too are easiest to care for if put in now. If you have a large garden, you might have room for a full-blown tree: a large standard of either an apple or a pear can spread 6m (20ft) or more. The specially trained varieties on dwarf root stocks, as I explained in April (see page 68), are usually easier to cope with, particularly as you'll need to grow at least two different varieties which flower at the same time to get a good transfer of pollen from one to the other, and so ensure a heavy crop on both. Look especially for varieties that have a good flavour, that crop well and are relatively disease-resistant.

Planting fruit trees

Both apples and pears need a sunny position, preferably with some shelter from frost – pears are especially vulnerable as they flower earlier. Prepare as large an area as possible, at least 90cm (3ft) across each way. Dig two spades deep, breaking up the subsoil and working in plenty of compost or rotted manure. Dig out a hole large enough to take the rootball comfortably at the level of the old soil mark – you can test this by standing the tree in the hole and laying a spade across from one edge to the opposite side to see if it lines up with the mark on the trunk. Remember to drive in a stake, if it is needed, before planting.

Place the tree in the hole and cover the roots with some of the excavated soil, working it down between the roots by jiggling the tree up and down a few times. Continue refilling the hole until you are half-way, and then tread it firm; return the rest of the soil and firm again. Fix the tree to its support with tree ties, water the soil thoroughly if the weather is dry, and finally mulch with an 8cm (3in) layer of compost or rotted manure to control weed growth.

Winter-pruning fruit trees and bushes

Pruning at this time of year largely consists of removing larger branches to open up the centres of bushes and standards, whether these are apples and pears or soft fruit such as red currants and gooseberries. All of them tend to produce too many branches and shoots in the middle of the plants, where they cross and overcrowd the centre blocking out the sunlight and inviting diseases.

You can tackle all kinds in the same way: cut out branches which

ABOVE The extraordinary inflated seedpods of bladder senna, *Colutea arborescens*, hang in clusters all autumn.

are dead or diseased, and any that cross or grow inwards, so that the centre is opened up to allow air to circulate and the sun to reach ripening fruit. With bush fruit you can also shorten the longer remaining branches by about a third to allow you to pick more easily.

If you grow your fruit in space-saving trained forms, you'll find that most of the essential pruning is done in summer, just when the weather's at its most inviting. All you need to do now is shorten the main stems and branches of trained forms such as espaliers by one-third of the current year's growth to encourage sideshoots to form.

Tying down fruiting shoots

There's one bit of training that doesn't need any cutting tools at all. Trimming back fruiting branches often results in a mass of new shoots just where you might not want them, and they're also likely to reduce the crop of fruit. These days growers tend to tie the shoots downwards, restricting the sap flow and encouraging further fruit buds. This method works for apples and pears, and is also the best way to deal with those long whippy branches that plum trees make.

All you need to do is tie a length of string near the end of the branch and pull it downwards until it forms a gentle arch, with the tip lower than the other end. Secure the string to the trunk or to a stake hammered into the ground. This needs to be done before winter sets in, while the branches are still supple; if you wait until the branch hardens up you risk breaking it.

FROST-TOLERANT APPLES AND PEARS FOR COLD AREAS
Eating apples: 'Ashmead's Kernel', 'Greensleeves', 'Jonagold', 'Katja' ('Katy'), 'Orleans Reinette', 'Suntan'. Cooking apples: 'Blenheim Orange', 'Golden Noble', 'Howgate Wonder', 'Lane's Prince Albert'. Pears: 'Beurré d'Amanlis', 'Conference', 'Doyenné du Comice', 'Gorham', 'Louise Bonne of Jersey', 'Onward'.

171

MISCELLANEOUS

Leafmould

Good gardeners look upon waste as an asset rather than a liability and, treated properly, autumn leaves are worth their weight in gold. I like to leave mine for a while to make a fiery tapestry of colour on the lawn, but when they lose their autumn hues they are gathered up and then left to rot down to make leafmould.

Leafmould is a wonderful crumbly brown material that looks like peat but contains much more goodness. It was greatly valued by old head gardeners as the 'magic ingredient' in potting composts, and it can still be used to replace peat in home-made mixtures. In the vegetable plot I also use it to run down seed drills if the soil's heavy and wet – it's pretty pointless sowing in wet cold soil but there are times when it's important to get on. A sprinkling of leafmould down the drill before and after sowing solves the problem, and the seeds nestle in a cosy haven, germinating strong seedlings that are raring to go.

Making leafmould

You can simply rake up the leaves with a spring-tine, rubber or plastic lawn rake, or in larger gardens you might find a push-along sweeper useful. However, they'll rot down quicker if they're cut up into small pieces, and you can do that easily by running the mower over them on the lawn or by putting them through a shredder.

An easy way to store the leaves while they decay is to make a wire-netting enclosure by banging four stakes into the ground at the corners and then wrapping these round with wire netting. Unlike compost, which is decomposed by bacteria, leaves are rotted mainly by fungi which are not nearly so fussy and need no extra heat, additives or complicated containers to get them going. Just tread the leaves down firmly as you go and leave them for at least a year.

A quicker way to rot them down is to mix them with some lawn mowings – you'll do that anyway if you mow them up off the lawn. Make sure the leaves are damp and you'll find that the grass will heat the material and speed up decay, especially if you store the leaves in

ABOVE A wire-netting enclosure is all that is needed to transform autumn leaves into valuable leafmould. Make a new one the following autumn as full decomposition takes more than a year.

bags. You can buy special ones with holes in the sides, stiff enough to stand open so you only need one pair of hands to fill them. Otherwise use plastic bin-liners with a few holes stabbed in the sides. Tie the tops of the bags, store them in a corner, and they'll make superb leafmould ready for use about the middle of next year.

Protecting plants against frost

Unfortunately you never know if the weather will be hard until it's too late, so take precautions now and protect any plants of borderline hardiness. Those that die down for the winter can be covered with a little loose straw, bark, bracken or conifer branches to keep the worst of the cold away. Evergreens can be covered when a really hard frost is forecast, but what you use makes a lot of difference: hessian sacking and old net curtains are ideal, or try 2–3 layers of fleece.

Polythene doesn't work if it's just draped over the plants because any leaves touching the material will still suffer, but it will do the trick if you can rig up a support to keep the sheeting off them. The tops of climbers that grow against a wall or fence can be protected with polythene if you pin a sheet to two poles long enough to reach above the plant to be protected. When hard frost is due, unroll the sheeting and simply lean the poles against the wall to form a tent over the plant; then roll it up again in the morning. It's well worth a little bit of effort to sleep easy at nights.

Protecting alpines

Alpines can cope with cold weather – in their natural surroundings most are tucked up in winter under a blanket of snow – but in our milder, lowland climate those with grey hairy or woolly leaves need a bit of coddling to protect them from wet weather, which can rot them or causes diseases such as grey mould. If you can provide good drainage with plenty of grit in the soil and as a mulch round the plants, you're half-way to success. It's also a good idea to cover the plants over for the winter with a bit of glass or plastic to keep them dry. You can do this quickly and cheaply as shown below. That way they're sheltered from the heaviest rain but there's still plenty of ventilation around the sides, which is vital for these cold-loving species.

bulbs of all kinds and spring-flowering herbaceous plants that will produce fine early blooms with just that amount of protection.

Watch the watering, though. Many plants will need very little while it's cold, and too much dampness under glass can encourage fungal diseases. Check regularly during winter, and if you find any infected leaves remove them pretty quickly before the problem can spread. And be sure to ventilate as much as you can on mild days – even a crack of air for an hour or so will help refresh the atmosphere and keep disease at bay.

And if you have an outside tap, make sure it's either cut off and drained for the winter or lagged with foam insulation.

BELOW Take no chances with outdoor container plants as winter approaches: snugly wrapped in sacking or similar insulation, their all-important roots will be safe from freezing.

PROTECTING ALPINES

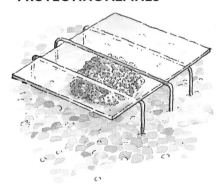

Make three large wire staples out of pieces of bent coat-hanger, and push two into the soil to provide legs to support the glass; the third one goes over the top to hold the glass in place.

Insulating the greenhouse

It's also worth trapping all the warmth you can in the greenhouse by insulating it. Bubble polythene fixed to the inside of the glass will retain a lot. If there's nothing growing under the staging – so light won't be needed there – cut polystyrene sheets to size and push them between the glazing bars to keep ground frosts out.

There's a heater in my greenhouse, but it's only set to come on when the temperature drops to a couple of degrees below freezing and is rarely used. And meanwhile the greenhouse is usually filled to the brim with container plants that would be at risk outside, as well as

PLANTS FOR
november

1 The large leaves of crimson glory vine, *Vitis coignetiae*, a self-clinging hardy climber up to 25m (80ft) high, make a rich display in autumn.

2 The dense white 3m (10ft) plumes of pampas grass, *Cortaderia selloana* 'Sunningdale Silver', last well into winter over its tussocks of hardy evergreen foliage.

1

2

3

3 Even in the depths of winter, *Lonicera fragrantissima*, one of the honeysuckle family, produces its sweetly scented blooms on bare spreading branches up to 1.8m (6ft) high.

4 Hardy spray chrysanthemums are indispensable border perennials with flowers in a wide range of mellow colours. They bloom over a long season, often after the end of autumn in sunny sheltered sites.

5 The single 8cm (3in) nodding bright yellow blooms of *Clematis orientalis* 'Bill Mackenzie' develop into large silvery seedheads, which last for months on vigorous stems 3m (10ft) or more high.

4

5

*T*his was the only month in which Geoff felt that he could leave the garden long enough for us to go away together on holiday. Unlike in November, we went further afield, to get sunshine rather than plants. But in fact Geoff never minded the weather – indeed, he loved it in all its guises: wet and windy, hot and still, silent and snowy. In spite of being a Leo, what he liked best was a crisp, cold, sunny day. Those were the days when I might catch him singing – anything from snatches of Frank Sinatra to a whole chorus from *The Messiah*. Singing was a shared interest – we met each other while carol singing, and for several years we travelled to the Albert Hall to sing in a 'Messiah from scratch' concert at Christmas. Geoff was such an unmaterialistic man that he was hard to give Christmas presents to, but records were always welcome – he loved listening to classical music and jazz – along with books and antique gardening tools. He was fascinated by old implements and methods, in why and how things were done. His interest in gardening was as broad as it was deep.

There is unexpected charm and beauty in the depths of winter: dormant apple trees trained formally on a series of arches are transformed into an inviting tunnel through the fresh snow.

december

key tasks for december

ANNUALS & BEDDING PLANTS
○ Sow pelargoniums early or buy 'plugs' to flower next summer, page 178

BORDER SCHEMES
○ Plan for winter colour in borders, page 179

BULBS
○ Start potting up lilies in batches, page 180

SHRUBS, TREES & CLIMBERS
○ Prune deciduous trees to shape, page 180
○ Shorten or tie in long stems to prevent wind damage, page 182

VEGETABLES & HERBS
○ Choose mini-vegetables for small gardens, page 182

FRUIT
○ Prune and plant blackberries, page 183

MISCELLANEOUS
○ Make a hotbed to force early crops, page 183

ANNUALS & BEDDING PLANTS

Growing pelargoniums from seed
I could never wax too lyrical about geraniums, or pelargoniums as we should call them to avoid confusion with hardy border geraniums. They've been the standard cottage garden pot plant since the year dot, and were often called 'window plants' because every cottage sported a few of them in flower on the windowsill. And they're terrifically versatile, flowering inside all winter and then, if you bed them out in borders or put them in containers, flowering outside all summer too.

If you're growing pelargoniums from seed, you need to sow them about now, and no later than mid-February. While growing from seed is fascinating, it does have two disadvantages: you need a propagator as the seeds won't germinate unless they are given a temperature of at least 18°C (65°F), and preferably higher; and it is expensive. Most seeds tend to be F_1 hybrids and so you only need two or three to fail, plus the cost of heating, to find that your plants are worth putting in the safe overnight.

You can, however, get the seedsman to grow them for you, so removing most of the risk. The majority of suppliers offer seedlings or young plants for potting on, and you can buy a pack of forty 'plugs' – tiny plants with an already established root system – for the cost of a couple of packets of seeds. But don't relax just because you've avoided the early sowing: if you're going to do it this way, you must send off for the plugs soon because they're usually grown to order.

BORDER SCHEMES

Planning for winter colour

If you look out of the window on a winter's day and see nothing but bare twigs, mud and rotting herbaceous vegetation, it's time to get things in hand. And there is little better to do on a raw, bitterly cold day than make plans. Even in the depths of winter, a garden should provide a view to lift the spirits and put a smile on your face, and this isn't difficult to achieve in a border, especially if you use the three-tier approach. This involves making a composition with a tree or two, a lower tier of shrubs or herbaceous plants, and underneath that a layer of low-growing plants.

The top tier

The best, and as far as I know, the only tree that will flower on and off throughout the cold weather is the autumn cherry (*Prunus* × *subhirtella* 'Autumnalis'). It is a small tree with semi-double white flowers, and there's an equally lovely blush-pink version called 'Autumnalis Rosea'. Or you could go for an evergreen such as *Cotoneaster* × *watereri* and its variety 'John Waterer', both with masses of long-lasting berries – they're really large shrubs, but can be pruned to make small trees.

The middle tier

There are lots of medium-sized shrubs which are interesting all through the winter. Dogwoods have brilliant winter-bark colours that are a special delight on sunny days. I'd certainly include the bright red-stemmed *Cornus sanguinea* 'Winter Flame' ('Winter Beauty') which has the bonus of fiery autumn foliage. Prune it hard in spring to encourage the bright young shoots. Don't miss out on daphnes, which produce flowers in February and continue until April, filling the garden with delicious perfume. *D. mezereum* is a small shrub with reddish-pink flowers and scarlet berries, while *D. odora* 'Aureomarginata' has soft reddish-purple flowers and, later on, creamy-yellow variegated foliage – this variety is actually hardier than the plain green form. The evergreen foliage alone of skimmias would justify planting them, but they also bear clusters of tight buds throughout winter. My favourite is

S. japonica 'Rubella', which carries large eye-catching clouds of red buds all winter until they open into white flowers in spring.

The bottom tier

Underneath the tree and shrubs, you can grow dwarf shrubs and herbaceous plants. Winter-flowering heathers, mainly *Erica carnea* varieties, go on right through from late January to April, and they don't need an acid soil which is good news for many gardeners. 'Myretoun Ruby' is one indispensable variety, a superb deep rose-pink that looks stunning beneath the autumn cherry. For an earlier show grow the rich carmine-red 'Eileen Porter', which will flower all winter.

Bergenias, sometimes known as elephant's ears, keep their round leathery leaves all winter, and some have the added bonus of superb winter colouring. *B. cordifolia* is one of the best species, especially the richly coloured 'Purpurea'; also consider the modern hybrids 'Abendglut' and 'Bressingham Ruby' which both have bright red flowers in early spring and glowing red winter foliage.

And of course, you can't be without the Christmas rose, (*Helleborus niger*), a lovely evergreen that produces delicate white flowers from late December to March. Around and beneath all these plants you can cram in bulbs such as February-flowering snowdrops, *Anemone blanda*, winter aconites, irises such as *I. histrioides*, scillas and the earliest cyclamineus daffs.

BULBS

Starting lilies in pots

I like to plant lilies in the garden about now. But very often they're not available this early, and by the time they do arrive the soil is likely to be too wet. So the solution is to pot them up temporarily until conditions improve, but there's no reason why you shouldn't leave them to flower in pots too.

Varieties such as the beautiful Asiatic or Mid-Century hybrids, especially short-stemmed kinds like 'Casa Rosa', 'Harmony' and 'Apollo', make an excellent display on the patio; the very dwarf Little Rascal and Pixie types, only 30cm (12in) or so high, are ideal container varieties. Sweet-scented *Lilium regale* was traditionally grown in large pots indoors for mass displays on special occasions.

If you're going to plant lilies out next spring, pot them up individually in ordinary 10–13cm (4–5in) pots and then keep these in a cold frame. Use extra-deep pots if possible for permanent potting, so bulbs are covered 15cm (6in) deep.

If you pot a few every month between now and early April, you should get a sequence of flowers up to the autumn. Remember to water and feed them regularly, and continue this after flowering until the leaves die down. Then renew the top 5cm (2in) of compost every September if you want to keep the plants flowering in pots.

RIGHT Even on a shaded house wall, pyracanthas produce huge crops of brilliant berries, golden yellow in the case of 'Soleil d'Or', while 'Mohave' is rich orange-red.

PLANTING LILIES IN POTS

Put a good layer of grit, gravel or broken crocks in the bottom of each pot, and cover this with 5–8cm (2–3in) of soil-based compost such as JI No. 2 or No. 3. Spacing depends on the size of the bulbs: you might get five smaller ones in a 20cm (8in) pot, but only three of other varieties. Fill the pots almost to the brim with compost, and keep them in a cold frame or in the garden, plunged up to their rims in soil.

SHRUBS, TREES & CLIMBERS

Pruning deciduous trees to shape

As soon as their leaves have fallen, deciduous trees can be pruned. This is the time of year when you can shape them up; and in small gardens you might also need to reduce their size slightly and thin the branches to make sure they don't cast too much shade. Before you get too secateur-happy, though, remember that hard pruning stimulates vigorous new growth, and simply sawing off thick

RIGHT Bright hoar frost embroiders shrubby branches and fern and epimedium leaves to create a magical winter scene around a weeping purple beech, *Fagus sylvatica* 'Purpurea Pendula', with its characteristic high-grafted mushroom-shaped head.

branches will result in a mass of weak sappy shoots next year.

The main rule is to open up the centre of the tree and remove branches that are crossing, damaged or overcrowding those you want to keep. Always cut back to a joint so that the shoot you trim back to can take over as a leader. Even then, keep an eye on the tree next spring and remove excess new shoots by rubbing them off while they're still small. Never remove more than about a third of the growth in any one year – and take your time: it takes seconds to cut bits off but years to grow them back again.

Preventing wind damage

If you're out and about with secateurs, take a look at your roses and other tall-stemmed shrubs, especially if they're growing in an exposed part of the garden. If the plants start rocking about in the wind, they'll work a hole in the soil around the stem. This will allow water to stand on the roots, which can cause rotting – in a snap frost it can also freeze the roots, which won't do the plant any good at all.

If there are long stems that look a bit vulnerable on buddleias or climbers such as vines, honeysuckle and ivy, cut them back by half, or tie them in before they get damaged by the wind. This also applies particularly to climbing and rambling roses, as well as to those vigorous shrub varieties that can make quite a lot of growth. It is only a holding measure, and you can finish pruning them properly in late winter or early spring. Don't waste the prunings, because there's still time to root them in the way I explained on page 156).

VEGETABLES & HERBS

There are often days when the sun shines, even if they are bitingly cold. Seize these moments to go out and check the kitchen garden; and, once out, you might even feel like doing something.

After a hard frost you should check any new plantings to make sure they haven't lifted, and firm them in if necessary. You could cut down the tops of Jerusalem artichokes, but leave the stems about a metre (3–4ft) long if they make a useful windbreak. You could also prepare a runner bean trench, one spade deep, and start filling it with weeds or vegetable waste, refilling it with soil in late March or April.

Planning to grow mini-vegetables

If you are armed with seed catalogues, the long evenings of December will give you wonderful opportunities to think ahead and make new plans for the garden. I always think that seedsmen are really selling us optimism. But you've every reason to be optimistic about growing crops even in a tiny veg plot if you use the latest 'mini' varieties. These can be grown closer together than normal kinds and are harvested while they're young and tender. What's more, they fetch a premium in the shops, so you'll be saving even more than you do with standard vegetables.

It's worth growing these varieties even if you've got a bit more room because, although they've been bred for harvesting while young, they can also be grown on to yield a more mature crop. That means you can gather them selectively over a longer season, with those left in the ground developing to full size. Nothing is wasted that way.

But to grow any crop well at close spacing you need very fertile soil, and I like to raise my mini-veg in deep beds that have been dug and manured to get the soil into fine fettle (see page 117). Then, every time you sow or plant a new crop, all you do is top-dress the soil with a general fertiliser and some garden compost. When you sow, you simply scratch shallow parallel drills with the tip of a garden cane and sow thinly in these; cover the seeds by drawing the back of a rake down the row, and tamp down lightly.

Most mini-veg can be sown in rows 15cm (6in) apart, with the seedlings thinned to suitable distances apart, from 1cm (½in) for leeks or 2.5cm (1in) for turnips, for example, up to 15cm (6in) for savoys and mini-cauliflowers. Try to arrange crops of similar height and shape side by side so that they don't shade each other and compete too much for light – they'll be jostling for space as they grow. One big advantage of this is that the soil surface is soon covered, which keeps weeds in check and also reduces evaporation in hot weather.

VARIETIES OF MINI-VEG
Kale 'Showbor' 15cm (6in) apart; savoy cabbage 'Protovoy' 15cm (6in); cauliflower 'Idol' or 'Lateman' 15cm (6in); carrot 'Amini' 1cm (½in); parsnip 'Lancer' 5cm (2in); beetroot 'Pronto' 2.5cm (1in); kohl rabi 'Quickstar' 2.5cm (1in); turnip 'Tokyo Cross' 2.5cm (1in); leek 'King Richard' 1cm (½in).

FRUIT

Growing blackberries

Now that it's getting harder to find a hedge, let alone a bramble twining through it in the wild, growing blackberries in your own backyard is an appealing option especially as the latest generation of compact varieties, 'Loch Ness' and 'Waldo', are thornless and produce large fruits with an excellent flavour.

You can grow these more choice varieties against a wall or fence, or free-standing on a post and wire support. Use 2.4m (8ft) fencing posts at the ends, with intermediate posts of the same height about 1.8m (6ft) apart. You'll need some strong wire stretched horizontally every 30cm (12in) from 90cm (3ft) to 1.8m (6ft) above the ground.

Now's the time to plant new canes, as well as to prune old ones. Plant canes 1.8m (6ft) apart in deeply dug soil with plenty of added compost or rotted manure, and after planting prune them hard to 30cm (12in) from the ground.

Blackberries fruit on canes they've produced the previous year, so pruning involves cutting out all those canes which have fruited, and then replacing them with the new ones produced this season. In the first year, train the canes into a fan shape on the wires, but leave a space in the centre. Then the new shoots produced the following season can be trained into this space while the older canes are fruiting. Once these have finished, they are cut out and the new ones that were bundled in the centre can be spread out in their place. That's all the care they need, apart from a lavish mulch after pruning each year.

MISCELLANEOUS

Making a hotbed

Gardeners a century ago were pretty lavish in their ways, but some of their less excessive ideas are still valuable today. The cold frame was one of them, and it should be used more widely; another Victorian brainwave was the hotbed, made inside a deep cold frame. It's something else that I think is due for revival, because it makes the best use of fresh horse manure that would otherwise have to be left in an unproductive heap for a year while it rotted down.

Fresh horse manure is certainly readily available in most parts of the countryside, if you keep an eye open for roadside signs. And even big cities have their share of stables where you are able to purchase a few steaming bags of the stuff.

To make use of it straight away, build a hotbed. You can make it in the open as a heap about 1.2m (4ft) square and 90cm (3ft) high, with the sides kept nice and square and the top quite flat. For best results, pile the manure into a wooden compost container which will help keep the heat in for much longer. Cover with a 15cm (6in) thick layer of 5 parts good soil, 3 parts mushroom compost and 2 parts coarse grit, all mixed well together.

Put a wooden cold frame over the top and leave for about 10 days while the fierce heat builds up and then starts to cool a little. At that point you can sow early lettuces, carrots, radishes, turnips, summer caulis and spinach for early harvest. When these have finished, plant the bed with bush tomatoes, melons, courgettes, aubergines, peppers or cucumbers to follow on in the summer. The heat produced at first will ensure fast early crops, the moist fertility will sustain the later summer ones, and at the end of the season you'll have a heap of well-rotted manure for the garden.

BELOW Making a hotbed in a stout wooden container confines the precious heat of the fermenting stable manure.

183

PLANTS FOR
december

1 One of the more vigorous bushy species, semi-evergreen *Cotoneaster* x *watereri* has distinctively textured leaves and heavy trusses of bright berries in autumn and winter.

2 Male forms of *Garrya elliptica*, the hardy evergreen silk-tassel bush, have conspicuous silvery-grey winter catkins. These are longest in the variety 'James Roof', which grows slowly into a dense 3m (10ft) shrub.

1

2

3

4

3 Very hardy and reliable even in exposed positions, the evergreen oleaster, *Elaeagnus* x *ebbingei,* is best known in this lustrous bushy variegated form 'Gilt Edge'.

4 Winter-flowering jasmine, *Jasminum nudiflorum*, is a favourite deciduous shrub for training on walls, where its leafless 3m (10ft) arching shoots bear a succession of bright yellow flowers until March.

5 Asian mahonias are vigorous hardy evergreen shrubs which prefer slightly shaded positions. *Mahonia* x *media* 'Charity' is a fine hybrid in this group, with long leaves and large upright-arching racemes of slightly fragrant blooms.

5

climate and the gardener

It is often said that the further north you go, the later spring arrives, and that on the whole gardeners in the North do things two or three weeks later than those in the milder South. But in reality the differences are not quite so clear-cut. For example, some of the earliest lettuces and tomatoes come from Lancashire and Sussex, two counties almost at opposite ends of the country. East Kent can experience frosts quite late whereas many London gardeners leave their geraniums out all winter, and in parts of Scotland frost is almost unknown. In fact, the difference between east and west can be as important as the north–south divide, while altitude and exposure are other potent influences on sowing, planting and harvesting dates.

Every garden is different and has its own local microclimate, which will only be revealed after a season or two of trial and error. In this book, recommended times for doing various jobs are based on years of experience at Barnsdale, a relatively 'late' garden in the east of the country. In Oxford you might manage things a week or so earlier, in Manchester a bit later, but the best guide is to watch and listen to your neighbours, who will know roughly when the first and last frosts are likely.

Observation and experiment are as important for successful gardening as following a monthly guide such as this, but there's always an element of unpredictability in our climate. Keep cloches and other forms of protection handy for a while after planting out, and take a few cuttings or make a second sowing as an insurance. Get to know the warmest and coldest parts of your garden, and keep an eye open for natural cues to do things. Nature does sometimes make mistakes, but when birds start nesting, hedgerow buds break or squirrels busy themselves storing food, you can be sure it's time for you to be doing something similar.

glossary

annual a plant which germinates, flowers, sets seed and dies within a year. The process can be spread over two calendar years, as when a hardy annual is sown in autumn to flower the following spring.

biennial a plant which makes most of its growth in the first year, and flowers and sets seed the next, after which it usually dies. Many vegetables are biennials, but most bedding plants grown as biennials are in fact perennials.

blind strictly used to describe a plant which has lost its growing tip, but often applied to bulbs that fail to flower because they are too young or overcrowded.

bottom heat warmth applied from below in a propagator or from a heated mat, to stimulate seeds to germinate or cuttings to root faster.

cane shorthand for a bamboo garden cane, but also used to describe the long annual stems of soft fruit such as raspberries and blackberries.

capillary matting woven material laid on greenhouse staging and kept moist so that pots and trays in contact with the matting can absorb moisture as needed.

catch crop a fast-maturing vegetable such as radish, lettuce or early carrots grown in ground that would otherwise stand empty for a few weeks between the harvesting and sowing of other crops.

cordon a plant such as an apple tree or tomato grown as a single stem and prevented from producing branches; cordons may be single, double or triple, and vertical or oblique (grown at an angle).

crown often used to refer to the upper portion of a perennial woody or fleshy rootstock of a plant which dies down in winter – rhubarb, peonies or asparagus, for example.

deciduous describes a shrub or tree which loses its leaves every autumn and is dormant until new leaves develop in spring.

dibber a valuable tool, made from a piece of dowel or a broken spade handle, used to make planting holes in the ground; the verb is to dibble.

disbud the removal of buds, either completely as when young strawberry plants are prevented from flowering, or selectively as when some flower buds on dahlias and chrysanthemums are removed to increase the size of remaining flowers.

drill a shallow channel scratched or drawn in the ground for sowing seeds or planting bulbs.

emergence the appearance of seedlings at the surface of the soil or compost, often the moment when less heat and more light are needed.

evergreen describes shrubs and trees that keep their leaves all year, a few old ones being shed continuously; in cold winters some of these plants may be semi–evergreen.

floret a small flower, one of several in a truss or spike – a delphinium floret, for example.

germination the moment when a seed starts growing; more heat may be needed than later, together with air, moisture and often darkness.

hardwood used to describe cuttings taken from the ripe woody stems of trees and shrubs in autumn.

hardy able to tolerate freezing, a relative term because there are various degrees of hardiness, and plants may be very hardy, fairly hardy and so on; half-hardy plants are sown in warmth and planted out after the last frosts.

heel a small piece of mainstem bark which is removed when pulling off a semi-ripe cutting, and which aids rooting.

heel in to temporarily bury and firm in the roots of trees and shrubs when planting is delayed; the last leeks and parsnips in spring are often moved and heeled in to allow cultivation of their bed.

herbaceous not woody; an herbaceous plant is one with soft top-growth, although the term usually refers to perennials that die down in winter.

humidity the amount of moisture in the air, an important quality under glass for cuttings and many soft leafy plants.

hybrid a plant which is the result of fertilisation between two different parents ('cross-fertilisation'); the first generation are known as 'first filial' or F_1 hybrids, the next generation as F_2. Random mixed fertilisation results in S_1 hybrids.

leader the main shoot at the top of a tree or the end of a branch.

mulch a surface layer of organic material, paper or plastic, used partly to feed plants and also to conserve soil moisture and suppress weeds; horticultural fleece is sometimes called a 'floating mulch'.

node the joint on a stem where a leaf stalk appears; the portion of stem between two nodes is called an internode.

offset a young plant or bulb produced at the side of its parent by division, and often removed as a method of propagation.

perennial a plant which grows and flowers each year; it is a relative term, many trees living for centuries, whereas the normally biennial foxglove may survive as a short-lived perennial for a few seasons.

pip a gardener's term for a small bulb, attached (as in garlic) to the main bulb by a short root, or formed in a seedhead, as often happens with leeks and other alliums.

piping a pink or carnation cutting produced by pulling the growing tip out of the lower stem.

pot up to transfer a seedling or plant to a pot for the first time; to pot on is to move the potted plant on to a larger container when its roots need more room.

rhizome a swollen underground storage root, as in many forms of iris.

root plate the disc at the base of bulbs and corms, from which the roots grow – easily damaged by rough handling.

runner a stem running above or just below ground, rooting at intervals and producing small new plants – strawberries, violets and buttercups all produce runners.

self-fertile able to produce seeds from its own pollen and cropping well when grown on its own.

semi-ripe (semi-hardwood or half-ripe) a type of cutting produced from a sideshoot which is just starting to ripen and turn woody at its base.

sideshoot a shoot growing from a main stem or branch, called a 'lateral' in technical books; a sideshoot growing from a sideshoot is a secondary sideshoot or a sub-lateral.

softwood used to describe a type of soft cutting prepared from the young growing tips of stems and sideshoots.

standard a form of tree or rose with all the branching growth at the top of a straight bare stem 90cm–1.8m (3–6ft) tall.

stipule the small leaf-like piece of tissue found at the base of leaf stalks on pelargoniums and some other plants.

stock plant a plant of any kind kept specially for providing cuttings and other propagating material.

stool as used by gardeners, this describes the rootstock of plants such as chrysanthemums when they are dormant; stools are usually kept for cuttings.

strike to treat a cutting so that it produces roots; a struck cutting is one that is rooted.

sucker an extra stem growing direct from the roots, unwelcome in grafted roses but also a means of propagating plants such as sumachs.

tilth the fine crumbly surface layer of soil after cultivation and preparation for sowing or planting.

top-dress to spread fertiliser, manure or some other 'dressing' on the soil surface without any cultivation.

vermiculite a treated mineral in the form of light translucent flakes, sterile and water-retentive, and useful for adding to compost or covering seeds.

index

Page numbers in *italic* refer to captions to photographs
Page numbers in **bold** refer to artwork illustrations

acknowledgments

The publishers would like to thank those photographers who gave permission for their photographs to be reproduced in this book.

All photographs are by **Stephen Hamilton**, with exceptions on the following pages:

John Glover: 16 left; 30; 36 below; 54-55; 61; 64; 68; 70 below right; 71 above; 106-107 Sleightholmedale Lodge, Yorkshire; 108-109 Glover; 117 The Croft, Cheshire; 120-121; 125 Savill Gardens, Windsor; 131 Preen Manor, Staffordshire; 132 above; 133 below; 147 above left; 147 below; 167; 174 below RHS Wisley; 175 above; 179.

Andrew Lawson: 18 Gothic House, Oxfordshire; 25 above left; 25 above right; 31; 37 above; 37 below left; 38-39; 43; 48; 56-57; 59 below right; 67 RHS Rosemoor Gardens, Devon; 70 below left; 76 Gothic House, Oxfordshire; 86 above; 99 Chilcombe House, Dorset; 102 below right; 103 above; 116; 127; 132 below left; 138 Gothic House, Oxfordshire; 141; 150-151 Eastgrove Cottage, Worcestershire; 153; 158 above; 162 below; 164-165 Barnsley House, Gloucestershire; 175 below left; 175 below right; 185 above left; 185 above right.

Marianne Majerus: 4-5

S+O Mathews: 180

Clive Nichols: 2-3 (designer: Rupert Golby) RHS Chelsea; 16-17 Wollerton Old Hall, Shropshire; 24 below; 37 below right; 44 (designer: C. Cordy); 45; 62 Beth Chatto's garden, Essex; 72-73 Chenies Manor, Buckinghamshire; 79 Barnsley House, Gloucestershire; 83 Ivy Cottage, Dorset; 96 Mrs Glaisher, Hildenborough, Kent; 104-105 Castle Howard, Yorkshire; 129 HMP Leyhill/Hampton Court Show; 133 above; 134-135 The Old Vicarage, Norfolk; 148-149 University Arboretum, Nuneham Courtenay, Oxfordshire; 174 above; 181 The Dingle, Wales; 184 right.

Hugh Palmer: 25 below Brook Cottage, Oxfordshire; 29 Erway Farm House, Shropshire; 92 Crathes Castle, Kincardineshire; 163 below Cherrybank Gardens, Perthshire.

Graham Strong/Clive Nichols Photography: 35

Multiple Sclerosis

A Guide for the Newly Diagnosed

Second Edition

Multiple Sclerosis

A Guide for the Newly Diagnosed

Second Edition

Nancy J. Holland, Ed.D., R.N.
Vice President, Professional Resource Center
National Multiple Sclerosis Society
New York, New York

T. Jock Murray, M.D.
Director, Dalhousie Multiple Sclerosis Research Unit
Halifax, Nova Scotia

Stephen C. Reingold, Ph.D.
Vice President, Research Programs Department
National Multiple Sclerosis Society
New York, New York

New York

Demos Medical Publishing, Inc., 386 Park Avenue South, New York, New York 10016

Library of Congress Cataloging-in-Publication Data

ISBN 1-888799-60-9

Printed in Canada

Dedication

Those diagnosed with multiple sclerosis today owe a great debt of gratitude to Labe C. Scheinberg, M.D. He opposed the voices who proclaimed defeat when faced with a diagnosis of multiple sclerosis, and insisted that much could be done to promote a productive and satisfying life, while limiting the negative impact of the disease.

Dr. Scheinberg is the champion of those with MS, from diagnosis throughout the disease course. He is the inspirational leader whose vision shaped this book.

Acknowledgments

Special thanks to several staff members of the National Multiple Sclerosis Society for their input and assistance with updating of this second edition:

Nancy Law
Cristina Lipka
Beverly Noyes, PhD
Ann Palmer
Alicia Soto

Thanks also to Jon Temme of the MS Society of Canada, and to our publisher, Dr. Diana M. Schneider, and editor, Joan Wolk, for their support throughout this project.

Contents

Foreword

The diagnosis of multiple sclerosis (MS) is often accompanied by a perception that life has become unpredictable and uncontrollable. Obtaining authoritative and accurate information about the disease and its management is the first step to regaining emotional balance and the feelings of control and empowerment.

As with many medical issues, the problem is *finding* such information. The Internet is full of information that is often misleading at best and totally false at worst, and the literature is full of material on "cures" and treatments that lack validity.

Multiple Sclerosis: A Guide for the Newly Diagnosed provides information that is both substantive and accurate. It has been developed by MS professionals with many years of experience in managing the disease, and is written with a straightforward and honest approach that provides all the information you need to begin to deal with this disease.

This is a new era in MS treatment. At no time previously have there been more ways to slow the disease process and manage its symptoms. The authors explore all of these in language that is understandable. They also recognize that there is a person behind the disease, and discuss topics such as choosing a health care provider and how to discuss MS with an employer. Things are changing so fast on the MS scene that one needs to keep up so as not to be left behind. While this book is written for the newly diagnosed, it clearly will also assist those previously diagnosed or simply interested in the latest information. I am proud to congratulate the authors on this excellent book!

Randall T. Schapiro, M.D.
Fairview Multiple Sclerosis Center
Minneapolis, MN

Multiple Sclerosis
A Guide for the Newly Diagnosed

Second Edition

1

What Is Multiple Sclerosis and How Is It Diagnosed?

IN THE MIDDLE OF THE NINETEENTH CENTURY, PHYSICIANS AND pathologists described a chronic neurologic disorder associated with scattered patches of scarring in the central nervous system (CNS)—the brain and spinal cord. The name *multiple sclerosis* comes from the "sclerosed" or hardened plaques of scar tissue located at "multiple" sites throughout the CNS. Nerve fibers (axons) in the CNS are covered with a *myelin sheath*, which provides an insulating function similar to that of the rubber coating around electrical wires. This insulation also allows nerve conduction to proceed at a rapid rate. Plaques damage the myelin around the nerve and disrupt the transmission of messages that communicate the desired action from the brain (message center) through the spinal cord to various parts of the body. An example is a signal from the brain to the legs to walk. Patients with changes indicating impaired function of the CNS often have a clinical history of episodes of neurologic symptoms that are related to the involvement of multiple areas of the spinal cord and brain.

In the mid-1860s, Professor Jean Martin Charcot at the Hôpital Salpétrière in Paris first described MS and its damage (lesions or plaques) in the brain and spinal cord in relation to the symptoms that separate MS from other diseases. He clearly defined the problems of MS and named the disease "sclérose en plaques," the name still used for MS in French-speaking countries.

Under the microscope the lesions or plaques are seen as areas in which the insulating myelin that normally surrounds axons is disrupted. There is an inflammatory reaction in these plaques, with some repair of fibers in older plaques and some scarring in very old plaques. More episodes and more plaques may appear as years pass. Although repair can still occur and may often be almost complete, the repeated myelin breakdown, incomplete repair, and accumulation of scarring lead to the clinical appearance of progression in most people with MS.

Once the disease was described and had a name, it was possible for physicians everywhere to recognize it. It became clear that MS was not uncommon but was in fact the most common serious neurologic disease in young adults. It followed a number of different patterns and courses, sometimes appeared more than once in the same family, and was more common in certain parts of the world and in Caucasian people.

As the physicians and researchers of today seek answers and learn more about MS, they uncover more questions and more things to learn. But we are learning more, there are more researchers working on the problem, and more research dollars are directed to solving it than ever before.

What Happens in Attacks of MS?

We have defined MS as a neurologic disorder characterized by scattered plaques of demyelination throughout the white matter of the central nervous system. Let's look in more detail at what those terms mean.

The multiple scars that give the disease its name are the end result of the patchy breakdown of the insulating myelin cover that surrounds nerves. Although the symptoms (numbness in a limb, blurred vision in one eye, or weakness in a leg) may suggest that one plaque has developed, there probably is more than one, and possibly many. More surprisingly, some plaques may develop and heal without causing any symptoms.

At first there is an inflammatory response in the plaque, with cells present that are often seen in immunologic reactions. This has led to the belief that the episode of demyelination, or *attack*, may be an immunologic reaction of the body to some material in the myelin sheath, such as a protein (see Chapter 2). Why this happens is not certain. We know of other conditions in which the body's normal defense mechanism that reacts to "foreign" material seems to regard the normal proteins of the body as foreign and reacts against them.

When the episode of demyelination is settling down, other cells clean away the debris and remyelination, or repair of myelin, begins. As a result, the symptoms that occurred during the episode of demyelination may improve or completely disappear, although some lingering damage may have resulted. However, the new myelin conducts nerve impulses somewhat more slowly than normal unaffected myelin. If a physician tests the speed of conduction in these nerves, they may be slower than normal nerves. This change has been used as the basis for tests to identify the disease, such as visual evoked potentials, brain stem auditory evoked potentials, and sensory evoked potentials. These are electrodiagnostic tests that measure the time for a message, such as a light seen by the eye, to pass from the eye to the brain for vision.

Episodes of demyelination accompanied by symptoms of MS may occur over many years. This is another hallmark of the disease—plaques that occur not only in multiple areas of the central nervous system but also in multiple events over time.

The Course of Multiple Sclerosis

The course of MS varies from person to person. We do not know why one person has a progressive course of symptoms and problems, while another has mild disease that produces little disability throughout the life span. Multiple sclerosis can have different patterns in people in the same family, and what pattern a person has seems to have nothing to do with anything we can measure in their bodies, their life activities, or whatever steps they take to manage the disease.

Despite this unpredictability, the course of MS can be classified into four types recently defined by an international survey of MS experts:

- *Relapsing-Remitting*—This form of MS is characterized by clearly defined acute attacks followed either by full recovery or by partial recovery but with some remaining symptoms. The periods between disease relapses are characterized by a lack of new symptoms, although the underlying disease process may be continuing.

  The term *benign* is used to refer to a small segment of people with relapsing-remitting MS who have a mild form of the disease and who remain fully functional in all neurologic systems 15 years after disease onset. This is the most difficult form of MS to "label" because it may require many years to see what pattern is developing. Many people with this form of the disease have mostly sensory symptoms. Because it is impossible to tell which patients may follow this course, decisions about drug treatment should never be based on the possibility that this course may occur.

- *Secondary Progressive*—The disease begins with a relapsing-remitting course. Within 10 to 15 years, approximately 50 percent of those with a relapsing-remitting course will enter a progressive phase, with a slow but steady decrease in overall condition. Patients may continue to have less frequent acute attacks or may stop having attacks altogether. It is not yet known whether treatment with one of the relatively new immunomodulating agents will decrease the number of people who develop this form of the disease.

- *Primary Progressive*—The disease shows slow worsening from its onset, without attacks but sometimes with occasional plateaus and temporary minor improvements. This form of MS is more commonly seen in people who develop the disease after the age of 40.

- *Progressive-Relapsing*—This pattern of MS shows progression from onset, but later on one or more attacks occur.

Remissions can occur at any time in the course of MS and can last for months or many years. Why they occur is not known, and we are not able to tell in whom they will occur or when. Remissions are more common in the early stages of the disease and in the relapsing-remitting type.

The Diagnosis of Multiple Sclerosis

It is often said that MS is a difficult diagnosis to make, but that is true only in some instances. Many patients who consult a neurologist can be diagnosed clinically without any doubt on the first visit. Other situations are more difficult, especially when a patient has minor complaints, shows no "findings" or abnormalities on examination, or has a symptom—such as numbness—that also is common in many other conditions, many of which are benign and transient.

The diagnosis of MS is made by a physician, usually a neurologist, who takes a detailed history of the patient's symptoms and complaints, followed by a thorough physical and neurologic examination. Although the disease is suspected and ultimately diagnosed by the clinician's diagnostic skills, two things can assist in the diagnostic process.

The first is a set of criteria for establishing the diagnosis, which were updated in 2001 by the "International Panel on the Diagnosis of Multiple Sclerosis," supported by the National Multiple Sclerosis Society and the International Federation of Multiple Sclerosis Societies (Table 1.1). Although the terms may sound very general, the patient suspected of having MS is classified by the physician as having "possible" MS or "definite" MS. When a neurologist says that a person has MS, it means that he or she has had more than one episode or attack of symptoms occurring in multiple areas of the white matter of the CNS; in some instances, instead of attacks, there will have been progression over a long time, again characterized by changes typical of involvement of many areas of the white matter in the CNS.

When a person does not demonstrate all the criteria for MS, he or she may be classified as having possible MS, on the basis that other conditions that might cause similar symptoms have been determined as unlikely, and additional features of the disease may become evident in time. Common examples of patients who are initially classified as having possible MS are those who present with their first symptom (thus, there have not been multiple episodes and they have not been progressive over a long time) or those who have had repeated episodes but always in one site (thus, not multiple in the areas involved).

The second helpful aid to the neurologist is a group of tests that may confirm the suspicion of MS. Remember, though, that the diagnosis is still a clinical decision, and there is no test that says definitively that MS is present. The test can only suggest changes that are compatible with the diagnosis, and the neurologist uses this to aid his or her clinical judgment. None are 100 percent accurate, but they are helpful in most cases.

Clinical Examination

The clinical examination has three major parts:

(1) *History.* The history includes not only the story of your symptoms and complaints but also your general health during your lifetime,

Evidence of more than one area of CNS (central nervous system) involvement (*dissemination in "space"*) and CNS involvement at more than one time (*dissemination in "time"*) are required for a diagnosis of MS.

Attacks	Lesions	Additional Requirements
Symptoms lasting at least 24 hours	Areas of involvement in the CNS demonstrated on neurologic examination	MRI—magnetic resonance imaging CS—cerebro-spinal fluid obtained by spinal tap VEP—visual evoked potential (non-invasive)
2 or more	2 or more	None
2 or more	1	*Dissemination in "space" shown by:* Multiple MRI lesions in specific locations or Positive CSF and fewer MRI lesions or Additional attack at different CNS site
1	2 or more	*Dissemination in "time" shown by:* MRI lesions or Second attack
1 (1 symptom or "mono-symptomatic")	1	*Dissemination in "space" shown by:* Multiple MRI lesions in specific locations or Positive CSF and 2 or more lesions consistent with MS **and** *Dissemination in "time" shown by* MRI or Second attack
Primary Progressive (progressive from onset)	1	Positive CSF **and** *Dissemination in "space" shown by:* Multiple MRI lesions in specific locations or 2 or more MRI cord lesions or Fewer MRI brain lesion plus 1 cord lesion or Positive VEP with brain lesions or Positive VEP with fewer brain lesions plus 1 cord lesion **and** *Dissemination in "time" shown by:* MRI or Continued progression for 1 year

Adapted from McDonald et al. Recommended Diagnostic Criteria for MS. *Ann Neurology* 2001; 50:121-127.

Table 1-1   New Diagnostic Criteria.

your operations and accidents, illnesses in your family, occupational information, and other details. This often is the most important part of the examination. The neurologist often makes the diagnosis during this part of the assessment, even before the neurologic examination or diagnostic tests, which are most often used to confirm the neurologist's suspicions from the history.

(2) *Examination*. To get a complete picture of your health and to better understand your symptoms, the neurologist performs a general physical examination that includes listening to your chest and heart, taking your blood pressure, and examining your muscles and skin, as well as a neurologic examination that includes examining your eyes, the cranial nerves to your head and face, your strength, sensation, and vibration over various parts of the body, your reflexes, and your balance and walking. Sometimes a patient is surprised to have his feet and abdomen examined when the complaint is of numbness in a hand. However, this overall examination provides a picture of your nervous system and is able to identify other conditions that might explain the symptoms you are experiencing.

(3) *Tests*. A number of tests can help to confirm that MS may be present and also can identify other problems that mimic its symptoms. Some patients so clearly have MS when they are assessed that no tests are necessary, or only one may be used to confirm the disease and rule out other problems that might be under suspicion. Following are only the most commonly used and valuable tests.

Tests

MAGNETIC RESONANCE IMAGING (MRI)

A few decades ago the MRI would have seemed like science fiction—a test that produces a picture of your brain as you lie inside a huge electromagnet that momentarily spins the molecules in your body. Minutes later the computer produces a remarkable picture of your nervous system that looks like a black-and-white photograph from an anatomy textbook. More remarkable for those who care for people with MS, the MRI is particularly good at detecting the patchy areas of change in the nervous system that occur with MS. It has become the most accurate and helpful test for MS, positive for changes consistent with MS in nine of ten people with proven MS.

The MRI examination is done while you lie on a table that moves inside a tubelike space in a large machine that holds a magnet. The person lies very still, and the magnet sends information to a computer that receives thousands of tiny bits of information and uses them to generate pictures. These images are like slices or views at many levels throughout the brain or the spinal cord, or wherever the scanner is set. No discomfort is associated with the procedure, and the scanners are becoming faster, so that the length of time for a scan decreases each year. A few people have some feeling of claustrophobia and dislike the closed-in feeling of the narrow space. Most people can tolerate it, especially when they know how important it is and when they have a clear explanation of the procedure and receive support and encouragement from the staff. However, anxiety experienced by some people can be easily reduced by mild sedation, such as diazepam (Valium®) 10 mg.

The MRI is an amazing technological advance that can help in the diagnosis of many diseases and also is helpful in research. However, there are some drawbacks to its completeness as a test for MS. Because it is so complex, the machinery, support systems, and personnel needed to operate them are very expensive. The cost of the test often is in the range of $500 to over $1,000—higher if more complex procedures are necessary.

Another drawback is that the MRI is not always positive or conclusive in patients with MS, especially if they are at an early stage in the disease and have had only a few or very mild symptoms. Furthermore, the test does not "show MS"; it shows changes that *could be* due to MS. We must remember that other conditions occasionally cause similar changes. That is why the clinical picture is most helpful and can indicate whether other problems should be considered or whether this is a typical story of MS symptoms, with typical findings of MS on examination, and with typical changes in keeping with MS on the MRI.

Finally, although the MRI can confirm the diagnosis, it does not tell us all the things you and we want to know, such as whether the disease is mild or advanced or whether it is getting worse (those are clinical features). Further developments in MRI techniques undoubtedly will allow us to answer many more of these questions.

CEREBROSPINAL FLUID

The cerebrospinal fluid (CSF) surrounds the brain and spinal cord and fills some cavities within the nervous system. A fine needle can be inserted into the lower back (below the end of the spinal cord) to remove a sample of this clear fluid for examination of cells, protein, and electrolytes; this is a *lumbar puncture*, also called an LP or a spinal tap. If the radiologist wants to see the outline of the space in which the CSF flows, a myelogram is performed, in which a dye is injected into the spinal canal and X-rays are taken. This procedure is done if compression of the cord by a disc or tumor is suspected.

A number of tests can be done on the CSF fluid, but the most useful in MS is to examine the proteins for the presence of *oligoclonal bands*; the protein is put on a gel and a current is passed through it in the laboratory to separate these bands. Approximately nine of ten people who have a well-established pattern of MS have bands in the CSF, but unfortunately this pattern is less common in early and very mild cases. The CSF is usually examined if the MRI is not conclusive but the clinical picture is still suggestive of MS.

Many people have heard that having a lumbar puncture is uncomfortable, but it usually does not cause much discomfort and often can be done on an outpatient basis. Unfortunately, about one-third of people get a headache when they sit up after the test, a problem that may last for days. Lying flat on the abdomen to facilitate closure of the puncture site and taking abundant oral fluids to replace CSF lost through testing should minimize this side effect.

EVOKED POTENTIAL STUDIES

The principle of evoked potential (EP) studies is simple. Nerves that have experienced demyelination conduct impulses more slowly than normal, even if they have healed and remyelinated. Evoked potential studies measure the rate and form of the impulse as it passes through specific nerves. The only evoked potential study that can strongly support the diagnosis of MS is the visual study.

Visual evoked potential studies assess conduction of messages through the optic nerves behind the eye. To stimulate the visual system, the person may be asked to watch a TV screen that shows a checkerboard or some other pattern that rapidly changes, producing a stimulus that passes through the visual system to the occipital cortex of the brain (located at the back of the skull) where vision is processed. Electrodes over the scalp measure the wave form and the speed of the impulse to determine whether one differs from the other or if characteristic changes consistent with a diagnosis of MS are present.

Watchful Waiting

Uncertainty is difficult to cope with, and many people would like answers to their problems, even if they are unpleasant. Definitive answers are not always possible.

In perhaps 10 to 15 percent of cases, the answer to the question "Is MS the cause of these symptoms?" remains uncertain even after all available examinations and tests have been done. By this time the neurologist will have eliminated other possibilities such as a tumor or a disc pressing on the nervous system. He often will know that MS could be causing the symptoms but that other conditions might also be responsible. This uncertainty can be upsetting, but the approach at this point must be one of "wait and see," with periodic examinations and visits to the physician if new problems appear or changes occur. In most instances, the diagnosis becomes clear over time. This requires patience by both the person with symptoms and the physician, but if they agree that they will wait together, the patient usually accepts the situation, having been reassured aboutthe absence of tumors and other worries. In some instances, the problem later turns out to be something other than MS, often a mild, benign, or treatable condition. It is better to wait than to be prematurely labeled as having MS on the basis of unclear evidence.

The Outcome

When a person develops MS, she naturally wants to know what this will mean in the long term, relative to life, health, and family. Unfortunately, uncertainty and unpredictability are characteristics of the disease, as well as of its pattern of symptoms and course. What we *can* say in general terms is that the outlook is improving year by year and will continue to improve. Even before there was therapy to change the underlying disease, the life expectancy of people with MS had been extended to within the normal range as a result of the development of treatments such as antibiotics for bladder and kidney infections and better therapy for many of the complications of the disease. Newly available treatments for the underlying cause of the disease undoubtedly will change the long-term tendency for repeated attacks, progression, and disability, but we still have a long way to go. Research is proceeding rapidly, and although it will never be fast enough or great enough for those suffering daily with MS, we are heading in the right direction.

2

What Is the Cause
of Multiple Sclerosis?

MULTIPLE SCLEROSIS (MS) HAS BEEN KNOWN AND STUDIED AS a distinct disease since the mid-1800s, but the cause of the disease (what scientists call the "etiology") remains a mystery. Although many theories abound as to what the root cause of MS is, none has been proved. Because understanding what causes a disease can lead directly to a better sense of how to prevent and treat it, research into the etiology of MS is one of the most active areas of exploration. Recent findings have brought us closer to a complete understanding of MS and have led to new therapies and new approaches for future treatments.

Recent Theories About the Cause of MS

Multiple sclerosis appears—or, as clinicians say, "presents"— as a neurologic disease. In other words, signs and symptoms of the disease can be attributed to problems in nervous system activity. Consequently, scientific work has focused on how nervous system problems in MS develop.

Autopsy studies of the bodies of individuals who had MS before death reveal the hallmarks of the disease in the *central nervous system* (CNS)—the brain and spinal cord. These include evidence of attack by the body's immune system, including inflammation or swelling of tissue, breakdown and loss of white matter or myelin surrounding nerve fibers and of nerve fibers themselves, and the appearance of hardened scars where myelin has been lost. Immune cells, such as T lymphocytes and macrophages—are present in the lesions. This is important because the CNS normally is immune "privileged" and immune cells usually remain in the bloodstream. In MS, however, such cells are able to penetrate the barrier between the blood and the nervous system—the "blood-brain barrier."

These immune abnormalities trigger a complex process of immune-mediated damage of myelin (primarily) and underlying nerve fibers (believed to be largely a secondary event) and cause a disruption of the proper flow of nerve signals from the brain and spinal cord to muscles and from sensory organs back to the brain and spinal cord. This brings about the typical neurologic problems in balance, gait, bladder and bowel control, numbness, pain, and other problems.

Many theories have been explored as to why the myelin of the CNS is attacked by a person's own immune system in MS. Some of these theories have been proposed simply because they can explain a number of other nervous system diseases with some similarities to MS. For example, congenital defects in nervous system structure or function have been considered, but there does not appear to be any direct link between such abnormalities and increased susceptibility to immune system attack of the sort seen in MS. A direct effect of a virus or bacterial infection on nervous system myelin has been proposed and intensively studied over decades because such infections can cause damage to the nervous system and do cause other nervous system diseases. However, such direct effects have never been proved to be involved in MS, and no single infectious agent has ever been unequivocally associated with its development. Scientists also have considered the possibility that some environmental toxin or even a dietary imbalance may be the cause of MS. Although toxic substances and diet can cause other nervous system problems, no research has supported such a cause for MS.

While years of investigation have not yielded data to support such causes of MS, research in these areas is still being explored by some scientists, and one often hears reports suggesting that one or the other virus or bacterium or chemical contaminant or heavy metal in the environment causes the disease. In spite of the attention and excitement drawn to such reports, further exploration usually has found the claims to have little if any scientific merit or relevance to MS. However, until the true cause of MS is discovered, rational, careful studies in these areas are still appropriate.

A More Likely Possibility: Immune System Problems in MS

Research on the cause of MS since the mid-1950s has focused more closely on the possibility that MS may be a disease of immune system function that becomes clinically apparent in symptoms that involve the nervous system. Many scientists have focused their research efforts on the hypothesis that MS is an "autoimmune" disease, in which elements of a person's immune system are misdirected and, instead of doing the normal job of defending our bodies against viral, bacterial, and parasitic infections, mistakenly turn against some part of the body—in this case against parts of the brain and spinal cord.

The concept of *autoimmunity*—a misdirected immune system attack against "self"—is by no means unique to MS. Diseases such as rheumatoid arthritis (RA), systemic lupus erythematosus (SLE), juvenile-onset or "type 1" diabetes (JD), among others, are also believed to be autoimmune in nature. Many of these diseases share some important characteristics: cells and/or antibodies of the immune system attacking and destroying what appear to be normal parts of a person's body; a tendency to be more prevalent in women than in men in nearly all autoimmune diseases; possible treatment through routes that control immune function; and other similarities.

The evidence that the immune system is involved in MS is fairly clear. First, people with MS seem to have clear-cut abnormalities in immune function compared with healthy individuals. These include, among other factors, evidence that specific white blood cells are present in the CNS that are primed to "recognize' and launch attacks against apparently normal components of the nervous system. In individuals with MS, there is clear reaction of white blood cells—called T cells—against proteins that compose CNS myelin. Interestingly, it has become clear since the mid-1990s that individuals *without* MS also have such T cells that react against myelin in their bloodstream. A key difference may be that in those without MS, such damaging immune cells remain in the bloodstream, separated from the CNS by the blood-brain barrier (BBB).

In MS, the BBB is broken or breached, allowing the immune cells to flow into the CNS tissue and initiate their damaging effects. Breaks in this important barrier can actually be visualized with contrast-enhancing (Gadolinium-enhanced) magnetic resonance images (MRI).

Additionally, in individuals with MS there appears to be an over-representation of cells and other immune system components that enhance immune responses and a relative underrepresentation of cells and immune mediators that suppress immune responses. Most notably, in tissue from individuals with MS immune system cells are clearly found in active lesions of the brain and spinal cord. These immune characteristics are not seen in individuals who do not have MS.

Although immune system involvement in MS seems clear, evidence that the problem is "autoimmune" is difficult to obtain in humans. Actual proof of autoimmunity requires that immune system cells that react against normal body tissue and cause damage in one subject be injected into a healthy subject and cause damage and disease there as well. Although this kind of experiment can be done in laboratory animals to prove autoimmunity, it obviously is not ethical to try to undertake such studies using humans to cause autoimmune disease in otherwise healthy people. Instead, evidence of the autoimmune nature of MS has been extrapolated from studies on laboratory animals with MS-like disease.

For many years, one of the most important avenues of immunology research related to MS has come from study of a laboratory disease of rats, mice, guinea pigs, and primates, called *experimental allergic encephalomyelitis* (EAE), a disease that has been proven to be autoimmune. While EAE is not MS and laboratory animals are not humans, there are many similarities in clinical symptoms and CNS lesion patterns between EAE in these laboratory animals and MS in humans. These similarities have led most scientists to conclude that EAE and MS have similar involvement of the immune system. Experimental allergic encephalomyelitis thus serves in many regards as a "model" for the study of MS, and in particular for studies on the very specific elements of immune function that might be involved in MS-like disease, lending credence to the belief that MS probably is autoimmune as well. It is important to note that EAE studies not only have contributed to our understanding of immune problems in MS but also have been used productively to test "proof of concept" for most current immune therapies now available for, or being tested in, humans with MS.

The Role of Genetics in MS

The possibility that MS may have a genetic component has been known for decades, based primarily on the fact that the disease sometimes seems to "run" in families. We know that MS is not directly inherited, but it is increasingly clear that a complex set of genetic factors helps to determine who may be susceptible to MS and who may not.

Observations that suggest a genetic factor in MS come from studies of many populations around the world.

First, approximately 20 percent of all individuals with MS have at least one additional family member, either in the same generation or in a different generation, who also has or had an MS diagnosis or symptoms that are characteristic of MS even if a diagnosis was never made. This suggests a possible genetic link, but the rate of "concordance" among family members is in itself not high enough to prove a genetic link and certainly not high enough to provide support for direct disease inheritance. However, results from a large-scale study in Canada in the 1990s indicated that the tendency for multiple cases of MS to occur in families is truly genetic and not due to any sort of shared environmental or dietary factor—another possible explanation for such family concordance.

It also has long been known that there are ethnic or religious populations in the world that are *genetically isolated*—they rarely or never marry or bear children outside their own group and thus have developed a relatively restricted and unique gene pool. Some of these groups rarely or never get MS. Examples include such religious sects as the Hutterites in Canada and such ethnic groups as Eastern European gypsies. While living in areas where there is a relatively high incidence of MS, these groups seem to be protected from MS. Genetically isolated populations are of great interest in disease research—not only those that seem to be "resistant" but also those in which disease may be prevalent. Such populations most likely have a more restricted pool of genes, raising the possibility that they can be used to more easily isolate disease-relevant gene factors. Studies on the genetics are under way in genetically isolated populations in locations such as western Finland and Tasmania, where scientists hope that new clues to MS genetics may be easier to obtain.

Related to this is the fact that there are racial differences in the incidence of MS. In North America, the disease occurs more commonly among Caucasians than among African Americans, even in the same community. Multiple sclerosis is almost never seen in Canadian Eskimos, even though the disease is quite common among Caucasian Canadians. In Africa, pure Bantus virtually never get MS, although Caucasians living in the same countries are susceptible. Also, MS is seen much less often—and in a clinical type quite different from that of Caucasians—among Asians in the Far East and in Asian Americans in North America, Europe, and Australia.

Even though there is clear increased susceptibility to MS in some families, many cases of MS are "sporadic." In other words, they appear in a family with no history of MS whatsoever. But even in "multiplex" families in which more than one case of MS may occur, the risk of disease is still quite low. In the United States, about one in 1,000 people have MS; when a family member (parent, sibling, aunt/uncle) already has the disease, the risk increases to 2 to 5 per 100, depending on the degree of relationship. This is an increase in susceptibility but still a relatively low risk. For twins, an important finding is that among nonidentical ("fraternal" or "dizygotic") twins, the risk resembles that for any other sibling; however, among identical twins ("monozygotic twins," who are genetically identical) the risk of both twins having MS if one twin has been diagnosed rises dramatically to as high as 30 percent, a clear indication of the importance of genetic factors.

While such information might one day provide us with the ability to predict susceptibility, it cannot yet help us. The risk rates are low even within families in which MS already exists. Inheritance patterns in MS are extremely complex and poorly understood. Large genetic studies have been undertaken in the United States, Canada, and the United Kingdom, taking advantage of the existence of families with multiple individuals who have MS and many who do not. From these studies we have learned that no single genetic factor is responsible for MS or even dominant in the MS genetic picture. Rather, there are many genetic factors that might contribute to MS susceptibility. There is no current identified single gene, and there is not likely to be one, that can be said to cause MS, as has been shown for diseases such as Huntington's chorea, Duchenne muscular dystrophy, and cystic fibrosis.

The fact that identical twins are not always "concordant" for MS (since both twins have an MS diagnosis only about 30 percent of the time) clearly indicates that, as important as genetic factors may be, other nongenetic factors contribute to determining MS susceptibility.

What Sets Off the Disease? Possible Environmental Triggers

For decades, studies of where MS exists in the world and where it is absent ("epidemiology" and "demographics") have suggested that some triggering factor in the environment must start the disease process. Data suggest that some factor—most likely infectious—must be encountered before the age of 15 in order for the disease process to be triggered later in life. Although somewhat controversial, this finding stimulated the search, over the last 45 years, for a virus or other infectious agent that causes, or at least triggers, MS.

Many common and uncommon viruses have been proposed as causative agents for MS over the past several decades. Many of these proposals have been based on the presence of virus in tissues from individuals with MS or, more often, the presence of immune system antibodies against viruses in the blood. In recent years, technology has become more sophisticated, and such searches include the use of polymerase chain reaction (PCR) analysis to detect protein "footprints" in blood, cerebrospinal fluid, and tissue, even if whole virus cannot be seen. In each case in which claims of a causative or triggering infectious agent have been made using such analyses, to date, further scientific work intended to confirm and expand upon data has failed to support the initial claim. Ongoing work, current as of 2001, continues to focus on human herpesvirus 6 (HHV-6) a common virus that causes roseola in infants and has been linked by some scientists to MS. A common bacterium, *Chlamydia pneumoniae*, which is responsible for "walking pneumonia," also has been linked to MS by some researchers.

Rather than focusing on a single infectious agent, many scientists now believe that individuals with MS have a heightened immune antibody response against a host of common and uncommon viruses and other infectious agents, and that past claims based on antibody responses against viruses are likely very misleading. While this has not stopped the search for a specific MS agent, it has made such a search and any claims that have resulted subject to skepticism in recent years.

With a new understanding of the importance of immunology in the MS disease process, many scientists have shifted their view of the role of specific viruses and other infectious agents in MS away from the search for a direct cause of the disease toward learning how an immune system response against an infectious agent may result in a later autoimmune disease. Increased attention has been paid to the possibility that many viruses, bacteria, and perhaps other pathogens could serve as a trigger for the autoimmune process that becomes MS.

Demyelination: The Cause of Symptoms

The damage done by an immune reaction against myelin and nerve tissue in the CNS might truly be considered the cause of MS because it is this process that results in neurologic signs and symptoms observed in the clinic and experienced by the individual with MS. As noted previously, immune system T cells normally in the bloodstream become activated against components of brain myelin. They cross the barrier between the bloodstream and the CNS, causing local inflammation in the brain and spinal cord in scattered places, but most often around blood vessels and cavities in the brain called *ventricles*. This process eventually results in inflammation and damage to the myelin insulation around nerve fibers and may result in damage and loss of nerve fibers as well. Lost myelin is extremely difficult for the nervous system to repair, and soon cells called *astrocytes* form scars where myelin previously existed.

Inflammation, loss of myelin and nerve fibers, and subsequent scarring result in reduced conduction of nerve signals within the CNS, out to muscles, and back from sensory organs. These conduction problems produce the symptoms that characterize the disease.

So, What Is the Cause of MS?

Multiple sclerosis is, to be sure, a complex disease that is just beginning to be unraveled. There remains no known single cause of MS, and it is likely that the disease is the result of a number of related factors. While symptoms come from problems in the nervous system, MS appears to be a disease of immune system function, most likely an autoimmune disease, which attacks the nervous system. Although the disease is not directly inherited, there is a genetic susceptibility. A triggering factor, or a combination of factors, seems to be involved, but no definite virus, bacterium, or other infectious or environmental agent has been identified. The ultimate consequence of the immune system problems in MS is the entrance of immune cells into the CNS, attack of myelin around nerve fibers, and eventual myelin and nerve fiber loss and scarring. The entire process results in the failure of nerve signals to operate properly, and this results in the well-known symptoms that are the hallmark of MS.

3

What Treatment Is Available?

THE MEDICAL MANAGEMENT OF MULTIPLE SCLEROSIS (MS) IS accomplished through a partnership of health professionals, the person with MS, and his or her family. Aspects of both symptomatic treatment and management of the disease course are addressed in this chapter.

People often say that there is no treatment for a disease when there is no "magic bullet," a simple cure that makes the disease go away, as penicillin may do for pneumonia. There is yet no "cure" for MS, but there are many treatments and approaches that will help you to understand and cope with the challenges, as well as many treatments and procedures to reduce its symptoms. Additionally, we are now in an era in which there are agents that lessen the number and severity of attacks, the progression of the disease, and the development of disability.

One of the most important first steps in dealing with MS is to learn more about it. You need to know what you can do to stay healthy and to reduce the problems that may confront you and your family. You are in control of much that is important in managing this disease. The fact that you are reading this book shows that you are already taking charge of one of the first things over which you have control—being informed and educated about MS.

Resources

Although your physician and other health care professionals will be able to offer many of the treatments and procedures discussed, you should begin by facilitating access to additional information through membership in the National (U.S.), Canadian, or other national MS societies. Some people are reluctant to join at first because they are uncertain of what commitment this might involve. There is none! Being a member will provide access to the best up-to-date information and help with issues and problems related to having MS. You can learn about ongoing research and important advances as they occur. Multiple Sclerosis Societies and their local chapters have many pamphlets on all important aspects of the disease (see Chapter 9).

There are many books about MS. Some are excellent, and others are not. Some are by professionals who manage the disease, some are by individuals who have successfully adapted to its limitations, and some are by enthusiasts for proposed new treatments. Consulting the MS Society will help to keep a balanced view because the publications it recommends have been carefully reviewed for both accuracy and usefulness.

People with MS often hear of possible treatments from friends and the media, and it is often difficult to distinguish those that are useful from those that are not (or that may actually be harmful). We strongly recommend that you check any suggested treatments made by people other than your physician or nurse with reliable sources, including your local chapter of the National Multiple Sclerosis Society or the books recommended in the "Additional Readings" section of this book.

Types of Treatment

Treatments in MS can be grouped into different categories:

- management of the acute attack
- treatment of the underlying disease
- management of symptoms

Management of Acute Attacks

When there is a change in symptoms over a few days or weeks, with the development of new symptoms or the worsening of old ones, the event may be a new "attack" of the disease. It usually means that new patches of inflammation and demyelination are occurring, in either new or old sites in the *central nervous system* (CNS)—the brain and spinal cord. These often are mild and cease after a few days or weeks. Treatment may be indicated if the symptoms are severe or continue to worsen. The swelling and inflammation in the plaques of demyelination can be reduced by high-dose intravenous (IV) methylprednisolone.

Some people may begin to recover soon after steroid therapy has started, but in others improvement may occur only slowly, even weeks after the treatment. As some spontaneous recovery is expected after most acute attacks, it sometimes is difficult to know how much was due to the treatment and how much would have occurred without it.

Not all episodes of new symptoms require therapy with IV steroids, but a number of treatment schedules can be used if indicated. There are some differences in the total steroid dose, the number of days of treatment, and the time between doses, but all are characterized by a high dose over a short period. This usually is given on an outpatient basis and generally is well tolerated, although some people experience emotional changes during the therapy and may have trouble sleeping.

If there is numbness in a limb, dizziness, or some other symptom that is annoying but not limiting in any way, your neurologist may decide to wait and see if the problem clears spontaneously, as it often does. An attack that has stopped progressing and is improving may be allowed to clear on its own. High-dose steroids help people to recover from an attack somewhat faster, but since they might recover just as well with time, decisions about treatment must be made on an individual basis. The repetitive use of steroids can have long-term effects that include cataracts and osteoporosis; therefore, their use should be reserved for more serious attacks that are not clearing spontaneously.

Although it is reasonable to rest when you have MS, especially during attacks, it generally is overdone and overrecommended. There is good evidence that you will be tired if you do not get a reasonable amount of rest (although some tiredness in MS, referred to as "MS fatigue," does not respond to rest), but there is little evidence that your MS will be worse with less rest. The fear that MS will become worse if you do not rest is without foundation and makes people fearful of doing normal things when they have symptoms. People may rest too much and thereby feel weary and weak, or stop work or neglect their responsibilities when they are capable of continuing these activities. A reasonable approach is to rest when you are tired and to develop a schedule that allows for a slower pace.

The best advice to people with MS is not "rest, with reasonable activity," but rather "stay active, with reasonable rest." The difference is placement of the emphasis. Slow down and rest more when symptoms and fatigue are a problem or when an attack occurs, but stay as active as you can and increase your activity again when the symptoms settle down.

Treatment of the Underlying Disease

Only recently have therapies become available that offer the promise of having an impact on the ultimate course of the disease. None of the currently available therapies will cure or completely stop the disease, but we have made a great deal of progress toward more effective treatment, with medications that reduce the number and severity of attacks and that will result in less progression and disability over the years.

These include three different interferon beta preparations and glatiramer acetate. They have been approved in many countries, and other agents will soon appear. These agents have been approved for use in MS based on extensive clinical trials. Most neurologists make their decision as to which drug is appropriate for a given patient based on that individual's disease characteristics.

Fairly good evidence indicates that the agents discussed in the following sections are helpful if they are used in the early relapsing stages of the disease, but evidence for their effectiveness if the disease moves to a progressive phase is unclear at this time.

It is important to recognize that these new agents help, but do not stop, problems or changes caused by MS. Some people who have taken them have greater expectations than the treatments can deliver and become discouraged and stop the drugs because they continue to have further problems. The hope is that over time you will be better than if you did not have the treatment, not that you will suddenly notice yourself improving.

Both the National Multiple Sclerosis Society of the United States and the Canadian MS Clinics Network have issued statements on the use of disease-modifying agents; these are excerpted here.

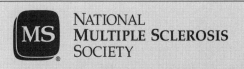

NATIONAL
MULTIPLE SCLEROSIS
SOCIETY

CLINICAL BULLETIN

Information for Health Professionals

Disease Management Consensus Statement

RECOMMENDATIONS

The Medical Advisory Board of the National Multiple Sclerosis Society has adopted the following recommendations regarding use of the current MS disease-modifying agents—Betaseron® (beta interferon 1 b), Avonex® (beta interferon 1 a), and Copaxone® (glatiramer acetate) (Rebif® is not currently available in the United States):

- Initiation of therapy is advised as soon as possible following a definite diagnosis of MS and determination of a relapsing course.
- Patients' access to medication should not be limited by the frequency of relapses, age or level of disability.
- Treatment is not to be stopped during evaluation for continuing treatment.
- Therapy is to be continued indefinitely, unless there is clear lack of benefit, intolerable side effects, new data which reveals other reasons for cessation, or better therapy is available.
- All three agents should be included in formularies and covered by third party payors so that physicians and patients may determine the most appropriate agent on an individual basis.
- Movement from one immunomodulating drug to another should be permitted.
- Most concurrent medical conditions do not contraindicate use of any of these therapies.

Consensus Statement of the Canadian MS Clinics Network on: The Use of Disease Modifying Agents in Multiple Sclerosis

The following statement relates to the currently available Health Protection Branch (HPB) approved medications for the treatment of multiple sclerosis: Avonex® (Interferon beta 1a), Betaseron (Interferon Beta 1b), Rebif® (Interferon Beta 1b) and Copaxone® (glatiramer acetate).

THE FOLLOWING ARE THE CRITERIA FOR CONSIDERATION OF THERAPY IN RELAPSING MS

- Patients must have "definite MS" as per Poser's Committee criteria.
- The course of disease must include clinical attacks.
- There must be evidence of ongoing "active" disease as indicated by either clinical history, repeated neurological assessments or advanced neuroimaging (MRI).
- The patient must be ambulatory with or without aid.

ADDITIONAL CONDITIONS

- Patients must agree to regular follow-up with the prescribing physician.
- Female patients must consent to practice appropriate contraception.
- There must be an incumbent mechanism to assure proper education before prescription, along with proper follow-up to assure compliance and monitor side effects with any recommended therapy.

IT IS FURTHER RECOMMENDED THAT

- All eligible patients be treated as early as possible in the course of their disease.
- All four currently HPB approved agents should be included in provincial formularies as each may have unique indications, and patients may demonstrate intolerance to one, but not another agent.
- Periodic review of patients be undertaken to evaluate efficacy in order to decide upon the appropriateness for continuing treatment, switching drug or discontinuing treatment.
- Each province establish a mechanism to evaluate any patient not fulfilling the above criteria, but whose physician feels warrants treatment.

THE BETA INTERFERONS

Interferons are naturally occurring proteins that are produced when the body reacts to a foreign substance or agent such as a virus. They belong to a class of molecules called *cytokines*, the hormones of the immune system. These cytokines are important regulators of the immune response to viruses and inflammatory conditions. Beta interferon seems to "calm" the immune system and is referred to as an *immunomodulatory agent*.

Beta Interferon-1b (Betaseron®)

Beta interferon-1b was the first medication to be approved for treatment of the MS disease process. The first studies of the drug were carried out on patients with established relapsing-remitting MS. They demonstrated a reduction in the number and severity of attacks, as well as a reduction of the number of lesions seen on the MRI brain scan. Longer term studies are showing some modification in the rate of progression of the disease as well, but these studies are as yet inconclusive. The drug is self-injected under the skin every other day, using a technique similar to the way a person with diabetes uses insulin. It does cause some side effects, which usually are manageable and tolerable. These include mild flulike symptoms after the injections, which can be relieved by simple analgesics and lessen with time, and skin reactions at the injection sites, which may persist for days or weeks. The flulike symptoms almost always disappear with time, but local injection site reactions may continue to occur.

Betaseron has been available only since 1993, so it is still too early to know how beneficial Betaseron® will be over the longer term, particularly in people who start on the drugs early in the course of the disease.

Beta Interferon-1a (Avonex®)

Beta interferon-1a has also been shown to be safe and effective. It is administered weekly by intramuscular injection. This medication also has been approved for the treatment of relapsing-remitting MS. In a recent study it was shown to delay a second attack of MS if used soon after a first episode. People who have had a positive MRI and one episode that looked like an MS attack are said to be "at risk" for having MS. As discussed in Chapter 1, one of the criteria for labeling someone as having "clinically definite MS" is having had more than one attack. The MRI may sometimes show slight brain shrinkage even early in the disease, and early studies suggest that this drug may slow or delay that process.

Beta Interferon-1a (Rebif®)

This drug is similar to natural interferon beta and is administered by the subcutaneous route three times a week, usually on Monday, Wednesday, and Friday. Rebif® is approved in 67 countries but is not yet available in the United States. There are two dosage forms available: 22 micrograms (mcg) and 44 mcg, which are provided ready to use in a prefilled syringe. The recommended dose in Europe is 44 mcg given three times a week in relapsing-remitting MS. This dose demonstrated reduced relapse frequency, slower progression in disability, and fewer lesions in the brain. The lower dose (22 mcg) given only once a week has shown some effect in delaying the second attack and hence the diagnosis of "clinically definite MS."

GLATIRAMER ACETATE (COPAXONE®)

Glatiramer acetate or Copaxone® is not an interferon. Rather, it is a *substitute antigen* that mimics myelin basic protein, an important component of the CNS myelin sheath and a major immune target in many people with MS. It is given at a dose of 20 mg subcutaneously daily by injection under the skin and is well tolerated by most people. Glatiramer acetate appears to inhibit the CNS immune reactions that are responsible for tissue damage and the production of MS plaques in people with MS.

The interferons show benefit on MRI parameters within a few weeks and on clinical parameters by three months. Glatiramer acetate also shows clinical benefit by three months, but appears to take several months to show its full benefit on MRI. It has been shown to reduce the number of attacks and to reduce the number of brain lesions seen on MRI in patients with relapsing- remitting MS. Side effects are transient, but they may include flushing, palpitations/tachycardia, chest pain, and dyspnea (difficulty breathing); it does not produce the flulike symptoms associated with the interferons.

OTHER DISEASE-MODIFYING AGENTS

In addition to the four drugs discussed, other agents sometimes are used for more advanced disease. Mitoxantrone and azathioprine are the most common of these and are discussed here because you may read or hear about them.

Mitoxantrone (Novantrone®)

Mitoxantrone is an anticancer drug that also is a strong immune system suppressant. It has been highly effective in suppressing the animal model disease EAE, and encouraging results have been reported in several trials, which showed a marked decrease in active MS lesions on MRI scanning and some reduction in the progression of MS. The drug was approved for use in MS by the U.S. Food and Drug Administration (FDA) in 2000 and generally is reserved for people with MS whose disease is seriously worsening. The long-term use of this drug is limited by the risk of serious cardiac complications.

Azathioprine (Imuran®)

Azathioprine has been available for many decades and has been widely used in Europe but less so in North America. There is some evidence that it reduces the number of attacks of MS and may reduce disability from the disease to some extent. The effect is modest at best, and in trials it took years to see benefits over those not receiving the therapy. It comes in pill form, is easy to use, and is inexpensive. However, there has been concern that this immunosuppressant might increase the incidence of certain malignancies (such as lymphomas) if it is taken on a long-term basis. Recent European studies have not shown such an increase, so its use is increasing. Regular blood tests are required when a patient is receiving this medication to detect early indications of liver dysfunction or effects on the blood counts. There are trials under way to assess the effect of combining azathioprine with an interferon.

Management of Symptoms

It is important to recognize that although a wide range of symptoms may occur with MS, a given individual may experience only some of them and never have others. Some symptoms may occur once, resolve, and never return. Because it is such an individual disease, it is not helpful—and may be misleading and frightening—to compare yourself with someone else, who often will have different symptoms, a different pattern of disease activity, and a different pattern of progression.

The most common symptoms of MS include numbness, fatigue, weakness, blurred vision, poor balance, and difficulty walking. As mentioned previously, you may experience one or more of these and never have others.

MOBILITY

Weakness

It is common for a person with MS to have symptoms of weakness in one or both legs. Initially this may be transient, lasting days or weeks during an attack, but in some people weakness develops over many years as a major symptom. Because the nerves in the CNS have important function in the motor control over muscles, patches of demyelination may affect these fibers and cause weakness in different muscle groups, most commonly in the legs. In some people, especially those who develop the disease after the age of 40, leg weakness and spasticity may be the only symptoms of MS, progressing slowly without any acute attacks.

It is common to develop weakness during an attack of MS, but sometimes weakness may be present all the time. The pattern of weakness can be asymmetrical, involving one limb or one side more than the other, or it can seem to be only in the legs. If it comes on in an acute attack, it is treated with IV steroids. If it is persistent, it is important for the neurologist to decide how much is related to weakness in the muscles, how much is due to *spasticity* or increased tone in the muscles, and how much is contributed by a change in sensation that make the limbs seem more clumsy.

If weakness is present, you should be encouraged to increase your level of exercise to strengthen the muscles. A physical therapist can help if you experience a lot of weakness, but if the weakness is mild, you can do an exercise program on your own. It is important to remember that any muscle can be strengthened. Just as "normal" muscles can be made stronger by exercise, weak ones also can be trained and strengthened by exercise. The muscles may not return to normal, but they will be stronger than they otherwise would have been, and that is always worthwhile.

If there is a lot of weakness in a limb, various aids, such as an ankle brace for a drop foot or a cane, may be necessary to help with walking until improvement is seen. Foot drop usually is first noticed when "tripping" over your foot occurs, causing the tips of shoes on the affected side to become scraped or scuffed. If weakness persists after treatment with steroids, a referral for physical therapy may be arranged so that the problems can be assessed, an exercise program developed, and any immediate problems treated.

You should continue a regular exercise program even after weakness has improved (see "A Note About Exercise" later in this chapter).

SPASTICITY

A complex control of muscle movements normally allows some muscles to contract and some to relax when a movement is carried out. This control can inhibit certain muscles and contract others when there is disruption to nerves in the CNS, resulting in the simultaneous contraction of many muscles, both the ones that help (agonists) and those that oppose the movement (antagonists). This causes the "tone" to increase in all the muscles, the limb to feel tight, and the limb movements to be slower and less smooth. It is more difficult and more tiring to walk with legs that have spasticity.

Spasticity can be reduced by exercise and by normal use of the muscles. It is important to perform stretching exercises of the spastic, tight muscles to prevent *contractures*, a state in which the tight muscle shortens. Each muscle should be stretched fully and held for a minute (See "A Note About Exercise").

A number of medications that are considered muscle relaxants do not work well in MS and can have side effects. An effective medication for spasticity and the symptoms that it produces (spasms, cramps, pain, aching) is baclofen (Lioresal®; as of this writing, production of the brand-name drug has ceased and only generic baclofen is available), which can be taken in different ways depending on the symptoms, their severity, and the person's tolerance to the medication. Because some people have painful spasms only at night and minor spasticity in the daytime, a nightly dose may be all that is needed. Others need relief from spasticity all the time, and a schedule of four doses a day is developed. Because all patients can reach a dosage level that seems too high, causing a general feeling of weakness and drowsiness, your doctor may start you with a very low dose, perhaps half a tablet (5 mg) twice a day, and slowly increase by adding a further half tablet every three days until symptoms are reasonably controlled. If symptoms are helped at a low dose, the dose is held there. If you develop side effects when the dose is increased, they may be eliminated by skipping a dose and going back to the previous level. Baclofen is very helpful in reducing the spasms and pain sometimes associated with spasticity, but it is only somewhat helpful in improving function limited by spasticity.

Tizanidine (Zanaflex®) is also an effective antispasticity agent that has effects similar to those of baclofen. It is especially effective for night spasms and sometimes is effective in reducing spasticity in patients who do not respond to other agents. Its use in combination with low doses of baclofen may produce an optimal antispasticity effect with fewer side effects. Tizanidine may cause a feeling of tiredness, and this can be minimized by slowly increasing the dose as this therapy begins.

Disturbances of Balance and Gait

Disturbances of gait and balance are common in MS because they can be caused by changes in different parts of the nervous system. A person may note that he or she does not walk or stand as steadily if experiencing incoordination, weakness in one or more limbs, numbness, dizziness, vertigo, or even visual problems. One of the most troublesome causes of gait disturbance is spasticity in the muscles of the legs. For some people, this is the most limiting problem of MS. Because so much of what we do involves being mobile, this problem causes the most disability and handicap in the disease over the lifetime of many (but not all) people with MS.

In many instances, difficulty in walking comes with the various symptoms of an attack of MS, improving or clearing as the attack settles down. In other instances, it is an ongoing problem. A person with MS may have few other problems except a gait difficulty that slowly increases over a period of years. This pattern is more common in those who develop the disease later in life.

Physical therapy can be helpful for gait difficulty, and a physical therapist can show you techniques of gait training, muscle strengthening, exercises, safety hints, and the use of mobility aids.

A Note About Exercise

Exercise is important for everyone, especially a person with MS. A program of range of motion exercises is one exercise program that you should do daily, or even more than once a day if your muscles are very stiff. Each joint is put through its full range of motion to keep it healthy and lubricated and to stretch and loosen the muscles that move the joints.

A simple exercise program that anyone can manage is the 10-10-20 exercise program, in which 10 general exercises are performed, each for 10 repetitions, for a duration of a 20-minute exercise period. The 10 exercises are general ones that improve overall fitness. They can be altered according to individual capacity and the need to overcome specific problems or weak areas. They can be individually designed by a physical therapist and modified as needs change.

Swimming has a number of advantages, although it often is more difficult to arrange on a regular basis. Swimming exercises most muscles, and some movements and exercises can be done more easily in water because the water supports the body during movement. The water should be cool because most people with MS are sensitive to heat and may be bothered by exercises that increase body heat or by warm exercise rooms. Function may be improved just by cooling in a swimming pool. Although swimming in the ocean can have the same effect, waves can easily put you off balance.

Relaxation techniques are useful and improve the enjoyment and rewards of a regular exercise program. They involve methods of learning positive relaxation of the mind and body, deep breathing, and mental imagery, combined with alternating contraction and relaxation of various muscles.

An exercise program should be regular and enjoyable. Anyone can carry out a boring exercise program for a few weeks, but not for a lifetime—which is what we all need to do. That is why many basements have a corner with almost new exercise equipment that has had little use. Some machines look terrific, but they are not very enjoyable to use, and sometimes we think that it is the machines (or physiotherapists) that are going to make us strong. YOU do the exercises, not the machine.

Exercise programs that many people enjoy include swimming, mat exercises, walking, and Tai Chi, but you must think about the exercises that you would find most enjoyable and can imagine still doing regularly years from now.

SENSORY SYMPTOMS

Numbness

The term *numbness* covers many alterations to the sensory system that affect sensation, particularly in the skin. People may experience numbness, but more often they feel tingling, pins and needles, burning, coldness, or other sensations that are difficult to describe. The disruption to the sensory nerves can be in the spinal cord, the brain stem, or the brain itself.

Tingling and numbness are "normal" symptoms that virtually everyone has experienced (a leg falling "asleep," dental anesthesia, cold feet in the winter), but these common occurrences are due to pressure, anesthetics, or cold to a peripheral nerve in an arm or leg, whereas MS affects only the myelin of the nerves in the CNS. It may seem as if the nerve in the leg is affected in MS, but in fact the demyelination is in the CNS, not in the peripheral nervous system. Numbness most often is felt in the ends of the limbs, the feet and lower legs, or the hands, but it can seem to rise from the legs up to the upper abdomen. Sometimes the numbness seems to have a level, as if a belt of numbness were wrapped around the abdomen; it also may be painful, with decreased sensation below the level.

Although numbness often is only a brief annoyance, it can cause other problems if it persists or only partially clears. You may drop things when your hands and fingertips are numb, even light objects such as paper, because you do not know how tightly you are gripping them. Because feeling in your fingers is decreased, you may need to use your vision to help recognize things that you could identify previously with your fingertips. You may have trouble identifying objects in your purse or pocket because numbness can decrease your ability to recognize a comb or a coin by its characteristic feel. You may not realize that good balance involves sensing information about the muscles and tendons in the limbs, which is carried to the nervous system by sensory nerves. If numbness is present in the legs, people use their eyes to maintain good balance. They notice, however, that they look down a lot when they walk and have difficulty walking in the dark and over uneven ground.

Numbness occasionally is accompanied by disagreeable sensations called *dysesthesias*, such as burning, "creepy-crawly" feelings, or sensitive skin (sensations similar to those felt when dental anesthesia is wearing off). These disagreeable feelings usually improve as sensation improves, but they sometimes require treatment. When numbness or dysesthesias occur as part of an acute attack, it usually improves with IV steroids. More persistent disagreeable sensations may be reduced by a tricyclic antidepressant such as amytriptyline (Elavil®). This medication is helpful in relieving sensory problems, even though depression is not related to these symptoms

Some sensation changes are described as pain, which is discussed later in this chapter. One of these is the symptom of an electric shock–like feeling in the back or limbs on flexing the neck. This occurs when there is some inflammation in the posterior columns of the cervical spinal cord, and the bending of the neck stretches these inflamed fibers, causing them to fire. The phenomenon is called *Lhermitte's sign*, named after the French neurologist who described it. It often is transient, clearing when the inflammation settles down, and can be made to clear faster with IV steroids.,

Facial Numbness

A common and upsetting symptom in MS is numbness on one side of the face. However, this is a minor symptom that usually clears without treatment. You might have a tingling feeling or a numbness, often described as similar to dental anesthesia, which at times can involve the gums and tongue. Symptoms around the face are perceived as more disturbing to people than the same degree of numbness elsewhere, such as the foot or hand, but in fact facial numbness often goes away in days or a few weeks. The neurologist may also find subtle differences to various sensations in the face on examination, of which the person is unaware.

Vision Loss

Different types of vision problems may occur in MS. *Optic neuritis* (sometimes called retrobulbar neuritis) is an episode of demyelination in the optic nerve behind the eyeball. Because it occurs in the nerve, a physician looking in the eye during the first episode may not see anything wrong. Later some scarring may occur in the optic nerve, and it will look pale in the back of the eye, seen by the doctor through a hand-held instrument called an ophthalmoscope. High-dose IV steroids is the standard treatment when one eye or occasionally both eyes are affected. Symptoms include blurred vision, loss of peripheral or "side" vision, and one or more black or "blind" spots. Total loss of vision in one eye may occur in some instances. Optic neuritis sometimes also causes pain in the eye, which clears quickly when steroid treatment is begun. Vision returns more slowly. It is common for individuals with relapsing-remitting MS to have one or more episodes of optic neuritis, although many people never experience this problem.

Another visual complaint people with MS may experience is a vague feeling that their vision is not as clear as it should be, even if a recent eye examination indicates vision to be normal. The problem may be with certain contrasts in the visual fields, or with color, which causes a mild change that usually is not detected on standard eye tests. When this occurs, text with sharp contrast is easiest to read. An unusual symptom is a decrease in vision associated with exercise (Uhthoff's phenomenon), probably related to an increase in body heat, which affects nerve conduction. Vision returns when the person stops exercising and cools down.

Some people with MS experience double vision and complain that they cannot see well. Actually, the vision in each eye separately may be normal, but the eyes do not focus together. Although it is annoying, double vision usually clears on its own or responds to IV steroids. It is rarely a persistent problem and can be temporarily relieved by patching one eye.

Another problem in eye control that may be experienced as a visual problem is *nystagmus*. When your physician asks you to move your eyes in different directions, she is testing eye movements and control. Nystagmus is a regular fine jerkiness of the eyes that may occur when looking to the sides, which usually is not noticed by the patient. Sometimes the eyes operate differently in that situation, with one having more jerkiness than the other. This causes a sensation that the environment is moving (oscillopsia) or looks double when looking to the sides. In some people the pupillary response to light is slowed, experienced as difficulty with bright lights, especially while driving at night. Glasses with photosensitive lenses usually compensate for this problem.

All that affects vision is not MS, and you should have regular eye examinations to see if you need glasses to correct the vision changes and eye problems that occur in all of us with age.

Pain

At one time it was believed believed that pain was unusual in MS. We now know that pain in one form or another occurs in more than half of all people who have the disease. It may take the form of an aching in muscles, shooting pains, jabbing facial pain, or discomfort from burning, tingling, or other sensory changes. The first step is to determine the specific cause of the pain. Not all pain is the result of MS, so other problems must be considered. Since pain problems in MS have specific treatments, as does pain from other causes, it is important to identify the underlying cause.

The spasms and cramps in the large muscles of the legs that occur when tone is increased by spasticity can be reduced by physical therapy, exercise, relaxation techniques, passive stretching, massage, and local cold. The pain associated with spasticity can often be effectively reduced with baclofen or tizanidine (Zanaflex®).

Remember that not all symptoms in people with MS are due to the disease and that any problems that cause pain in anyone else also can occur. Joint pain, back pain, abdominal pain, headaches, and other problems may be due to conditions that have nothing to do with MS and should be investigated and treated just as they would if MS were not present.

Facial Pain

A type of nerve pain that can occur in the face, called *trigeminal neuralgia*, is characterized by a sharp, jabbing, knifelike pain, usually over the cheek and sometimes over the eye on one side. Although it can occur as an isolated syndrome in the elderly, it often indicates the underlying demyelinating process of MS in a younger person. Several types of pain occur in the face, including temporomandibular joint (TMJ) pain, tension headache, and migraine. If trigeminal neuralgia is the cause, it is treated with a group of medications that decrease the nerve firing. The initial treatment usually is carbamazepine (Tegretol®), to which most people quickly respond well. In the few people who have unacceptable side effects, baclofen, diphenylhydantoin (Dilantin®), or gabapentin (Neurontin®) is substituted.

A small number of people do not tolerate these medications, lose the beneficial drug effect, or do not respond to them. In such cases, a surgical procedure may be considered. It usually is done on an outpatient basis by a needle procedure through the face into the trigeminal (fifth cranial) nerve. This is usually successful. Trigeminal neuralgia associated with MS is due to the presence of a plaque in the connections of the fifth cranial nerve in the brain stem. Although it can cause severe facial pain, trigeminal neuralgia usually is successfully managed. It is not uncommon for the problem to return months or years after it has been controlled, but treatment can be restarted if it does.

Hearing Changes

It is unusual for people with MS to notice any change in hearing other than that seen in the normal population, but MS can on occasion cause a decrease in hearing. More commonly, a subtle change can be noted on specific testing of the hearing system, but without producing noticeable symptoms. Significant hearing change due to MS is rarely a problem, and when acute episodes of hearing loss do occur, full recovery can be expected.

ELIMINATION

Bladder Control

The most common symptoms of bladder involvement in MS are the need to urinate *often* (frequency) and the need to urinate *now* (urgency). If these symptoms are particularly troublesome, involuntary wetting (incontinence) can occur because of difficulty getting to the bathroom in time. Many people manage this by being aware of their symptoms and taking opportunities to urinate regularly. Markedly restricting fluid intake, which seems to be a logical method of dealing with the problem, is actually a bad idea; your kidneys and bladder need a continuous flow of fluids to excrete wastes and minimize the opportunity for infection.

If frequency and urgency are a more serious problem than you can manage by simple measures, medications such as oxybutynin chloride (Ditropan®), propantheline bromide (Probanthine®), tolterodine tartrate (Detrol®), or flavoxate hydrochloride (Urispas®) may control the problem. It is important to determine that urinary retention is not present before these medications are initiated. A number of problems with the bladder can occur in MS, each of which needs a specific approach to management. If simple measures and these medications are not sufficient to control the problem, a urologic assessment is needed to see if other approaches are required.

It is important to know that bladder problems are common in MS and can be managed with simple measures in most cases, but they also can lead to serious complications if untreated. Urinary infection in men should always be explored further, and recurrent urinary tract infection in women also requires investigation. If burning or painful urination occurs, especially when the urine is cloudy and has a foul odor, you probably have a bladder infection and need to be in touch with your physician right away.

Bladder symptoms sometimes can be reduced by drinking about eight glasses (eight-ounce) of fluid daily, limiting citrus juices (orange, grapefruit, and tomato), and adding cranberry juice or cranberry tablets several times daily.

Bowel Control

Bowel control problems (primarily constipation) are less common than bladder problems, and in most cases they also can be managed by simple methods. The first step is to maintain a regular bowel schedule.

Try to have a bowel movement each day after breakfast because establishing a regular daily pattern avoids constipation and a tendency to irregular bowel movements as a result of inactivity. Each day take the time to sit and try at the same time—don't wait until you feel like going to the bathroom—try to develop a regular reflex timing for bowel movements. Your diet should be high in fiber, including a serving of bran each day, and there should be adequate fruits and vegetables in your meals. Drinking enough fluids is also critical, as dry stool is the most common cause of constipation.

Another factor in bowel health is exercise—this helps maintain good bowel function in everyone, but it is especially important when you have MS. Loss of bowel control is a more serious problem and can be managed by altering diet and some exercises. A consultation with a gastroenterologist may be needed because this problem can discourage a person from taking part in many social and family activities.

OTHER SYMPTOMS

Fatigue

People with MS may notice two patterns of fatigue. One is a feeling of tiredness and weakness that occurs with increasing exercise or other physical activity. For instance, walking may be fine at the onset, but your legs may become increasingly heavy and tired after walking a long distance, with some dragging of the feet. Strength is recovered and you can continue again after sitting down and resting for a brief time.

Another kind of fatigue is a general feeling of exhaustion, which can be more annoying and limiting. This can be mild or severe, intermittent or continuous. You may experience this type of fatigue quite suddenly during a normal day, which may come over you like a wave, making it difficult to continue with whatever you are doing. More commonly, a general fatigue is present no matter how much or how little you do. It may be aggravated by overdoing activity or getting less sleep, but it may be present even if you do nothing and have had a good night's sleep. When we ask people with MS to list the symptoms that bother them the most, fatigue usually is at the top of the list; it also is the most common.

Most people learn to modify their day in ways that allow them to manage fatigue, such as taking brief rests or even occasional naps. Others say that they cannot do this because of the nature of their work or responsibilities, and they push through the fatigue without its causing any problems. It simply makes you tired to overdo it when you have fatigue; it does not worsen your MS. The most common problem from overdoing things is to be more tired. It is common for people to say they can push through their work or task but that they pay for this effort with several days of increased fatigue. Sometimes the fatigue will characteristically appear at about the same time of day, allowing for some restructuring of activities if your work or other schedules permit.

Most people with MS say that the fatigue they experience feels abnormal, unlike the normal tiredness that everyone experiences. Most neurologic diseases are not associated with this pattern of tiredness, although a number of other autoimmune diseases do exhibit this unusual fatigue. Because it is so "different" and so common in MS, it is surprising that it was not recognized as a characteristic symptom of MS until recently. By a serendipitous observation it was found that amantadine (Symmetrel®) taken twice a day is helpful in reducing fatigue in about half the people who experience it. Another medication that may be helpful is modafinil (Provigil®), a drug originally developed for narcolepsy. It has not been available long enough to assess its long-term value. There are some early reports that high doses of enteric-coated aspirin (ECASA) (Entrophen®) may be helpful, but caution must be used with long-term high doses.

Tremor

Everyone has some tremor (to see the normal physiologic tremor, put a piece of paper on top of your outstretched hand). Multiple sclerosis may be accompanied by different types of tremor, ranging from annoying to fairly disabling. There are a variety of approaches to controlling them, some of which people learn on their own. For example, bracing the forearm against the side or on a hard surface reduces arm and hand tremor. Another variation is to have a method of immobilization that is used for some specific task, such as writing, but is removed when the task is completed. Physical and occupational therapists may use *patterning*, repeating movements to make them smoother and more automatic. Adding weights to the limb may reduce tremor, and adaptive equipment can be useful.

Medication is only partially effective, and some of the drugs tried in the past seemed to give only limited assistance and caused side effects. Perhaps the only drugs that may have a significant effect are beta blockers such as propranolol (Inderal®). Mild sedatives and tranquilizers may help, but they probably are only worthwhile when you have some other need for a sedative, such as tension or anxiety, which aggravate tremor. Stereotactic brain surgery has been used in selected cases, but this is unusual and carries significant risk.

Vertigo

Vertigo is the sensation that many people call "dizziness," but since that term can mean different things, it is necessary to explain exactly what you feel. Vertigo has the sensation of movement, whether it seems that the room is moving or turning or that *you* seem to be moving. If it is severe, the room seems to be spinning, or you may feel like you are tipping or falling or that the floor is coming up to meet you. This sensation usually is due to a disturbance in the vestibular system of the middle ear or its connections within the brain stem and brain. In MS the problem most often is in the nerve connections in the brain stem. It usually is transient, lasting hours or occasionally weeks; it is unusual for it to last much longer. If it persists, it can be treated by stimulating the vestibular system or suppressing the vestibular reflexes with medication.

If the onset of vertigo is acute and lasts for many days, it can be treated by IV steroids, but it usually settles by itself. When vertigo is worsened by movement, as it often is, paradoxically the problem can be reduced by purposely stimulating the vertigo. Thus, positional exercises can be done using a simple method on a soft surface such as a bed. The vestibular system is stimulated by falling onto the bed to one side three times (the vertigo lessens each time), then to the other side, and then backwards. There often is a position of comfort when a person has vertigo, with fewer symptoms when lying on one side and more symptoms when lying on the other side, and with the head supported at a certain angle. Sedatives are helpful, as is diazepam (Valium®), which suppresses the vestibular reflex.

Vertigo can be mild, experienced as a slight swimming feeling in the head. Mild nausea and poor concentration often are associated with this. Again, positional exercises and an exercise program are more helpful than sitting still, which is the natural tendency.

Seizures

Seizures are not common in MS; they occur in approximately 6 percent of patients. They usually are effectively treated with common anticonvulsants such as phenytoin (Dilantin®) or carbamazepine (Tegre-tol®). An unusual type of "seizure" is a localized spasm that is more like a major muscle spasm than an epileptic seizure and often occurs on one side of the body. Such spasms also respond to medication such as car-bamazepine.

Facial Weakness

Facial weakness can occur suddenly in MS, although it is uncom-mon. When it does happen, especially early in the course of the disease, it may resemble Bell's palsy, a benign form of acute facial palsy that often follows a viral infection. Both Bell's palsy and the facial weakness of MS respond to steroids. In MS no treatment may be needed if the weak-ness is mild or is already rapidly improving on its own.

Alternative and Complementary Therapies

For many centuries there has been an approach to curing and healing illness and symptoms that has been separate from the medical profes-sion. At any time and in any century these have taken hundreds of forms. Some are commonsense approaches that the "wisewomen" and elders in the community used to treat minor problems without the necessity of calling a doctor. Aside from these home remedies, there are therapists who offer treatments that are outside the mainstream of medicine. They include herbalists, psychic healers, reflexologists, homeopaths, natur-opaths, and many other therapists who pursue an approach based on belief or ideology rather than a scientific approach based on question-ing, testing, changing, and advancing.

Believers in alternative medicines usually do not want their beliefs tested. The treatment is not based on science or data, so they may argue that science is not an appropriate way to assess its value. This reaction against traditional ways of evaluating therapies complicates the ability of the medical community to sort out effective therapies from ineffec-tive ones.

Some therapists offer methods that do make people feel better, including massage and other physical therapies, and that is good, but it should not be confused with a specific therapy that is claimed to cure MS or reduce MS disease activity. Therapies that impact general health fall within the "wellness" concept and are considered "complementary" rather than "alternative" measures.

Are alternative therapies safe? That depends. Many are safe and may even make people feel better. Others, particularly remedies that are unapproved and unregulated and which may contain mysterious and changing ingredients, can cause serious side effects and even death in some instances. Alternative therapies, home remedies, and herbal treatments often are thought to be safe because they are "natural," but that is not justified—many are not safe and many are not natural. There often is little information on their safety or benefit. People take such substances at their own risk. Some alternative medicines have made people very sick; they also can react with medications that are being taken for other reasons.

What are you to do when you hear from a friend, another person with MS, or the media that something may be a treatment for the disease? Talk to your physician. He or she will not mind discussing a newspaper clipping or other source of a "therapeutic claim." Your physician will be able to tell you the pros and cons of most therapies. Another helpful source is your local MS Society, which should have information on anything you have read or heard about. Finally, consult *Alternative Medicine and Multiple Sclerosis* and *Multiple Sclerosis: A Guide to Treatment and Management* (see "Additional Readings" at the end of this book), which provide information about hundreds of therapies used by people with MS and are claimed to be useful in treating MS and its symptoms, explaining what each is about, what evidence there is for its use, and whether it is recommended.

In commenting on alternative therapies, we do not wish to be discouraging, but we do want people with MS to take only medications and therapies that have been demonstrated to be safe and effective. We recommend that you find evidence that this is the case before you try anything.

What Is Ahead in Research for New Treatments?

As described in Chapter 7, research is now progressing at a pace we have not seen before. It is natural to hope for a sudden "breakthrough" in MS, a discovery that will solve the problem, but this rarely occurs. More often research adds a new bit of knowledge that leads to the next questions, which, when answered, add still more knowledge and lead to more research and more answers. This eventually translates into better understanding, better treatment, and, hopefully, ways to prevent the disease.

Newspapers may like stories about dramatic breakthroughs, but the world of research and medical advances is of one step leading to the next, eventually leading to the answers we are seeking. It is a long and painstaking process, but it is the way progress actually occurs.

People with MS and those who care for them are more hopeful than ever as we see improvements in care, new advances in neuroimaging and diagnosis, better control of symptoms, new medications that change the disease, and an increase in our understanding of the underlying genetic and environmental mechanisms in the disease. Just as people with MS have reason to hope, so do those of us who work to find the cause and cure of the disease and to bring better care to those with MS and their families—and never before have we had such good reason to hope.

4

Practical Guidelines

THERE ARE MANY THINGS YOU CAN DO TO STAY AS HEALTHY AS possible, take control of your life, and cope with the challenges that multiple sclerosis (MS) may bring. The disease is not in control of you—*you* are in control of your life, your attitudes, your relationships, your approach to problems, your interests, and your activities. The best way to take control is to obtain more information and learn more about MS.

This chapter discusses some things you should do and some things you should not do. For example, you should get more information about MS; you should make sure you have an opportunity to ask questions about the disease; you should exercise; you should try to live a normal, active life, adapting to any limitations; you should work to improve your relationships; you should express a positive attitude; and you should have regular medical assessments.

The things you should not do are actually fewer in number. For example, don't withdraw from life and friends; don't stop exercising; don't expose yourself to a hot environment; don't try every drug, herb, therapy, and procedure that you hear about without first getting reliable information about the scientific evidence, possible benefits, and side effects; and don't feel ashamed or diminished because you have MS.

Should I Learn More About Multiple Sclerosis?

MULTIPLE SCLEROSIS IS A DISORDER OF THE CENTRAL NERVOUS SYSTEM. Many things are known about it, and many advances are being made. There still are many unanswered questions, but it is important to learn more about the questions that are being asked by researchers and the theories that are being tested.

The best initial source of information is the MS Society. In the United States, call 800-FIGHT-MS to reach the National MS Society, and in Canada call 800-268-7582 (see Chapter 9 for the number of the nearest office of the MS Society of Canada).

What Should Others Know About Multiple Sclerosis?

IT IS IMPORTANT FOR YOUR FAMILY, FRIENDS, AND COWORKERS TO UNDER-stand MS. Initially you may feel that you do not want anyone to know that you have MS. That is understandable, but it is essential to tell the people you love, and others when necessary, so that they can understand and help you deal with the disease. Most people are pleased and surprised at how supportive and understanding others are when they are informed. Many people may have guessed that something was wrong but did not know what to do or say. Until they know the truth (see Chapter 6), employers may not understand your need to take time off or to rest, and they may think you are not working well. Decisions to inform should be made on an individual basis, but in general disclosure is a good idea.

Once family and friends are aware of your diagnosis, they might benefit from literature that would allow them to better understand MS. In particular, your family should understand your symptoms and problems so they can be helpful and supportive. This is not possible if they are unaware of your MS and how it makes you feel.

Who Can Answer My Questions?

IT IS IMPORTANT TO HAVE YOUR CONCERNS ADDRESSED AND YOUR QUESTIONS answered. Sometimes people are afraid that they might ask too many questions or that their questions might not be clear. Make a list of the questions you want to ask. Call the MS Society or bring the questions to your physician on your next visit. You probably will find that they are questions most people ask and that they are not new to the staff. If there is no clear answer to a question, it is important to find that out as well. Each new piece of information will add to your overall understanding of MS.

What Can I Learn from Other People Who Have Multiple Sclerosis?

PEOPLE WITH MS SOON LEARN THAT IT IS A COMMON NEUROLOGIC DISorder and that there are many others in their community who have the same disease. It often helps to talk to others who share the challenges and problems of coping with MS, but there are some cautions. You cannot compare yourself with others in terms of the type of disease, the course, or the symptoms. Multiple sclerosis is an individual disease, and you probably will find that the features of your MS are quite different from those of the next person. It may seem puzzling that there are so many individual patterns for the disease, but that is actually fairly common in other diseases as well. The variety of symptoms of MS is great, so the apparent variations in individuals seem great as well.

One way that people with MS can benefit from each other is in selfhelp or support groups. These take various forms, but they usually are small groups that meet in homes or in community facilities to talk about and better understand MS. The object is always to take a positive approach and to take control over everything that you can manage so that you can help yourself and others. The MS Society has information on support groups, including how to join one or how to start one.

When Is Information Not Helpful?

MISINFORMATION IS NOT HELPFUL AND CAN CAUSE MUCH TROUBLE AND distress, not to mention wasted time and money. If someone says that mercury in dental fillings causes MS, check it out from those who know—staff at the MS Society, someone in the MS clinic in your area, or your physician—but don't go to the dentist and have your fillings removed. If someone tells you that ginseng cures MS, check it out. If someone says there is a doctor in a clinic somewhere who has a cure for MS, call the MS Society, not your travel agent.

What About My Activities?

People with MS should lead normal and active lives within the limitations of their symptoms. This means that we encourage activity more than rest, staying active and involved rather than withdrawing and dropping out. We want people to remain productive and working. It is understandable that symptoms and problems may make this harder for you, that doing things may take more time and energy, but it is still better to do it than not to do it.

People with MS are happiest and at their best when they live normally and carry out the activities they enjoy. There are no absolute limitations—if you feel like climbing a mountain and do not have symptoms and problems that limit you, go for it! Unfortunately, MS does cause symptoms that may limit activities to some extent. It requires adjustment so that you can continue to do as much as you can, in the time you need, and in the way you can manage. If you work at managing your problems, coping with any limitations, and keeping a positive attitude, not only can you do many of the things in life you want to do, but also you may accomplish much more than others without MS, as they often do not use these positive skills to deal with life.

What About Exercise?

SIMPLY PUT, EXERCISE IS GOOD FOR EVERYONE. WHEN THE DIAGNOSIS OF MS is made, you should set about getting yourself in the best shape that you can, both mentally and physically, in order to manage any challenges that come with the disease. We all benefit from regular exercise, and it is even more important for the person with MS. If fatigue is a problem, you should arrange your exercise for times when fatigue is less bothersome, schedule it in periods with breaks, or redesign the type and pattern of exercise so that you can still do it.

In general, the best exercise is one that you enjoy so that you will still be doing it in six months and six years. Exercise should be a lifetime habit for all of us, including people with MS, even if the exercise program needs to be modified at times. Decide what you like to do and would enjoy doing almost every day. Try to involve others in exercise as well. Exercise programs in the community have a tendency to motivate you to participate regularly; they also have an enjoyable social aspect.

Can I Overdo It?

IT WOULD SEEM LOGICAL TO BE CONCERNED THAT OVERDOING THINGS might cause attacks of MS and worsen the disease and that we should rest and avoid strain and work. This is *not* good advice. There is no evidence that doing a lot, exercising, or even overdoing activities or physical exercise has any deleterious effect on MS. True, it may make you tired for the next day or so, but there is no evidence that it worsens your MS. Some people "push through" their fatigue, which also may make them tired the next day but does no harm.

It might be tempting to blame overactivity for the development of a new attack of MS or a new symptom, especially if it happened a day or a few days later, but a careful accounting of strenuous events, stressful events, and the occurrence of attacks would show that this probably is coincidental. Don't worry about activity; be reasonable, keep active, and do what you can.

How Much Should I Rest?

BECAUSE FATIGUE IS A MAJOR PROBLEM FOR MANY PEOPLE WITH MS, A reasonable balance between maintaining your normal activities and taking brief rests is appropriate. People usually find their own balance of activity and rest, and in this way they keep up their activity, work, and other responsibilities.

It is important to recognize that the fatigue in MS is not "normal" tiredness that follows too little sleep or a long, hard day. The fatigue in MS is often an abnormal sensation; it is unrelated to the amount of sleep and activity and it feels different. It can occur in waves and may seem overwhelming at times. Adapting the level of activities is often successful, and some medications also may be helpful (see Chapter 3).

Do not rest too much. *Activity* is a more important watchword than rest in MS.

What About Stress?

ALL PEOPLE EXPERIENCE STRESS IN THEIR LIVES. BEING GIVEN A DIAGNOSIS of MS is stressful. Having to see yourself and your life in a different light, with greater uncertainty, is stressful. But marriage, raising children, doing our jobs, and the "daily-ness" of life also bring stress. The central point is not whether stress is present in your life (it almost always is), but your response to it. People can, and do, react differently. Some see stress as a problem to be solved. Some respond emotionally, collapsing in tears, becoming depressed, or lashing out angrily at others. Some are initially upset, but then set about overcoming or dealing with the stress. Others do not believe it is possible to deal with it and give up. It is not the stress; it is our reaction to it that makes the difference.

When people react to stress in a nonproductive way, they often state that anyone would react the same way. That actually is not true, but some people are unable to see any other way of reacting. Fortunately, by analyzing such events, you can learn how to react more positively. It is not easy and sometimes requires counseling, but a person who reacts ineffectively to stress can learn how to respond better. It does mean that you must recognize that your responses could be more productive before you can work at it or seek help.

Can I Develop Better Coping Skills?

WE ALL HAVE CERTAIN PATTERNS OF COPING. SOME OF US REACT MORE intellectually to problems and stresses, while others react more emotionally. Most of us have a combination of the two; it is the *balance* of intellectual problem-solving responses and emotional responses that is important.

It is natural to feel upset when something stressful happens. It is *not* normal, however, for that to be the only response. There is a point at which we must think clearly and objectively about what the stress is all about, how we can analyze it, and how we can most effectively deal with it. That combines the appropriate emotional and problem-solving aspect. You can improve these coping skills by improving their components. When a stressful event has passed, you can analyze how well you responded: whether your emotional response was appropriate and balanced, and whether the steps you took were the most effective and efficient ones for solving or dealing with the problem. Such analysis often gives you a different perspective, particularly if it is done in an honest fashion and enables you to see how you could respond more effectively the next time.

How Can I Maintain a Positive Attitude?

THE MOST IMPORTANT FACTOR IN DEALING WITH MS—OR ANY CHALLENGE in life—is a mature, positive, and good-humored attitude whenever possible.

Some people struggle harder than others. There is no question that a positive attitude is of great importance because a negative person cannot tolerate very much adversity. Multiple sclerosis does not make you positive or negative; you already had an approach to life before you developed the disease. Multiple sclerosis can challenge your approach, your positivity, and your good humor, however, so it is important to make an even greater effort to overcome difficulties in a way that makes you feel good and improves your relationships. People like to be around those who are positive and good-humored. We can understand those who are negative and turn their frustration on others, but they do not manage well, are more unhappy, and do not learn to take control of the things they can manage.

What About My Relationships?

GOOD RELATIONSHIPS ARE HELPFUL TO ALL OF US, AND THEY BECOME EVEN more important when we have difficult challenges to deal with and overcome. One important aspect of taking control of your health and your future is to strengthen your relationships. It has a positive effect on you when you do everything you can to improve your relationships with your spouse, your children, your family, your friends, and everyone with whom you come in contact. It may seem simplistic, but it actually is one of the most important things you can do. Our relationships with others are central to our happiness and state of well-being, and it is rewarding to begin to improve them.

Should I Tell People I Have Multiple Sclerosis?

IT IS NATURAL THAT YOU MAY HAVE FELT UNCERTAIN ABOUT TELLING PEOPLE— even your family or close friends—when you first were told that you have MS. It is hard to recognize that something about yourself has changed, and it is worrisome to think that it may change relationships and how people regard you. Eventually you will come to recognize that you are still the same person, that the people who love you will continue to love you and support you, and that others generally are understanding and helpful. Sometimes they may try to be *too* helpful, as most people do not want the relationship to be altered or to be treated differently. All of these feelings, plus some embarrassment about "having an illness," make many people want to hide the diagnosis. They think "maybe if I pretend the problem doesn't exist, it won't exist."

It is a good rule to be honest and open in our relationships and interactions. Of course, like all health matters, the fact that you have MS is a private and confidential matter, so who you confide in is a personal choice. It is common to keep the information within a small circle initially, especially because everything may be calm and stable for many years. A problem begins to develop when symptoms cause difficulties that are visible to others, but they have not been made aware that you have a health problem. At that point others may wonder, worry, and speculate about what is happening, and their speculation can be more harmful than the truth.

It also is worth considering that people feel excluded and not trusted when they are kept in the dark yet know that something is being kept secret. There are some instances when keeping a medical problem a secret can be a serious offense or can cause serious problems. You cannot lie about having a medical problem when answering questions on insurance forms or other official documents. There are only a few instances when it is proper to ask such questions, but in such instances you must answer truthfully.

What Happens When It Is Hot?

MOST PEOPLE WITH MS FIND THAT THEY ARE MORE HEAT-SENSITIVE. IT DOES not occur with everyone, but most people notice that they become weak or dizzy, or even feel sick, in a hot bath, on a hot humid day, or in a warm environment. They also notice the opposite—they feel better and function better when it is cooler, when they are swimming in cool water, or when they move from a warm room to a cool room.

Remyelinated and partially damaged nerve fibers may function less well when body temperature is elevated, and, conversely, the nerves function better when temperature is lowered. This tends to be a transient phenomenon that does not produce a lasting effect. However, it can produce marked weakness, and patients often describe themselves as feeling like a "dishrag" or "wiped out" on a hot day. This response to heat was once the basis of the *hot bath test*, which was used as a test for MS before modern diagnostic tests were available. Although it is suggestive of MS, it is not accurate enough to be an important test.

You may wonder whether becoming weak in a hot environment will make you worse, but the phenomenon is transient and disappears as soon as you cool off. We do recommend that you avoid such an environment because you will feel less well, function less well, and have more symptoms when it is very warm. Air conditioning often is required in summer months to maintain reasonable temperature control and is considered medically necessary for tax purposes (a letter from your physician is needed). Avoidance of sunbathing, saunas, and hot tubs is strongly advised.

Should I Change My Diet?

THE DIETARY APPROACH TO THE MANAGEMENT OF MS HAS A LONG HISTORY. It is difficult to perform clinical trials on diets, but there was interest and some suggestion of a positive response from studies of diets that are low in animal fats (essentially a low-cholesterol diet) and with a supplement of a vegetable oil such as sunflower seed oil or evening primrose oil. A few of these studies showed some positive benefit; one large study showed no benefit. There also was some suggestion that people with early and mild disease benefit the most. Many people use the simple approach to diet of lowering the amount of animal fat and supplementing it with a vegetable oil because it is a healthy diet and everyone in the family can potentially benefit from such a diet. Many more complex diets have been recommended in MS, which have little logic or justification and are so complicated that people give them up after a short time.

The most important point is to stick to a balanced, healthy diet, maintain normal weight, and limit your intake of animal fat. This is a good dietary recommendation for everyone.

Should I Sleep More?

HOW MUCH YOU SHOULD SLEEP IS BASED ON YOUR NORMAL PATTERN. Some people require eight or nine hours a night, whereas others require only five or six hours. The average is $7\frac{1}{2}$ hours of sleep, and the measure of effectiveness is how rested you feel in the morning. You should not change your sleep pattern because you have MS. Since fatigue is a major problem for many people, there is a tendency to think that you will be less fatigued if you sleep more; even with normal or greater sleep hours, you will still tend to feel tired during the day if fatigue is due to MS. Surprisingly, oversleeping often makes people feel more tired. It is worth remembering that many factors can decrease the quality of sleep, including alcohol and many drugs.

What If I Need Surgery?

THE ANSWER TO THIS QUESTION IS SIMPLE. IF YOU NEED SURGERY AND THERE are good indications for surgery, you should have it. If you do not need surgery, you should not have it. This is a good rule whether you have MS or not. There does not appear to be any increased risk to people with MS who undergo surgery. In the past there was concern that the stress of surgery might precipitate MS attacks, but the number of attacks of MS that occur in those circumstances is the same as that which would be expected in an average population of people with the disease, and no more. This relates to the previous point that there is little evidence that stressful events precipitate attacks of MS, whether they involve surgery, anesthesia, trauma, or major life events. The most important rule is to be assured that surgery is truly indicated and necessary. This rule is not different because you have MS.

Is Pregnancy a Risk?

THE OBSERVATIONS ABOUT MS AND PREGNANCY ARE NOW FAIRLY CLEAR. Pregnancy does not appear to increase the incidence of attacks of MS; in fact, some data suggest that disease activity decreases by up to 70 percent during this period. However, there is an increased number of episodes of symptoms or attacks in the six months following delivery than would be expected in a six-month period. Those episodes should be treated and managed like any other episode of MS. Pregnancy has no long-term effects on disability or disease progression.

Two other aspects of pregnancy and child-rearing must be considered. First, there is a small but real genetic risk for MS in a family, in the range of 2 to 5 percent for a first-degree relative. This is greater than the risk in the normal population, but it clearly is low. More significant, raising a child is a lifelong responsibility, and people with MS must recognize that their health during the time that they will need to carry out this responsibility may be uncertain. One cannot predict health status in 10 years, for example. This probably is the major factor that governs the decision about having a child. Recognizing the risks and problems, each couple must determine for themselves this very personal decision. An excellent resource on this topic is the book *Mother to Be: A Guide to Pregnancy* and *Birth for Women with Disabilities* (see "Additional Readings").

Will Multiple Sclerosis Affect My Sex Life?

BECAUSE MS AFFECTS THE CENTRAL NERVOUS SYSTEM AND THE NERVES THAT control various functions in the body, the complex and sensitive control system for sexual function also can be affected. Early in the disease there may be no physical effect on sexual function, but the enjoyment of sex may be affected by your emotional state. Worries, depression, or altered feelings about yourself can affect your relationship with others and the normal emotions associated with sexuality. Thus, sexual function may be affected by psychological factors, and this possibility needs to be considered. More often there is a physiologic basis for the difficulties, which often are seen in conjunction with bladder and bowel symptoms. For men, the most common problem is achieving or maintaining an erection, which can be helped by medication such as sildenafil citrate (Viagra®). Women may experience decreased vaginal lubrication, which can be accommodated by synthetic lubricating products, such as Astroglide®.

What About Driving?

DRIVING IS ONLY A PROBLEM WHEN SYMPTOMS OR LIMITATIONS MAKE IT risky or unacceptably difficult. Vertigo, double vision, or a temporary loss of vision would not permit you to drive safely while you are experiencing such difficulties. Problems with leg weakness or incoordination would limit rapid and accurate use of brake and accelerator pedals and would make driving unsafe. It may be possible to return to driving when symptoms improve, but it is wise to depend on the assessment of your physician when there is any question about this. Most rehabilitation facilities can assess whether a person can drive safely.

When a problem is more long-standing and renders driving unsafe, it may be possible to adapt the controls on the vehicle to allow a person to drive. The most common adaptation is alteration of the controls so that they are operated manually.

Although a person may be anxious to continue driving and willing to take some chances, feeling that they are "all right to drive," greater consideration must be given to others who may be at risk, including passengers and pedestrians.

Should I Move?

SOME PEOPLE READ THAT THE INCIDENCE OF MS VARIES IN DIFFERENT PARTS of the world, that it is more common in temperate climates and rare in very hot climates, such as near the equator. They ask if it would be helpful if they moved to a hot climate; the answer is no. In fact, they might find the heat a problem because it tends to make people with MS feel worse. We also believe that the geographic patterns probably have other explanations, such as the distribution in the world of people who have the genetic characteristic that might predispose to MS.

Will I Be Different?

IT IS NATURAL TO WONDER HOW MS WILL CHANGE YOU. YOUNG PEOPLE see themselves as healthy and do not visualize themselves with a serious disease. When you are given a diagnosis of a medical condition, it is natural to begin to think of yourself differently, and you may have to readjust your self-concept. You are still *you*, but it requires you to see that a different element has entered your life. Many things change as you go through life—some good, some not so good. What is necessary is a positive approach to challenges and determination to move ahead.

What About Other Questions I May Have?

WE COULD NOT POSSIBLY ANTICIPATE ALL THE QUESTIONS YOU MAY HAVE about what to do and not to do, but we have tried to anticipate the most common questions. You will have many more questions, and they should be asked of your physician, other health care professionals, or staff at the MS Society. It is always better to ask a question, even if you are uncertain about exactly how to ask it or if you think it sounds "silly." It is better to ask a question than to wonder or worry in silence.

We recommend the book *Multiple Sclerosis: The Questions You Have— The Answers You Need* as a more detailed guide to many of your questions (see "Additional Readings").

5

Coping with Multiple Sclerosis

BEING DIAGNOSED WITH MULTIPLE SCLEROSIS (MS) CAN CREATE turmoil in every area of a person's life. In some ways, life will never be quite the same again. Even in the absence of impairment, the worry—or effort to camouflage worry—is always there. The diagnosis often precipitates a roller coaster ride of emotions, including fear, optimism, despair, and hope. The time following diagnosis can be challenging and confusing. This chapter will help you to bring perspective to the emotional turmoil and help you think about ways to ease the distress and continue with your life.

The Crisis of Diagnosis

People have a variety of reactions to hearing the diagnosis of MS for the first time. Some experience a combination of fear and panic when first confronted with the news. These feelings may quickly be replaced by denial, a refusal to believe that this could possibly be happening. "There must be some mistake!" is an almost universal reaction to the diagnosis, often followed quickly by feelings of anger and resentment. Lisa's story provides an example of some of these feelings. When asked about her initial experience with MS and the diagnosis, she replied:

> I was having a multitude of symptoms that I didn't understand, such as tingling and numbness in my hands and arms and legs. I was having trouble feeling the ground when I was walking. I couldn't see very well out of my left eye—it was almost like looking through an oily film. A whole bunch of odd things were happening that I didn't understand. When I finally got the diagnosis, I was really scared. I didn't know what MS was or what would happen to me. I was afraid of the whole thing.
>
> Later I was angry—very angry. Then I decided there was no way I could really have this disease. In fact, I was second-guessing the doctors—going from one to another asking what was wrong with me. All I could think of was that can in the grocery store that you throw your loose change into—you know, the one with the picture of someone in a wheelchair. It was probably a good year before I even started to accept the fact that I have MS. There was no way I could have it—I'm too active and I do so many things. And I can't stop doing them.

The diagnosis actually brings a sense of relief for some people, especially those who were beginning to wonder if they were "going crazy" or if the symptoms were "all in their head." These fears are sometimes reinforced by physicians who, in the absence of clear physical abnormalities, believe that emotional problems may be causing imaginary or exaggerated symptoms. A small study by Loveland (National MS Society, Health Services Research Report, 1993) found that women presenting with early symptoms of MS were significantly more likely than men to get this type of response from their doctors and that men's descriptions of physical symptoms generally were given more credence by their physicians.

Relief is also experienced by those who imagined a more distressing, or perhaps fatal, explanation for their symptoms, such as cancer. Freed from the fears of a malignant tumor, they feel confident that the symptoms they are experiencing can be successfully managed.

Jim, who was diagnosed with MS in 1988 after a long and frustrating search for some answers, spoke about fear and relief at finally learning his diagnosis:

> It took me four years to get a diagnosis. I was scared to death when I heard "MS." I didn't even know what MS was. But I was also relieved. When you're used to not having a label for all the strange things that are

going on and suddenly the problem is identified for you, that alone is a relief—all this finally has a name.

Regardless of the initial emotional response, the diagnosis of MS creates a crisis for the individual and the entire family. The person who has been diagnosed may experience a sense of isolation, despite efforts of family members to offer support. Lisa mentioned this experience:

Even though people wanted to help, I was the one who had to learn to live with it and had to learn what I needed to do to live with it. You have to make your choice of how you're going to live your life. You have to do it because it's your disease and nobody can do it for you or make it go away.

Family members are also immersed in their own concerns about the future and the impact that MS will have on their lives. The positive aspect of this type of crisis is that it provides an opportunity to assess future plans and a powerful motivation to take actions that support those plans. There is an opportunity to affirm the values and strengths of the individual and the family and all the good things that remain intact in spite of MS. In order to go forward, it is important to know that you can successfully move through the difficult emotions and continue to pursue your goals and dreams. A professional counselor—psychologist or social worker—can be a helpful ally to the person with MS and family members in working toward a positive outlook for the future.

The Adjustment Process

The initial variable reactions to the diagnosis of MS inevitably give way to a feeling of deep sadness. This is related to the addition of a serious chronic illness to one's identity and self-image. Chronic illness forces each person to confront the frailty and vulnerability of the human condition in a personal and immediate way. One also faces the painful reality of society's negative attitudes about disease and disability. This process involves grieving for one's former self-image and integrating the realities of MS into one's identity. Sadness, anger at the disease, and self-absorption are experienced during this time.

Grieving is necessary for a person to move forward, just as it is following the loss of a loved one. Unlike the grieving we associate with death, the grieving process in chronic illness tends to ebb and flow with the symptoms and physical changes that occur over time. Grief may be postponed, but it can never be totally avoided. Sometimes these feelings may be channeled inappropriately, such as anger at one's spouse or children or at health professionals who cannot cure the illness. It is important for everyone involved to understand this grieving process and to communicate their care and support.

The period of intense grieving may last from a few weeks to several months, with gradually diminishing intensity. As it subsides, at least for the time being, one can again begin to focus on and enjoy special relationships and daily activities. Ideally, there is a gradual acknowledgment of the permanence of MS in one's life, while maintaining a sense of continuity between the past and the future as well as a commitment to maximizing quality of life.

Depressive feelings are to be expected as part of the initial grieving process or in response to subsequent changes or losses imposed by the illness. Over the course of the disease, however, individuals with MS are at greater than average risk for depression. They need to be able to recognize when some kind of treatment intervention would be beneficial. Symptoms of significant depression include ongoing and pervasive sadness, loss of interest in or enjoyment of important activities and relationships, feelings of hopelessness and despair, sometimes including suicidal feelings or thoughts, and changes in sleeping and eating patterns. Intervention is recommended if any of these symptoms continue for an extended period of time or seem to be worsening. It is important to realize that relief from depression is readily available. Counseling and/or antidepressant medication are successful in relieving its symptoms. Seeking help for this problem demonstrates an understanding of its significance, not personal weakness or deficiency.

Jim comments on his experience with depression:

> I was pretty depressed, so I went to see a psychologist. She was connected with a rehabilitation facility, so her primary interest was working with people who are chronically ill or disabled to help them find comfortable ways of living and thinking about themselves. It was a perfect match because that's just what I needed at that point.

One hallmark of MS that must be addressed as part of the adjustment process in its "unpredictability." When several focus groups were held by the National MS Society to identify what aspects of the disease people found most troubling and challenging, the resounding answer was the unpredictability of the disease course and the uncertainties related to future ability/disability. What symptoms and impairments might occur, when would new symptoms appear, when would they go away, or would they go away? Amy, who was diagnosed eight years ago, addressed this issue:

> *I think not knowing what will happen is the hardest thing for people when they're diagnosed with MS. They totally freak out and wonder 'what's this disease going to do to me?' They have to realize that what happens to someone else is not necessarily going to happen to them. And if it does, well, you will have to deal with it.*

Flexibility is a key element in living with the unpredictability of MS. Goals need to be assessed and revised, with a "plan for the worst, hope for the best" outlook. A college student named Leslie was pursuing a career in horticulture, which necessitated spending a fair amount of time in greenhouses. Her early symptoms included heat sensitivity, with temporary blurred vision and extreme fatigue when she was exposed to warm temperatures. Although this problem remitted, any future recurrence would have prevented Leslie from performing her job. After careful thought, she switched to teaching, an occupation that heat sensitivity or most other possible MS symptoms would not prevent her from continuing. Similarly, the purchase of a new home should involve consideration of issues of mobility and accessibility. Many people with MS are not significantly bothered by problems with walking. However, since mobility impairment is a problem at some point for a fair number of people with MS, it is simply good planning to consider this possibility when choosing a home, even while being reasonably optimistic that serious walking difficulties will not occur.

Coping Strategies

Coping strategies reflect an individual's personality and usual style of interfacing with people and events. By adulthood, strategies have been selected and refined through an unconscious process; most of us do not consciously choose and evaluate our coping mechanisms. However, it becomes important to look at those coping styles critically so that they can be boosted when necessary and modified or discarded when they are counterproductive. The following are examples of two types of strategies.

Denial is ignoring or minimizing the seriousness of the situation. We all engage in denial about the moment-to-moment possibility of accidental death. Intermittent denial may be useful in the early stages of adapting to MS because it enables people to deal with the immediate symptoms they are experiencing without having to contemplate all the possible problems that may occur in the future. Denial is *not* useful if these potential problems are ignored when making important life planning decisions such as purchasing disability insurance, buying a home or an automobile, or making career decisions. One of the most serious consequences of continued denial is avoidance of disease-modifying therapy. The availability of interventions that can have a favorable impact on the disease course for many people with MS is a very positive factor supporting hope for the future.

Denial can also interfere with obtaining optimal health care. Yes, a bladder infection may indicate underlying MS pathology and should be evaluated in light of that possibility. The numbness and tingling in your fingers may not be carpal tunnel syndrome, commonly associated with extensive computer use. Acknowledgment of your symptoms and paying proper attention to them will ensure that the physicians involved in your health care will provide you with the treatments you need and will not perform surgeries (e.g., for carpal tunnel syndrome or herniated disks) or prescribe treatments that are unnecessary or even harmful.

Intellectualization is focusing on available factual information to the exclusion of feelings and other psychological issues. A certain amount of intellectualization makes it possible for people to learn about the disease, assess its impact on their daily lives, and make use of their problem-solving abilities to meet the challenges imposed by MS. Intellectualization becomes excessive when it consumes enormous amounts of energy; some people expend so much effort collecting and analyzing information that they have little or no energy left to deal with their emotional reactions to the disease or with the feelings and reactions of those around them.

Looking at these two examples, the strengths and weaknesses inherent in some coping strategies can be seen. Denial is useful in allowing a person to get on with his or her life, but it is detrimental if it interferes with obtaining optimal treatment or with life planning issues. Intellectualization is useful in obtaining essential information, but it is harmful when it is used as a means to block feelings about the disease that should be expressed. The blocking of emotional awareness and expression can interfere with long-range coping efforts.

Interpersonal difficulties may arise when two people who live together and must cope with MS have conflicting coping styles. A person who copes by talking through feelings and events or by reading all the literature on MS may encounter resistance and even anger from a partner who is trying desperately to maintain denial as a way of dealing with the disease. In some situations, counseling is useful to help a couple recognize each other's coping styles and provide mutual support. An excellent resource on this topic is *Multiple Sclerosis: A Guide for Families* (see "Additional Readings").

Education About Multiple Sclerosis

While some individuals are more inclined than others to seek information about something that is stressful to them, one of the most effective things a person with MS or a family member can do to facilitate adjustment to MS is to learn about the disease—what to expect and what can be done to relieve physical symptoms and promote psychological health. People with MS have indicated in National MS Society surveys that information about the disease and its effects is their most important need. Education about MS is available through a number of sources, primarily MS health care providers and the U.S., Canadian, and other national MS Societies (see Chapter 9).

Keep in mind, however, that adults can choose to learn in a variety of ways and may choose to do so in different settings or at different times. For some, devouring every available piece of written material is the most desirable strategy. These individuals compare different sources of information, analyzing and sorting varied opinions, to create a personal perspective. The result is a sense of "ownership" over the information and its gradual integration into personal philosophy and decisions about day-to-day activities. Other people prefer a group setting that provides opportunities for the immediate testing of new ideas and feedback from peers and/or professionals.

Such group educational programs are widely available through the U.S., Canadian and other national MS Societies. The National MS Society in the United States has a mail program, called "Knowledge Is Power" for people who have been recently diagnosed with MS. The program consists of a series of modules on topics of interest sent on a predetermined schedule to people who request this service. This mail series can be obtained by calling 1-800-FIGHT-MS.

Another component of the educational process relates to reports of possible treatments or "the cure" for MS. Given the variability and unpredictability of the illness over time, it is not surprising that diverse therapies have been heralded as having a significant impact on MS. When symptoms remit—as they frequently do quite naturally over the course of the disease—whatever treatment or activity is being used at the time is given credit for the improvement. Since dramatic improvement and long periods of remission are common occurrences in MS, even without any therapy, it is important to be prudently skeptical when evaluating therapies that claim to benefit people with MS. Only those treatments that have been evaluated for safety and efficacy in carefully designed and controlled scientific studies provide documentation of benefit. Other therapies, generally outside the usual medical interventions and called "complementary" or "alternative" therapies, should also be carefully evaluated. Some of these claim a boost to the immune system and are not appropriate for people with MS, who already have an overly active immune system. Any non–physician-prescribed therapy that claims to reduce MS disease activity or any therapy that claims to cure MS should be avoided. *Alternative Medicine and Multiple Sclerosis* is a comprehensive guide to this topic (see "Additional Readings").

Choice of Health Care Providers

The choice of health care providers is a critical decision relative to long-term management issues. People with MS generally have a normal life expectancy, and management of the disease is a lifelong process. The physician who manages the symptoms and disease course will interact with the other physicians involved in your health care, such as your internist, gynecologist/obstetrician, cardiologist, or any other medical specialist whose services you might require during your lifetime. Members of your chosen health care team will also provide you on an ongoing basis with information that you will need to make important life decisions relating, for example, to job choices, family planning, or the selection of an MS treatment option. Choose your health care providers carefully. Investigate your physician's board certification (neurology, family practice, or internal medicine), experience with MS, hospital or medical center affiliation, and reputation in the community. In most cases, you will need to have a relationship with an internist or family physician to monitor your general health and a neurologist to manage your MS. The local chapter (United States) or division (Canada) of the MS Society, as well as other national MS societies, can suggest several physicians in any given community who have experience in the management of MS, as well as MS specialists in certain geographic locations.

Support Networks

Family and friends provide the major support for the person who has MS. Their caring and concern are vital, especially during the difficult times following diagnosis or when a flare-up of symptoms occurs. A "sorting out" of friends and relatives may be necessary because not all people with a close relationship are able to be supportive in the same way. One person may be comfortable listening to concerns and providing emotional support, while another may find it easier to assist with more concrete activities, such as a ride to the doctor's office. Another friend or relative may be a great problem solver, helpful in finding solutions or identifying resources in troublesome situations. At the same time, a person's ability to help should not be too narrowly or rigidly determined, especially without discussing it with him or her. It is important for all those who provide support to know how important their contributions are to the person with MS.

People with MS may find it especially helpful to talk with other people who have the disease. This interaction helps to demonstrate that people with MS do indeed continue productive and satisfying lives despite the intrusion of the disease. A physician or other health care provider may be able to provide the name and phone number of someone who is willing, even eager, to talk about his or her personal experiences with MS.

Many chapters of the National MS Society have "peer counseling" programs that train selected individuals with MS to be helpful to people who have questions about the disease. They are available to answer questions, discuss issues, and relate their personal MS successes and failures. In some areas, the peer counselor is available for a telephone conversation; in other areas, the counselor may also be available at local MS center (medical) sessions. Amy commented on her experience with a peer counselor:

> *Having that one-on-one interaction, having someone to talk to who understands, who has gone through similar experiences—that was really important to me. She was a source of strength and kept helping my self-image to stay in shape.*

Some people find a group setting most helpful because they can benefit from the experiences of a number of people with MS. Group members also feel good about the group interaction and support, which is much like a family support network. In an MS support group, MS temporarily feels "normal" because it is the common experience of all members. This normalization of MS is extremely supportive of the overall adjustment process. Instead of feeling isolated, the person in a support group sees MS as one component of a full and diverse life, which can be managed with an understanding of the disease, support of family, friends, health professionals, and peers with MS. Some support groups are led by a counseling professional, such as a psychologist or social worker, while others are "self-help" and are led by one of the group members.

Disclosure

Disclosure about one's illness—whether to family members and friends, new acquaintances, or employers and colleagues—is a significant issue for most people living with MS. Many people are uncertain how much information they want or need to disclose, especially because there often is no visible impairment and some of the symptoms caused by the illness can easily be attributed to a less serious cause. Considerations about disclosure at the workplace are discussed in Chapter 9.

The first and most important group or people to consider are your family members. They are the easiest to make recommendations about, but sometimes the most difficult group to tell. Close family members need to know about your MS—what to expect and what they can do to help. In general, parents, siblings, and other close adult relatives should be told calmly and directly about the diagnosis. They need to begin learning what MS is and what is known about your prognosis and limitations.

Children also should be told about the diagnosis. Even very young children are aware when something is wrong and tend to imagine the worst possible scenario. They need to be given some concrete information about the disease that they can relate to and understand (e.g., that Mommy will be extra tired sometimes, may have trouble walking, or will need to hurry to the toilet). They also need to be reassured that Mommy is not going to die and that she will be able to take care of them. Children need to know that, although the parent may not be able to be as physically active as before, the family will work together to solve any problems that arise. Parents should also explain that no one can "catch" MS the way a cold can be caught from another person, that the children did not cause the MS, and that they have no control over making it better or worse. Parents tend to underestimate the impact of MS on their children; they are at least as affected by their parents' emotional state and the emotional climate within the household as they are by any physical limitations imposed by illness. *Multiple Sclerosis: A Guide for Families* provides a comprehensive discussion of this topic (see "Additional Readings").

What to tell friends and acquaintances may need to be determined on a case-by-case basis. How much you choose to tell will depend very much on the relationship you have with another person. Informing your friends will allow them to provide the emotional support you need and will relieve you of energy-consuming efforts to conceal the problem.

Disclosure also is an issue for people who are dating. When is the best time to tell, and how much should be revealed? As with other questions about MS, no single answer suits every individual or situation. In general, you have no obligation to talk about your MS before extending or accepting an invitation for a date. Nor should you feel any need to discuss MS before you have decided whether you like a person. Once you have decided that a relationship is worth pursuing, the following guidelines may be helpful:

- Remember that secrets and half-truths do not make a firm foundation for a healthy relationship.
- Think about when you would like to know important health-related information about the other person.
- Keep in mind that revealing your MS may become increasingly difficult as your investment in the relationship increases.

Wellness Orientation

In contrast to a *disease orientation*, which focuses on minimizing the impact of the chronic disease on all aspects of your life, a *wellness approach* looks at achieving the positive state of maximal health despite the presence of a chronic illness. Jones and Kilpatrick, in the *Families in Society Journal* (May 1996), propose a definition of wellness as the state of harmony, energy, positive productivity, and well-being in an individual's mind, body, emotions, and spirit. This model encompasses interpersonal relationships as well as relationships with the environment, the community, and society in general. The wellness orientation is comprehensive in its promotion of mind-body unity within the individual, as well as integration of the individual within the community and society as a whole.

A practical example of a wellness orientation is the practice of aerobic and general conditioning exercises, which have an orientation different from that of traditional physical therapy designed primarily to address disease-imposed impairments. Nutritional programs designed for general health (e.g., the prevention of heart disease and certain forms of cancer) go beyond traditional dietary measures that target specific MS-related problems such as constipation and urinary infections. Resources in this area include *Living with Multiple Sclerosis: A Wellness Approach* and *Alternative Medicine and Multiple Sclerosis* (see "Addditional Readings").

Practices such as yoga, meditation, and Tai Chi also fall within the wellness concept and are sometimes categorized as "complementary therapies" that work along with—rather than against or in place of—traditional medical therapy. The term *complementary therapy* is new and not clearly defined, with the result that certain nonmedical therapies are considered unproven, speculative, or even dangerous by the medical community. However, there is growing support by medical professionals for a wellness orientation and for selected aspects of complementary therapies. It is hoped that this shift in attitude will lead to more controlled studies of the risks and benefits of some of these therapies. Lisa again comments on her experiences, focusing on wellness behaviors:

> I learned to watch fats and learned more about what I should eat. Now when I finish school, I usually go straight to the swimming pool and exercise for 30 to 40 minutes.

In following a wellness approach, it is important to remember that one cannot directly impact the disease process through health-promoting behaviors. People must recognize that their control over MS is limited and that the disease may become active in spite of the health practices they have initiated. People should feel good about the wellness activities they pursue in order to enhance their general health and well-being, but they should not feel guilty or blame themselves when a relapse occurs. Although a wellness approach cannot control the unpredictable nature of MS, it *can* enable you to improve your health and devise creative ways to continue activities that are satisfying and enjoyable.

Similarly, people often believe that they can control their MS if they simply try hard enough to "fight" it. Those who engage in this kind of thinking tend to experience a sense of failure when the disease worsens. Assuming this kind of personal responsibility for disease progression is both harmful and self-defeating. Your energy—emotional and otherwise—is better channeled into pursuing wellness, always recognizing that the goal is an overall improvement in general health rather than control of the disease process.

Individuals who struggle to control their MS sometimes feel that they are losing the battle or "giving up" if they begin to use an assistive device. These devices actually extend your abilities by conserving energy, promoting safety, and reducing effort. For example, those who fatigue easily or struggle to be ambulatory with a cane or crutches will find that their activities become severely limited. All their energy is used simply to get from one place to another, leaving little or no effort to do or enjoy whatever activity had been planned. Struggling to get to the supermarket may mean that there is no energy left to shop. People with MS should use whatever techniques, tools, or devices are available to maximize and extend their activities and opportunities. Someone who is comfortable walking for short distances may choose to use a motorized scooter on a trip to an amusement park, shopping mall, or museum. A worker in a large office who normally uses a cane might also choose to use a scooter to conserve energy and enhance productivity. The effective use of assistive devices is an important extension of the wellness philosophy. These tools should be seen as a means of maintaining a full, productive, and enjoyable life rather than as a symbol of defeat.

Parting Thoughts

Lisa relates her personal philosophy:

> If I had never had MS, I would never have traveled the way I did. I took a year off after I was diagnosed and traveled all around Europe. I decided I was going to do things while I could because I didn't know when something might be taken away from me. And I think one thing I've learned from MS is to do things while I can. It's a lesson for everyone. We should all live each day to the fullest, because we never know when something might happen to take it away.

Jim relates what gets him through:

> I would say that I have a lot of support from my family and friends. That probably helped me through. I had quite a few conversations, talks,

heart-to-heart discussions with different people and that helped me quite a bit. Also, I'm somewhat religious and that helped.

Mary speaks about giving up denial:

I am not crazy. I have this disease, I have done nothing to deserve it and there is nothing I can do about having it. I just have to begin to take each day, one at a time, do my best and accept whatever comes. The sheer honesty of admitting that I have an illness is a great weight off my mind. I am more attentive to details in my life, and more willing to do what my body tells me to do, instead of fighting against it. I have found a new calm I had not known before.

A religious or spiritual orientation has been linked with successful coping in a number of studies. It seems that religion helps some people find meaning in their illness or at least put it into a meaningful context. Amy also refers to spirituality, as well as her own personal characteristics, as a support:

Since I grew up in a single parent household, I always had to draw on my own resources. So I worked real hard on that—and on my own sense of spirituality. I just had to—I've always depended on myself. I've always demanded a lot from myself and I guess I just drew it from within.

Amy refers to a key aspect of the coping process—a person's inner strengths. With an adult-onset disease, coping strategies have already been tested in other areas, creating a base on which to build. These strengths surface as the sense of crisis recedes. Amy has more advice for dealing with MS and with life in general.

Another thing is to laugh—to have a sense of humor. Don't take things so seriously. If you don't have a sense of humor, it's all for naught, you know. Life is too short. It can just really drag you down if you let it— you can't let that happen. Just try to take things one day at a time. One day at a time and "slow is fast enough," you don't really have to be in that much of a hurry. Take your time and take it easy and don't be afraid to ask for help.

6

Employment Issues
and Multiple Sclerosis

MOST OF US SPEND THE MAJORITY OF OUR WAKING HOURS AT work and have a serious personal investment in and commitment to employment-related activities. Our self-image and identity often are drawn from our occupation or professional status. One of the first questions asked when getting to know someone is "What kind of work do you do?" From a practical perspective, the income we receive as wages is necessary to purchase goods and services to maintain our particular lifestyle. Work that is not associated with direct financial remuneration—such as parenting, homemaking, and volunteer activities—also contributes to self-definition but usually without the lifestyle consequences. These activities, however, *will* have a financial impact if they must be replaced by the paid work of others. Given all of these factors, it is not surprising that anything that potentially threatens the ability to continue employment or other productive and rewarding activity generates concern and anxiety. A diagnosis of multiple sclerosis (MS) certainly presents this kind of distressing situation.

The good news is that most people who discover that they have MS can and should continue working, usually in their current capacity. The immunomodulating drugs that have become available in recent years may help you to continue your employment status, although this factor has not been systematically studied. We do know that many people with the relapsing-remitting form of MS (attacks and remissions) experience fewer and less serious flare-ups when taking one of the disease-modifying therapies. Symptoms experienced during a flare-up of the disease may or may not interfere with your ability to function at work, but in most cases your prior activity level can be continued.

Exacerbations may interfere with your usual work activities, but these episodes occur only on the average of one to two per year in the relapsing-remitting form of the disease. Progressive MS may require some changes in work activity, but disease limitations appear at a slow enough pace to allow for necessary modifications. It is important to be open with your employer about changes or adaptations you need in the work environment or routine that will allow you to continue to be fully productive. Employers already have made changes that are linked to *prevention* of disability, such as ergonomic desk chairs and hands-free headsets for the telephone. When put in this context, it likely will be easier for your employer to understand the benefit to productivity and the win-win situation for both of you.

A person with a recent diagnosis of MS may not quickly or easily arrive at a comfort level with the disease and work-related issues. The emotions surrounding this unpleasant news are likely to engulf work areas as well as almost all aspects of your day-to-day life. Even when most physical symptoms have cleared, unpleasant and troubling invisible symptoms may remain. Problems such as fatigue, numbness, or pain can increase anxiety and interfere with actual job activities. Symptoms such as urinary urgency and frequency may cause embarrassment. Impaired balance can be socially distressing because of its association with drinking.

These factors are mentioned only to highlight the emotional turmoil that a person newly diagnosed with MS may experience. This is *not* the frame of mind to have when making critical decisions about work. *Take your time!* Be sure that you have accurate and sufficient information on which to base a decision and that you are emotionally prepared to look objectively at the entire situation—know all your options and their ramifications. Speak with others who have successfully managed MS and/or with a counselor who is experienced in helping people with MS think through the important issues related to employment.

With this background in mind, the following critical points must be emphasized:

- Employment and other productive activities must not be abandoned unnecessarily because of fear and/or misinformation.
- Help is available to assist with work-related decisions and to implement the steps necessary to keep working.

Myths About Multiple Sclerosis

A number of myths or false beliefs make adjustment to MS more difficult. These misconceptions are held not only by a segment of the general public but also by an alarming number of health professionals who do not have extensive experience with MS and/or are unfamiliar with the professional literature. Some of them have a direct impact on the work experience. They include:

- *Stress.* At various points in the history of MS, stress was thought to worsen the disease and escalate the disease process. Scientific studies have examined this issue in detail, and results have failed to support the role of stress in either the onset or the progression of MS. Advice to quit working, get help to care for children, and curtail volunteer activities is misguided if it is based only on the diagnosis of MS. Specific symptoms may have an impact, but they need to be evaluated individually and carefully because problems may be self-limited or responsive to symptomatic therapy.
- *Activity.* It was formerly believed that physical activity was detrimental to people with MS. The directive was to "take it easy," stop all physical exercise, and rest as much as possible. Bed rest was the primary recommendation for this erratic and unpredictable disease. The major public figure to challenge this notion was Olympic ski medalist Jimmie Heuga, who could not accept a life of inactivity. We now know that Jimmie was right and that activity and exercise are actually beneficial to the well-being of people with MS. It follows that work-related activity should not be curtailed unless dictated by specific, long-standing symptoms that have not responded to therapy.
- *Incapacitation.* Before MS was routinely recognized in its early stages and in mild cases, the common belief was that it would

inevitably, and usually quickly, lead to serious disability that would interfere with the ability to perform daily activities, including employment. It is now known that this is not true—most people with MS can remain active and involved.

Disclosure

The decision to communicate—or not to communicate—the diagnosis of MS in the workplace is complex and important and deserves careful consideration. Disclosure when interviewing for a new job poses different issues from disclosure when you already have an established position.

It is important to be aware of both legal and practical considerations, whether you are seeking a new job or maintaining a current one. In the United States, people with disabilities are protected by the Americans with Disabilities Act (ADA), which became law in 1990. The definition of "disability" is complex, but it clearly encompasses MS regardless of whether symptoms are present. This is due to the possible *perception* of a disability. A diagnosis of MS carries such a possible preconception since an employer could potentially discriminate based on the association of MS with disability. The ADA prohibits employers from asking about or considering a diagnosis or general limitations in hiring and promotion decisions and only allows questions about ability to perform key components of the job. A job applicant or employee need only be armed with information related to key job components and need not be concerned about responses to disease or disability-related questions as long as the capacity to perform the job is not compromised. It is important to think about the essential or key elements of your current or prospective job because nonessential functions may legally be delegated to or traded with other employees.

In a similar manner, Canadians are protected by the Employment Equity Act (Bill C-64) passed in 1995, which replaces the previous Employment Equity Act (EE Act). This legislation eliminates employment barriers experienced by women, Aboriginals, and visible minorities, as well as people with disabilities. In a news release at the time of passage, Art Eggleton, president of the Treasury Board, described how employment equity was being advanced while the talents and expertise of all Canadians were being promoted. Among the areas of concern that prompted this most recent employment antidiscrimination legislation was the severe underrepresentation in the workplace of people with disabilities. Both the private and public sectors are covered by Bill C-64. The act makes use of the Canadian Human Rights Tribunal (to be named the Employment Equity Review Tribunal when hearing employment equity cases). It also confirms the mandate for Human Resources Development of Canada to conduct research, provide labor market data, and administer programs to recognize outstanding achievement in employment equity. Both appeal procedures and enforcement measures are addressed.

In addition to legal considerations, people with MS are often concerned about health insurance, life insurance, and disability insurance. A prospective or current employee needs to explore policies relative to diagnosis of a chronic disease or occurrence of disability. "Preexisting condition" clauses must be carefully investigated, as well as "caps" (lifetime limits on expenditures for a particular condition or for an individual's total medical expenses) and related categories that potentially limit the availability of medical and health services because of MS or another chronic condition. These factors may or may not be disclosure-related, depending on prior documentation of diagnosis and extent of information required for ongoing insurance coverage.

The noninsurance, nonlegal aspects of working with MS often are more difficult to assess and address. Such considerations include anticipated employer and fellow employee support or lack of support, possible growth freeze if limitations are imagined by the employer, and personal emotional investment in efforts to acknowledge or deny issues related to MS. Colleagues, including supervisors, often rally to support a fellow worker with a health problem and pull in resources such as "matching gifts" or volunteer incentives. Disclosure relieves the stress of covering up real needs and concerns and mobilizes team spirit and support. You also need to disclose necessary accommodations. An employer is required to make arrangements to help an employee perform "essential job functions." These accommodations must be "reasonable" in that they must be affordable and must not impose undue hardship on the employer.

There also are compelling reasons not to disclose: subtle or not so subtle pressure to resign, to accept lesser job responsibilities, or not to apply for promotion or expanded responsibilities. People have reported a "dead-end" feeling if a the supervisor has clearly communicated lack of support for further advancement.

Resources

You probably do not need this information now and may never need it. However, you should be aware that such information exists at the time of diagnosis so that you can obtain appropriate assistance at the first sign of difficulty and avoid larger problems altogether. Modest effort early on can prevent serious situations later and support your smooth career development.

Literature is available from the National Multiple Sclerosis Society in the United States (800-FIGHT-MS) and the Multiple Sclerosis Society of Canada (416-922-6065). Several publications are particularly helpful: "ADA and People with MS" (Cooper, Law and Sarnoff, 2000), which gives details about your protection under the law in an easy-to-read style; *Should I Work? Information for Employees* (2001), which gives a general overview of employment issues that might concern people newly diagnosed with MS; and *Information for Employers* when disclosure has occurred.

Occasionally, "accommodation" is needed. An accommodation may involve a change in scheduling, a parking space closer to the building entrance, or an office closer to the bathroom. Occasionally, equipment or a structural change such as a ramp may be needed. This is less often the case but usually is accomplished with minimal effort and cost when dealt with directly when the need is first identified. Resources on this topic include *Multiple Sclerosis: Your Legal Rights* and *Employment Issues and Multiple Sclerosis* (see "Additional Readings").

The National MS Society has a mail program for people recently diagnosed with MS, called "Knowledge is Power," which can be accessed by calling 1-800-FIGHT-MS. Society chapters also have periodic educational programs for people recently diagnosed with MS and their families and include issues relative to employment. Each state has a vocational rehabilitation office; the number can be obtained through the telephone directory or information assistance. Look in the blue government pages of the telephone book under "State Government" and look under one of the following headings:

Department of Vocational Rehabilitation
Department of Rehabilitation
Department of Human Services
Department of Social Services
Department of Social & Rehabilitation Services
Office of Vocational Rehabilitation.

Some important resources include:

- *Technical Assistance Centers*

- *National Institute on Disability & Rehabilitation Research*
  1-800-949-4232
  202-205-9151(voice), 202-205-9136 (TDD)

- *Equal Employment Opportunities Commission (EEOC) District/National Office*
  800-669-4000 to speak with an agent
  800-669-EEOC (3362) for written information
  800-669-6820 (TDD)

- *Architectural & Transportation Barriers Access Board*
  800-USA-ABLE (872-2253)
  (202) 272-5434 (voice)

Other resources in Canada include:

- *Canadian Council on Rehabilitation and Work*
  410-167 Lombard Avenue
  Winnipeg, Manitoba R3B OT6
  204-942-44862

- *Universal Design Institute*
  University of Manitoba
  Winnipeg, Manitoba R3T 2N2
  204-474-6450

- *JAN—The Job Accommodation Network*
  West Virginia University
  P.O. Box 6080
  Morgantown, WV 26506-6080
  (800) 526-7234

7

Research in Multiple Sclerosis: The Search for Answers

RESEARCH IN MULTIPLE SCLEROSIS (MS) BEGAN IN THE MID-1800s as simple descriptive studies that examined the symptoms of the disease and its effect on nervous system tissue. It has evolved into a specialty area of basic and clinical research that incorporates virtually every discipline of modern biotechnology, ranging from the most up-to-date molecular laboratory techniques; to studies of population, socioeconomics, and psychology; and to the testing of new therapies for their safety and efficacy.

Scientific research is a specialized discipline. Scientists are trained not only in their area of specialty research but also in the discipline of scientific inquiry. Simple "observation" is a form of scientific inquiry that is most useful in initial studies. The observation of biological processes and how they may change, for instance in disease, can help generate important new theories about disease cause and treatment, which can then be tested in more rigorous fashion.

In its most rigorous form, scientific research involves the testing of specific theories or hypotheses using controlled laboratory or clinical techniques that have the greatest likelihood of providing meaningful answers. A *hypothesis* is a tentative assumption that a scientist seeks to prove or disprove in the course of investigation, using state-of-the-art technology to get answers.

Most modern MS research is related to four major hypotheses about the disease and its cause (see Chapter 2): (1) that it is an autoimmune disease; (2) that it occurs in genetically susceptible individuals; (3) that it is triggered by some infectious or environmental factor; and (4) that it results in inflammation and loss of the white matter (myelin) and underlying nerve fibers of the brain and spinal cord, bringing neurologic symptoms and the associated socioeconomic problems long recognized to occur with MS.

Research in Immunology

While MS is recognized as a disease of the brain and spinal cord of the central nervous system (CNS), it is widely believed that the characteristic neurologic signs and symptoms of MS are caused by an immune system disorder that causes damage to CNS tissue and disrupts the normal activity of the CNS that controls movement, sensory perception, thinking, and emotional functioning.

The immune system is a highly complex organ of the body that includes lymphocytes (T cells), antibodies, a host of regulatory substances that circulate in the blood called *cytokines*, and many other key players. Normal immune function protects the body from injury and disease caused by infectious agents—bacteria, viruses, parasites, and the like—by mounting an attack against the "invaders" and clearing them from the body. Our own body tissues generally are protected and *not* subject to attack by our immune system.

Although there is some disagreement, most scientists working in the field of MS believe that the disease is caused by an abnormality in which a person's own immune system fails to distinguish foreign invaders from normal tissue in the body. As a consequence, the immune system attacks normal body tissue, resulting in inflammation and tissue damage that is often permanent. This "self-attack" of the immune system against body tissues is termed *autoimmunity*. Autoimmunity, then, is considered to be the true root cause of MS and, as such, is the largest area of research in MS worldwide. Understanding immune function in the disease will help pinpoint its cause and result in innovative therapies.

Immunologic research related to MS has progressed over a number of years from identifying immune cells in the nervous system, where they do not normally belong, to understanding how immune system components are regulated and become dysfunctional in autoimmune disease. We are now in a position to marshal this vital information about immune system function and dysfunction into the development of potential new therapies for MS.

Studies have been undertaken in healthy individuals to better understand normal immune system functioning, in individuals with MS to understand what goes wrong in the disease, and in individuals with other autoimmune diseases—such as rheumatoid arthritis and juvenile-onset diabetes—to understand what they can tell us more generally about immune system abnormality.

In addition to human studies, immunologic research in MS has been greatly aided by work on the laboratory animal model disease *experimental allergic encephalomyelitis* (EAE), an autoimmune disease of the brain and spinal cord in laboratory rats, mice, guinea pigs, and primates that has many characteristics in common with MS. Studies of animal models for MS and related animal model diseases for other human autoimmune disorders have greatly facilitated our understanding of basic immune system function and what goes wrong in autoimmune diseases. They are a practical, relatively rapid way to obtain answers to difficult questions.

Because MS involves the immune system, for several decades physicians have used powerful drugs that suppress immune function by decreasing the growth and proliferation of immune cells. Many such therapies tested for MS—such as cyclophosphamide, azathioprine, and even procedures such as total body or total lymphoid irradiation—have global or widespread immunosuppressive effects, potentially leaving a treated patient open to a variety of infections and complications, which made these therapies of questionable value in terms of "cost versus benefit." More specific immune therapy approaches have been desired for many years. Thus, pinpointing the immune problems in the disease more exactly has long been a goal, with the belief that such information could lead to highly specific therapies aimed at those immune system components involved in the disease, while leaving the rest of the immune system intact and functioning.

The search to understand the specific immune responses involved in MS has been an important focus of research in recent years. This includes exploring what makes an immune system that is normally directed against outside invaders become misdirected against normal body tissues (mistaking "self" tissue for "foreign" invaders); searching for the actual target of immune responses in the brain and spinal cord (the "antigen" that triggers immune attack); and determining the nature of T cells and antibodies that are primed to attack this target.

Another promising avenue of immunology research seeks to understand how and why immune system cells and antibodies move from the blood stream into the CNS. Work in this area is essential if we are to complete the picture of MS and develop treatments that prevent such "trafficking" and stop the disease in its tracks.

Not all hypotheses and studies are successful in MS research (or in any other branch of research). For example, in the late 1980s, with considerable background information on immune responses in EAE in mice, scientists reported evidence that there were relatively few potential disease-causing brain antigens—targets of the disease process—in myelin around nerve fibers. They also reported that they were able to identify T cells specific to those antigens and, they believed, to the MS disease process. With this information, a number of scientists and pharmaceutical companies began to design specifically engineered antibodies (immune system proteins produced in the laboratory that have an ability to target and neutralize specific proteins) and synthetic peptides (parts of proteins) aimed at preventing immune system attack against the CNS. In the animal model for MS, EAE, disease could be prevented entirely, and improvement was seen when disease was already present before treatment using such interventions.

Such information generated enormous excitement and many hypotheses for treating MS in humans. However, the immune response against myelin in humans turned out to be much more complicated than in the laboratory animal model disease. We know now that there are multiple myelin antigens involved in immune system responses in humans, and different people may have different antigen responses. Over time, there tends to be a shifting in immune responses so that the target of the immune response in myelin may change in the course of disease in a given individual. This means that specific T cell treatments aimed at taking advantage of the originally proposed "restricted" immune responses in MS are not likely to be effective for a wide spectrum of patients with MS, and treatments effective at one time in the disease may not continue to be effective.

One consequence of these disappointments has been a focus in immunology research in MS on chemical messengers called *cytokines*. Cytokines are produced by immune and other cells that regulate immune system activity. Many scientists believe that they may be important "final pathways" involved in all immune responses and that by manipulating cytokine activity it may not be necessary to understand specific immune cell responses in MS to combat the disease. Early studies showed that some cytokines make EAE or MS worse and that others may make the diseases better. Interferons, which are one type of cytokine, are an example of this dichotomy: interferon beta has been shown to be beneficial for treating MS, while there is evidence that interferon gamma makes the disease worse, at least at certain stages of the disease. Work under way continues to gain a better understanding of the cytokine "networks" that are involved in MS and to learn how to block "bad" cytokines and enhance the effects of "good" ones—all to the ultimate goal of providing safe and effective disease treatments. However, even in such more detailed analyses of immune networks, the outcomes are not always predictable. For example, an important cytokine called tumor necrosis factor alpha (TNFα) was found to be involved in damage to nervous system tissue in animal models of MS and believed to be functioning abnormally in MS itself. Blocking action of TNFα in EAE prevented or improved disease. However, in preliminary clinical studies in humans with MS, use of such TNFα blockers caused an increase in MS-related lesions in the brain, a clear indication that this approach could not be easily used in MS and might in fact be harmful.

While most work in MS immunology has focused on the T-cell response, a different kind of immune molecule produced by B cells, termed *antibodies*, are increasingly believed to be important in MS pathology as well. Antibodies have been found in MS lesions in the brain and have been linked to disease pathology in certain forms of EAE. These studies have been essential in pointing out a new direction not only in fundamental research in MS but also in treatment: certain kinds of immune therapies that can "improve" T cell–mediated disease can actually make antibody-mediated disease worse, and vice versa. Therefore, a better understanding of the relative roles of T cells and antibodies in disease pathology in different individuals, and perhaps at different stages of disease in the same individual, has important treatment implications and the potential to unveil key aspects of the underlying disease phenomenon.

An important adjunct to the issues of genetics and immunology is the role of hormones in MS. It is well known that MS is more than two to three times as common in women as in men, a gender bias that is seen in many diseases considered to be autoimmune in nature. And it is well known that pregnant women with MS tend to have stabilization or improvement in their disease in the second and third trimesters of pregnancy, only to experience a higher risk for a disease exacerbation in the first several months after delivery. This phenomenon has been linked to the role of estrogen hormones in pregnancy, and the need for the immune system to be suppressed in pregnancy to prevent a "rejection" of the fetus, which is recognized as being foreign by the mother's immune system. This is because its genetic makeup, a combination of the genes of the mother and the father, is fundamentally incompatible with the mother's immune responses. Hormone regulation of immune responses in MS has been an important area of MS research in recent years. Estrogen hormones actually can improve EAE, the animal model of MS. This key new aspect of our understanding of MS immunology led in 2000 to clinical trials in women with MS designed to determine whether the use of estrogen hormones can help mediate disease in women who are not pregnant. Additional evidence also suggests that testosterone, a male hormone, may be equally important in its impact on immune function, and this also may result in a new treatment approach.

Genetic Research

Understanding genetic factors in MS is a relatively new and rapidly expanding field, resulting in vast amounts of new information. Basic population studies tell us that specific groups of people in the world may be protected from MS and that others may be more susceptible (see Chapter 2). Genetic research has become highly "molecular" in nature as scientists race to uncover genetic factors that underlie the disease and may help determine who is susceptible to developing MS. The race to reveal the total human genetic code—completed at the end of 2000— will help enormously in unraveling the complexities of diseases with genetic components. While the gene code race focuses on the "normal" human genome, with that in hand, the ability to search for discrepancies that may be related to disease will be enhanced significantly.

The possibility of specific gene therapies is no longer the stuff of science fiction, even though its application to human disease is far from straightforward today. And for gene therapy to become a potential in a disease like MS, we need to understand completely the genetic factors that underlie the disease and devise ways to "correct" any defects that may be present. We are a long way from this goal and, given the nature of the disease, it may not be possible to achieve at all.

A more immediate consequence of such genetic work may be the development of techniques to more readily determine susceptibility to MS in the general population and in families in which the disease already occurs. Genetic factors may even one day provide some clues to the prognosis for any individual with the disease, helping to predict the type of MS that a person will have and even its severity.

An interesting consequence of genetics research has been a boost to the belief that MS is autoimmune in nature. Immune function is under strict genetic control, and the genes of people with MS that control immune function are in some ways different from the immune system genes of healthy individuals. Among these are genes involved in helping the immune system determine which body tissues are its own ("self") and which substances are foreign—a bacteria or virus or even a transplanted liver or kidney from a genetically different donor. This ability to distinguish between "self" and "foreign" allows the immune system to mount an effective response against foreign substances but not against tissues or cells that are part of its own body. Genes controlling this recognition process are called human leukocyte antigens (HLA genes), histocompatibility genes, or major histocompatibility genes (MHC genes). Based on both early population studies in which HLA "typing" was done on blood samples and more recent results from whole genome screens of individuals with MS in the United States, Canada, and the United Kingdom, the HLA genes are, to date, the strongest link that we have to an MS genetic factor.

A second important gene type that may be involved in MS controls structure and function of "receptors" on T cells of the immune system. Such receptors are essential in determining the target of immune responses. Although still controversial, some evidence suggests that T-cell receptor genes in people with MS may be different from those in people without the disease, resulting in a somewhat aberrant interaction between immune cells and potential targets of immune attack. Much work recently has focused on T-cell receptors and on the interaction between these immune cells, myelin antigens, and self-determining HLA molecules.

Thus, at their most basic level, genetic studies are helping us to know more about the immune nature of the disease, how much of the disease susceptibility may be related to genetic problems in immune system function, and how much of it may be related to other nonimmunologic factors or even to environmental or infectious factors.

Infectious Disease Research

Genes and the immune system are clearly involved with MS, but what event actually triggers the development of MS in people who are susceptible? That is where infectious disease research comes into play. Over decades, most such research has focused on the possibility that one or more viruses may be responsible for triggering MS, but new understanding of the possible role of bacteria is expanding our view of infectious processes in MS.

Virus infections can cause diseases with characteristics similar to those of MS, and certain viral diseases in laboratory animals also result in myelin damage. For decades there has been evidence that certain viral infections, particularly upper respiratory tract viral infections, may set off acute exacerbations of MS in individuals who already have the disease.

Researchers have hunted for a specific identifiable virus related to MS, not only with the hope that this will result in a relatively simple explanation for disease but also with the hope that combating such a virus will result in a safe and effective preventative or treatment. However, the search for "the" MS virus has been relatively unfruitful. Several dozen common and uncommon viruses have been postulated to be specifically related to MS, based on either epidemiology studies, the presence of higher levels of antibodies against a given virus in individuals with MS, or, more recently, evidence from very sophisticated polymerase chain reaction (PCR) analysis that can detect the "footprint" of a viral protein even if the virus has been long eliminated by the immune system.

In virtually every case of such claims, however, follow-up studies intended to confirm a relationship to MS have been unsuccessful; most such claims have been determined to be due to inadequate experimental sampling or laboratory contamination. Nonetheless, there remains the possibility that specific infections may be related to MS, and virologists who focus on this disease are at the forefront of ongoing searches. Interestingly, in recent years, most of the focus has been on viruses that are very common in the general population—not necessarily isolated only in individuals with MS—such as human herpesvirus 6 (HHV6), which causes roseola in infants, and to which virtually everyone in the population has been exposed.

In recent years, attention also has been drawn to a possible role for a bacterial infection. This has focused mostly on the bacterium *Chlamydia pneumoniae*, an equally common infection known to cause "walking pneumonia." Reports have claimed an association with this bacterium in individuals with MS and its presence in MS tissues. At the time of this writing, these results remain preliminary but promising and add to the possible view that not only viral infection, but also perhaps infection with bacteria, may be linked to MS.

If such a common virus or bacterium is responsible for MS, one must ask why the disease is not more common—since virtually everyone has been exposed to these agents. This is where *genetic susceptibility* may have its impact: while infectious factors and genetic factors may be necessary for MS to develop, neither alone is sufficient for MS to develop.

Many investigators believe it is likely that no specific virus, bacterium, or other infectious agent will be found to be related to MS. Rather, they are concentrating on research that explores how a susceptible person's immune system reacts to a variety of viral or other infections, or how immune function is tied to hormonal and other factors that might explain the initiation of the MS process. Studies in the mid-1990s amplifying earlier studies on MS-like disease in animals helped to explain how an immune system that has lost its ability to distinguish "self" from "non-self" tissue can be tricked by certain infectious agents into mounting an attack against a person's own myelin. The "trick" might be a very close similarity of molecular structure between some viruses, bacteria, and myelin itself, so that an effective immune response mounted against a key infectious agent might result in a "cross-reaction" based on molecular mimicry with myelin. This "mistaken identity" may explain much of the origin of MS and help to determine how the disease can be prevented from occurring in susceptible people.

Glial Cell Research

The symptoms of MS are directly due to inflammation and breakdown of myelin and cells that make myelin—called *oligodendrocytes*—in the brain and spinal cord of the CNS. Most likely as a secondary process, nerve fibers that are wrapped by myelin also are often damaged in MS. The biology of oligodendrocytes and other such glial cells in the CNS is therefore a vital and expanding area of research. This includes study of how oligodendrocytes develop and form myelin in early stages of life, how they are affected by immune system responses, how the nervous system responds when myelin is lost, how scars are formed when myelin is lost, and what the potential is for myelin regeneration and recovery.

Basic biochemical studies of myelin using increasingly sophisticated techniques have closely analyzed the tissue in people with MS, and such studies are used to determine if there are any abnormalities in the myelin or oligodendrocytes that might make these tissues and cells vulnerable to immune system attack. Much traditional biochemistry repeatedly demonstrated that myelin, or white matter, is "normal" in individuals with MS, suggesting that the autoimmune attack in MS is truly a question of immune cells not recognizing normal "self" tissue. By the mid-1990s, a new technology stemming from magnetic resonance imaging (MRI), called *magnetic resonance spectroscopy* (MRS), began to show that normal-appearing white matter in the brains of people with MS may actually have subtle abnormalities. It is not clear if this is directly related to a cause of the disease or whether it is an early, previously undetected result of the disease process. Such studies show not only the power of newer technologies but also the need to constantly reassess scientific beliefs and facts. We still need to consider, therefore, that there may be inherent abnormalities in white matter and myelin in individuals who develop MS and that the immune response directed against such abnormal tissue may be more appropriate than we previously believed—that is, they are not truly "self."

For many decades it was believed that myelin in the CNS could not be regenerated after it was damaged or lost in adults. This belief was shattered by the finding in the early 1980s that there was a degree of new myelin development in individuals whose brains showed extensive immune system damage and scarring due to MS. This myelin regeneration was weak, slow, and insufficient to overcome the devastation caused by the disease, but it provided new hope that myelin could be repaired.

Primed by this relatively recent knowledge that damaged CNS oligodendrocytes can regenerate and form new myelin, many laboratories are focusing on ways to enhance myelin growth and development in animals and in humans. In most cases of MS, particularly early cases, myelin insulation around nerve fibers is damaged or lost, but the underlying nerve fibers that control functions are intact and probably would be able to function essentially normally if their insulation were restored. This could result in a degree of functional recovery if remyelination could be achieved.

Some experimental approaches scientists are taking to meet this challenge include identifying the early stage myelin-making cells in the nervous system, called *oligodendrocyte progenitors*, that are capable of forming new tissue after immune system damage; using "growth factors" to stimulate more rapid and efficient myelin growth; modulating immune system functions by blocking special immunoglobulins and antibodies that may be inhibiting myelin growth; and transplanting myelin-making cells from healthy donors or from healthy parts of a person's own nervous system to diseased or damaged nervous system sites.

These studies have been largely limited to experimentation in laboratory animals with genetically deficient myelin or animals in which specific myelin lesions have been experimentally produced. Studies using certain immunoglobulins to suppress a theorized immunologic inhibition of myelin grown have been done in humans with MS, with mixed results; more work is planned. All of this research provides hope that myelin regrowth and functional recovery for individuals with MS may be possible in the future.

It is vital to recognize two key problems: (1) as long as the immune system problems responsible for myelin destruction remain unchecked, any efforts at myelin regeneration will be sabotaged by the ongoing disease process; and (2) for some individuals, especially those with advanced MS, it is clear that there is damage not only to myelin but also to vital nerve fibers. Nerve fibers that are damaged are unlikely to be able to function again, even if myelin insulation has been restored. Thus, research focusing on myelin regeneration must move hand-in-hand with efforts to stop the underlying immune system process.

Clinical Research

Clinical research directly involves individuals who have MS. It is aimed in a number of different directions. Studies in basic immunology, virology, and glial biology, in laboratory test tubes, or in animal models of MS, all become applied in the clinic to help us translate such fundamental disease information into studies of people with MS. Clinical trials (see Chapter 8) focus on testing the safety and efficacy of new drugs and agents developed to treat MS and its symptoms.

Another important area of clinical research is the refinement and development of new techniques for diagnosis. Such techniques can be used to follow disease progress, particularly the relatively new imaging techniques based on magnetic resonance technology that allow direct observation of lesions in the brain and spinal cord (MRI and related technologies). New developments in analysis of blood, cerebrospinal fluid, and urine also have importance in diagnosis and in monitoring the results of experimental clinical studies.

While new treatments are being developed to help reduce the symptoms and progression of MS, helping individuals and their families cope with the disease, obtain the best possible medical care, and function at the highest possible level in society are essential aspects of research in the areas of psychosocial studies as well as health care delivery and policy research.

Understanding the psychological and emotional aspects of MS has become a major focus of research in recent years, as we realize that the brain pathology (as well as day-to-day stress) of the disease creates problems in cognitive (intellectual) and affective (emotional) function. Increased information in these areas is leading to new techniques to help with coping and rehabilitation, as well as specific interventions that can be applied in a clinical setting.

Although not limited to MS, the problems of access to care and services for people with chronic disease are increasingly unwieldy and are becoming the focus of high-quality health care delivery and policy research. Data gathered from such studies have a direct impact on altering public perception of chronic disease and on changing for the better legislative policy, entitlement programs, and societal policy for all people with disabilities.

Research in MS is broad-based and comprehensive, involving all aspects of basic and applied sciences related to biomedicine. Funding for this research traditionally has come from governmental agencies, MS societies in many countries around the world, and, more recently, pharmaceutical and biotechnology companies. To date, the results have been a significantly increased understanding of the disease, new and specific therapies, and significantly enhanced quality of life for people with MS. Basic and applied research are needed more than ever before to close the gaps in our knowledge of MS and move us closer to full treatment, prevention, and cure.

8

Searching for Treatments: The "Ins" and "Outs" of Clinical Trials

RESEARCH ON MANY FRONTS RELATED TO MS IS AN ACTIVE AND vigorous undertaking. In the long run, all biomedical research in MS—be it the most basic or the most applied—is intended to gather information about the underlying disease process and is ultimately directed toward developing new therapeutic agents that may be safe and effective. Testing new drugs or devices in "clinical trials" of agents developed through basic and clinical research is itself a major focus of MS research. The outcome of such research can be treatments that can alter the disease course, prevent the disease from occurring, or improve function in people who already have MS, which together might constitute a functional "cure" for MS. The ultimate research experiment, therefore, is the *clinical trial*.

A clinical trial is the scientific study of the efficacy and safety of a drug or device for a given disease on people who have that disease. As scientific studies, clinical trials are complex, time-consuming, and expensive. They must be done as carefully as any other scientific experiment to ensure that the study results are accurate, reproducible (repeatable by other scientists yielding the same results), and broadly applicable outside the original study population. Poorly done clinical trials that result in misleading conclusions are wasteful at best and potentially dangerous for the intended population needing the treatment.

The Special Problems of MS Trials

PLACEBO EFFECTS

While care must be taken to ensure the quality and integrity of any clinical trial, MS clinical trials are particularly difficult to undertake. People with MS generally are highly motivated to search for a treatment or cure for their disease, and this positive motivation can actually interfere with the objective assessment of any drug or device. This often occurs because of a phenomenon known as the *placebo effect*—the tendency to improve simply because of participation in a clinical trial even if no active drug is being administered. A largely psychological phenomenon, the placebo effect is based in the faith that a given intervention will work even if there is no evidence to support such faith. Working with a sympathetic physician who also strongly believes in the value of an experimental treatment can help to reinforce such tendencies.

Placebo effects probably have some true basis in the physiologic responses a person can have as a result of experiencing increased hope or excitement in the prospects of helping to find a truly useful therapy. These physiologic effects are poorly understood, but they can have an impact on sense of well-being and can even seem to cause improvement for a short time. This is particularly the case when results of treatment rely on self-reporting of symptoms or physical state by a treated patient, rather than on the more rigorous objective assessment of performance by an examining physician or laboratory findings.

While important and potentially useful, such placebo effects must be carefully separated from a true therapeutic drug effect. Any useful drug for MS must have an effect that is greater than the placebo effect.

THE NATURAL DISEASE VARIABILITY OF MULTIPLE SCLEROSIS

The high degree of variability in MS makes the design of clinical trials difficult. In any individual, the disease may go through seemingly spontaneous remissions and worsening, which are unpredictable in occurrence, severity, and duration. Spontaneous stabilization in previously progressive disease or a spontaneous remission of symptoms could easily be confused with a drug effect in a treatment program, even if the drug is having no impact whatsoever.

The disease may be very different from individual to individual. While symptoms of MS can be cataloged, no two individuals experience the same problems in the same ways. Because of this variability, clinical trials for new treatments must include provisions to overcome the natural disease variability that is seen over time and within and between individuals. A true drug effect must be separable from the natural variability in disease course.

UNDERSTANDING THE PREDICTED DRUG EFFECT

Drugs and other agents tested for MS generally have a mode of action that is more or less understood. In fact, agents usually are chosen for testing in MS because the known mode of action bears some relation to what we know about the disease. However, drugs may have different effects on different MS disease types. Agents that may be predicted to alter the frequency or severity of acute attacks of MS may have no benefit on longer-term progression of disease. Thus, clinical trials for acute attacks in MS must include only individuals with well-defined disease relapses or the results at the end of years of exploration will be uninterpretable. By the same token, results of a study testing the ability of an agent to stop progression of disease would be muddied by the inclusion of patients with relapsing-remitting disease and no progression.

In the end, trials must be designed to answer questions on the particular type of disease or symptom for which the new agent is predicted to have an effect. The inclusion of individuals with different disease types or without the appropriate symptom problem may result in an incorrect conclusion.

Finally, some drugs may seem to cause improvement but actually only have indirect effects on the disease. Agents with *psychotropic* effects, such as antidepressants, can help enormously in day-to-day coping with MS for patients who have depression associated with their disease, and such individuals likely will feel and perform better. This could be mistaken for an effect of the medication on the underlying disease process when there really is none at all. Understanding the true effect of any drug on the disease process requires a detailed knowledge of the drug's action and careful clinical assessment of effects on the disease.

Availability of Safe and Useful Therapies

Since 1993 several new treatments for MS have passed the approval process for marketing by the U.S. Food and Drug Administration and by drug regulatory authorities in countries around the world. Relapsing-remitting MS has no fewer that four agents that have been found to be at least partially effective in this form of disease, and progressive and worsening MS can now be treated by one or two agents based on regulatory approvals. More agents are being developed for all forms of MS to provide additional therapeutic options when agents already exist and to find new treatments for types of MS that still remain untreatable.

The availability of treatments actually complicates the search for new therapies in MS. One hopes that new treatments that are being tested will be at least as good but hopefully better than (more effective, fewer side effects, easier to use) those already available. However, the ethics of treating patients in a placebo-controlled study may be questioned since a portion of those enrolled—those who are placed in a placebo group in the trial—would be asked to forego effective treatment for the duration of the new study.

This dilemma has resulted in questions about the ethics and practicality of undertaking placebo-controlled trials for forms of disease for which effective treatment is already available, a topic that has been specifically addressed in the Declaration of Helsinki, an international agreement that sets out guidelines for all human research. As an additional complication, placebo-controlled trials generally are the most efficient and the least expensive to conduct. Alternatives to such trials—such as testing new treatments against available therapies or in combination with available therapies—are attractive but have additional cost and practical considerations.

These and other problems associated with MS clinical trials can best be overcome by extremely rigorous experimental design for the studies. The generally accepted methods of study are time-consuming and expensive, but they hold the best chance of obtaining a clear-cut answer about the efficacy and safety of any agent in MS.

Multiple Sclerosis Clinical Trial Study Design

SCIENTIFIC RATIONALE: A PRIMARY REQUIREMENT

The first and perhaps the most essential step in the consideration of any new drug or agent for its therapeutic potential in MS is that it should have a strong scientific rationale for being tested in this disease. Based on our knowledge of the MS process and on experimental studies of the drug in the laboratory, in animal disease models for MS, or in human disorders with similarities to MS, a physician or scientist will conclude that a drug may have a potential role in the treatment or management of MS. Drugs or any other substance or device without a scientific rationale related to the cause of MS should not even be considered for disease testing because they likely will have no impact on disease outcome and will be wasteful of the time and effort of participating individuals with MS and their physicians, as well as the financial resources required for the study. Many "alternative" therapies can be faulted on this first criterion: a lack of bona fide rationale for even being considered in a disease such as MS.

"PRELIMINARY" OR PHASE 1 STUDIES

Given a strong scientific rationale from basic and laboratory animal research, human trials almost always begin with toxicity or safety studies in a very small number of people with the disease. This is called a "preliminary" or *phase 1* clinical trial. In such early experiments, physicians usually have little sense of whether the candidate agent is safe for use in humans—the most vital consideration in any medical intervention. In these earliest studies, usually only a few very seriously ill people are asked to participate because these people may find the potential risk of any new agent to be worthwhile given the grave nature of their disease. If such studies demonstrate that the agent is safe, a physician may pursue further studies to get a sense of possible efficacy.

"PILOT" OR PHASE 2 CLINICAL TRIALS

"Pilot" or *phase 2* studies usually involve larger, statistically relevant numbers of patients (often 20–100 or more) with a disease type and severity that seem appropriate to the known or hypothesized drug effect. Key issues in such a study are (1) determining the effectiveness of the drug in halting progression, reducing relapse rate, or improving symptoms and function; (2) obtaining additional information about toxicity and safety; and (3) refining knowledge about the best possible dose and route of delivery (i.e., oral, by injection, etc.).

Such pilot studies aim to be objective in obtaining the required answers. Thus, patient performance on drug may be compared with predrug status (so-called "longitudinal studies") or against the known performance of a similar group of individuals not receiving treatment (a "historical control" study). Even better, they should be compared with an identical group of patients who are on a parallel "control" track but obtaining sham or placebo treatment (a treatment that looks identical to the actual drug or therapy but is therapeutically inactive) when ethically and practically possible or with patients who are being actively treated with the best available therapy for that form of disease.

Because MS can change over time, even with no treatment intervention, longitudinal studies and studies using historical controls usually are unsatisfactory because it is impossible to know whether changes during the trial are due to the test drug or to underlying disease changes that may have occurred anyway.

True objectivity is enhanced if both the patients and the physicians who periodically check for efficacy are "blinded" or "masked" to the treatment status of individual subjects. In other words, neither knows which group of patients is receiving the experimental drug and which group is being given control treatment. Such "double-blinded" studies are hard to achieve, given the fact that many test agents have side effects that may be "unblinding" to the patient or examining physician. But rigorous efforts at blinding are essential to reduce the likelihood of false results due to psychological responses to the clinical trial itself or to biases about anticipated treatment outcomes among either physicians or patients.

Increasingly, phase 1 and 2 studies are combined into a "phase 1/2" study to speed the initial assessment of toxicity and efficacy. Magnetic resonance imaging (MRI) is now used as a key outcome in such studies, and often the primary outcome. Since available therapies for MS all show the ability to reduce accumulation of new lesions detected by MRI, often the first step an investigator takes in evaluating a new treatment is to determine if it, too, can reduce new lesion formation, or at least not result in increased lesions. This is applicable in trials in which the expected impact on therapy might be on disease pathology that can be detected by MRI examination. In such studies, MRI has largely replaced clinical assessment as the primary mode of analysis in early phase clinical trials.

Results from such phase 1/2 studies, which often can take several years to obtain, may or may not show statistical benefit to people receiving drug compared with people receiving control therapy, or unacceptable levels of side effects. The agent usually is abandoned as a possible therapy if there is no benefit, or if there are uncontrollable or dangerous side effects. On the other hand, if the possibility of benefit remains after the study or if early indications of benefit are actually seen and side effects are minimal or acceptable, a further, larger clinical trial, usually with a focus on change in clinical status and lesion formation detected by MRI, will be undertaken to confirm and expand the studies.

"DEFINITIVE" OR PHASE 3 CLINICAL TRIALS

"Definitive" or *phase 3* trials usually are the final step toward making a decision about the value of a proposed therapy. As in the previous trial stage, the key questions concern efficacy and safety. Large, statistically determined numbers of participants are essential, and the study often is conducted at a number of different sites (so-called "multicenter" trials) and often is international in scope to ensure that the drug can be used in an equivalent fashion by many physicians in many care settings. Rigorous adherence to blinding of patients and examining physicians as well as careful random assignment of patients into treatment and control groups are essential to ensure objectivity. At the conclusion of the study period, when the blinding code is broken and the performance of drug-treated patients can be compared with that of the control group patients, there should be sufficient information to determine if the tested agent is truly safe and effective.

Recent definitive clinical trials for MS have included as many as 1,500 individuals, have involved 50 to 100 participating centers, and have taken multiple years to complete. These are the "gold standard" studies from which physicians and patients may have the best confidence that the results are sound.

There are variations in the these study designs, often depending on the amount of information available about a new drug from the laboratory, from use in other diseases, or from prior use in MS. Not all new agents go through a test phase in animal models of MS (e.g., interferons were not studied to any extent in animal models of MS because significant amounts of safety data from humans with other diseases were already in hand), and in some cases phase 2 and phase 3 studies are combined into a single large phase 2/3 study when sufficient information is available from previous studies on dosing and route of delivery. However, the elements and data described are required to determine true benefit and safety. These are also the elements and data required by the U.S. Food and Drug Administration and similar regulatory bodies in many countries, which closely monitor clinical trials at every step. It is ultimately the regulatory authority's assessment of the efficacy and safety data and the care with which a study is done that determines whether any agent may be marketed as a treatment for MS.

"POST-MARKETING" OR PHASE 4 STUDIES

Once governmental regulatory approval has been granted and the agent can be marketed and advertised as a treatment for MS, there often is a series of further studies, which are termed "postmarketing" or *phase 4* studies. These usually are designed to collect information on further adverse reactions to the agent, to explore the use of the drug for different forms of disease (e.g., an approved drug for progressive MS might be tested in relapsing-remitting disease in a phase 4 analysis), or to test the effects of the drug on related disorders (e.g., testing the efficacy and safety of a drug approved for MS on rheumatoid arthritis).

In some cases, regulatory authorities mandate phase 4 studies to collect data that were missing in the definitive analysis and that are important in understanding the use of the new medication. Sometimes the outcome of these mandated phase 4 studies can determine continued marketability of new agents. Should data become available that change the original understanding of the safety and efficacy of the new agent and compromise its use, regulatory authorities may remove the treatment from the market.

Financing Clinical Trials

Drug studies are time-consuming and expensive. Such studies most often are supported financially by pharmaceutical and biotechnology companies that invest significant "research and development" resources in these experiments. Grants from the federal government or voluntary health agencies, such as the National Multiple Sclerosis Society, also may fund part or all of the cost of clinical trials. It is rare (and often considered unethical) to request that a patient who volunteers to participate as an experimental subject be asked to pay for that privilege.

Who Participates in Clinical Trials?

The decision for any person with MS to participate in an experimental clinical trial is an intensely personal one and is highly subjective. Since there is always the potential for risk of any untested agent, a potential study participant must be fully informed by the treating physician, who must include a clear assessment of the potential risk factors in the study. Informed consent, including close personal discussion with the physician and nurse as well as required written permission from the study participant, are legal requirements that protect the rights of all participants.

A true sense of altruism, coupled with a sense of adventure, often characterizes those who volunteer to participate in such studies, since participation in either treatment or sham group ultimately may help tens of thousands of people with MS. The clinical trial volunteer is a real pioneer and a true hero.

Why Can't Some Patients Participate in Clinical Trials?

An unfortunate dilemma occurs when a person decides that he or she wants to participate in a clinical trial and finds that it is impossible. A frequently asked question is, "Doctor, why can't I be in your clinical trial?"

Clinical trials generally are limited to a relatively small number of individuals, who must be located geographically close to the clinical center(s) where the study is undertaken. Since most studies require intense and frequent clinic visits at specific predetermined times throughout several years, difficulties in travel from home to the clinic may be considered in determining whether someone will be accepted into a study.

The design of trials is such that generally only one type of MS— say, relapsing-remitting disease—is involved in the study. This excludes people with any other form of disease. Even within the group of interest, further restrictions, called inclusion and exclusion criteria, will be enforced in virtually all studies: disease limited to a certain duration or a certain level of disability; restricted age of participants; exclusions based on prior medications or participation in previous trials of agents for which there might be dangerous or confusing effects with the new experimental treatment.

For any particular test drug, other restrictions also may apply, depending on the known characteristics of the test medication. There may be prohibitions against pregnancy if an agent might cause harm to a fetus; individuals with other medical conditions not related to MS that may be affected by known characteristics of the test medication may be excluded. These practical factors often can result in an eager patient being refused a place in a new clinical trial.

If this should be the case, disappointed individuals may take some solace from the realization that positive findings from a clinical trial eventually will benefit many, many more people than could ever hope to participate in the initial studies. Everyone will benefit from the time and effort invested by the few.

Where Can I Learn About Ongoing Clinical Trials?

Finding out about clinical trials in MS should be a joint project of the patient and the physician. The network of physicians who organize and run studies in MS is ever-growing, and in consultation with a personal physician, an interested patient usually can learn of any pending studies locally or in nearby communities, often with the assistance of the local branch or chapter of the National Multiple Sclerosis Society, Multiple Sclerosis Society of Canada, or their over 30 affiliated member organizations around the world.

In summary, the ultimate research in MS is the development and testing of new therapies for use in the disease. Clinical trials, designed to objectively test efficacy and safety, are difficult and expensive to undertake. While people with MS are always needed to participate in such research, the decision to volunteer often is a difficult and personal one, and the practical restrictions involved in conducting clinical trials in MS often exclude many people who would gladly participate. In the end, basic and clinical scientists, patients who participate in clinical trials, pharmaceutical companies, and governmental and voluntary health agencies focused on MS worldwide are all partners in ensuring the development of new treatments for individuals affected by MS.

9

How Your Multiple Sclerosis Society Can Help

PEOPLE WITH MULTIPLE SCLEROSIS (MS) HAVE NEEDS AND CON-
cerns relative to their diagnosis, many of which are shared
by family members and close friends. The issues vary for each
individual according to time since diagnosis, degree of impairment, and family and work situations. Other factors such as
personality characteristics, previous life events, and learning
and coping styles also have an impact. The family physician
or neurologist is a frequent source of information. While this
is certainly appropriate, a medical practice is not an adequate
resource to accommodate the extensive non-medical needs of
those with MS, their families, friends, and other concerned
persons such as employers, teachers, and health professionals.
In North America the primary resource for addressing non-
medical MS-related needs are the National Multiple Sclerosis Society in the United States and the Multiple Sclerosis
Society of Canada. This chapter provides general information
about the U.S. and Canadian Societies, as well as the specific
ways these organizations can help you.

Overview of the National Multiple Sclerosis Society

The National Multiple Sclerosis Society (NMSS) is the only non-profit organization in the United States that supports national and international research on the prevention, cure, and treatment of MS, with more than $310 million expended to date. Equally important, the Society's goals include the provision of nationwide programs to assist people with MS and their families and the provision of information about MS to those with the disease, family members, professionals, and the public. Programs are designed to help people with MS to maintain their independence and lifestyle, with "state of the art" health care and other support systems available. The Society's mission—to end the devastating effects of MS—addresses the negative impact of the disease in the present through education and services and into the future through research and advocacy.

The Society was founded in 1946 by Sylvia Lawry, whose brother had MS. In her search to learn more about the disease, she found that only two scientists in the country professed any interest in the disease. Ms. Lawry placed an advertisement in the New York Times seeking any information about successful treatments for MS. A number of people who were also touched by MS responded. They had no news of a cure, but asked that Ms. Lawry share whatever helpful information she received. And so the National MS Society was born. It has grown to more than 760,000 members, including over 280,000 people who have MS. More than 140 local units provide varying levels of assistance and education. The home offices in New York City, Denver, and Washington, D.C. direct MS-related research and advocacy, provide some specific services, and provide support, structure, and guidance for chapters. Policies and national priorities are established by a National Board of Directors, composed of business and professional leaders with a special interest in MS. The Board is assisted by a nationally representative group of individuals with MS, the National Programs Advisory Council. Each local chapter is governed by a Board of Trustees. Staff at both national and chapter levels work in partnership with volunteers and the community to implement the necessary and desired programs. There is an ongoing process of identifying needs and eliciting feedback regarding the value of programs. This involves people with MS, their families, and the professionals who serve them, and provides direction for Society activities.

Philosophy of Programs

The NMSS and its chapters are committed to empowering people with MS to live as independently as possible within the limits of their disabilities, and to the maximum of their capabilities within the least restrictive environment. This goal is achieved through programs, services, and activities that:

- Promote and support knowledge, health, and independence
- Inform and educate people with MS and their families, professionals, public officials, and the general public about MS
- Provide support programs that help people with MS and their families cope with the changes and challenges that MS presents
- Help people gain access to community resources and quality, specialty health care
- Stimulate changes and developments in the community and public policy beneficial to people affected by MS
- Fill gaps in community resources

The Society believes that all people with MS and their families in the United States should have access to certain basic programs and ensure this through its chapter certification process.

All people with MS are offered services without discrimination, Access is not affected by a person's race, color, religion, age, disability, or sexual orientation, or the individual's relationship with a chapter. Chapters do hold "targeted" programs to meet the needs of specific groups, e.g., education programs for those newly diagnosed, young professionals' groups, gay/lesbian network, etc.

The confidentiality of members with MS and their family members ("clients") is strictly maintained. Client status is indistinguishable on the general membership list, and clients receive general Society mailings, including solicitations for support, unless a clear request to the contrary is made.

Who Are Served?

The Society's mission reflects our dedication to "end the devastating effects of multiple sclerosis." At the center of chapter programs are people who have MS. But others are affected as well. NMSS clients are any and all who come to the Society for information and/or professional assistance. The secondary focus of our programs is the MS "family circle"—spouses, children, parents, relatives, and significant others. Coworkers and close friends are included in this circle as well. Family members and significant others can also utilize chapter programs.

The NMSS is the leading source of information on MS for the general public. It also provides education to health professionals, service providers, and community agencies. Although not a direct service to people with MS or their families, such information and education can have significant impact on quality of life, increasing access to quality health care and community resources and promoting understanding from others.

Quality of Life Goals

The NMSS organizes services under three main Quality of Life Goals: MS Knowledge, Health, and Independence. Specific services are addressed within this framework.

Knowledge	*Health*	*Independence*
• Knowledge of MS by clients, families, professionals, the public	• Physical health • Emotional health • Family and social support	• Independent living • Accessibility • Employment • Long-term services

KNOWLEDGE

The National Multiple Sclerosis Society facilitates acquisition of essential knowledge about MS by providing information and education to clients, families, professionals, and the public.

Knowledge of MS by Clients and Families, Professionals, and the Public

Information about MS is the first and most frequent request the NMSS receives from people with MS. Client surveys consistently request more information about MS: symptoms, diagnosis, programs, treatment, research, and related issues such as employment, health insurance, disability rights, and family issues.

Seeking information about MS is usually a first step in the coping process. Getting accurate up-to-date information can assist you to make informed decisions, become aware of needs and resources, and take some control over this unpredictable and complex disease. One of the main functions of the NMSS is to serve as the repository of the most current and accurate information on MS.

- Information can be obtained by calling 800-FIGHT-MS (1-800-344-4867). Selection of the first option connects the caller to the closest chapter. He or she can then request information on the topic of interest.
- Internet Web site with updated information about treatments, current research, and programs (http://www.nationalmssociety.org).
- Knowledge Is Power educational program (serial mailings) for people newly diagnosed with MS and their families, available through all chapters or on the website.
- Moving Forward group educational program for people newly diagnosed with MS and their families, available through most chapters.
- Education programs on various topics throughout the year.
- Annual national education program
- Booklets, articles, and information sheets on MS-related topics (see "Resource Guide").
- Lending library of books, audio- and/or videotapes, with mail access, through your local chapter.
- *Inside MS* national quarterly magazine, and chapter newsletter quarterly or more often.

HEALTH

The National Multiple Sclerosis Society helps people with MS to achieve optimal health physically, emotionally, and in their relationships.

Physical Health

People with MS must deal with concerns about physical impairments related to the disease and their impact on general physical health. NMSS programs and services address physical health needs by:

- Promoting "state-of-the-art" MS health care and facilitating access for people with MS through formal affiliations with MS clinical facilities and professional education programs;
- Providing referrals to neurologists, physical therapists, and other medical/rehabilitation professionals knowledgeable about MS;

- Swimming and other exercise programs sponsored or co-sponsored by some chapters, or referral to existing programs in the community
- Wellness programs in some chapters.
- Affiliation with local MS clinical facilities to facilitate access to, and coordination of, health services.
- Participation in local and national advocacy issues related to physical health, e.g., health insurance reform, through Action Alert Network. (call your local chapter to join, or sign up on the Society's web site).

Emotional Health

Emotional health is a state of psychological well-being, which includes an individual's adaptive capacities. It is demonstrated by successful interactions with others and with the social environment. Difficulties with adaptation in a chronic illness are normal and respond favorably to a variety of interventions.

Although NMSS chapters are not primarily mental health agencies, we can help individuals and their significant others in their adaptation to chronic illness. Chapters provide short-term counseling, defined as "reflective listening and problem solving." The social isolation that often results from having a chronic illness can be reduced through peer relationships and group programs that bring people together.

Assistance with problem solving:

- "Someone to Listen" peer support program, which meets the second most requested service—to speak with another person who has MS. "Peers" are specially trained to provide information and support to the person with MS
- Local counselor/therapist referrals
- Self-help groups—leaders have often received group leadership training through the Society
- Peer support programs

Family Support

Families of people with MS are important to the National MS Society, which has formally adopted the Family Service America, Inc. definition of family: "A family consists of two or more people, whether living together or apart, related by blood, marriage, adoption, or commitment to care for one another."

This definition highlights the inclusion of all varieties of family configurations. The NMSS recognizes the enormous, ongoing stress that the entire family experiences, as well as the critical support provided by the family to the person with MS. Programs emphasize the strengths of the family and bolster these strengths by offering education and other means of support and assistance.

The NMSS sponsors a variety of family programs combining education, counseling, and social activities (in some chapters); social events such as holiday parties; "Children with MS" program, which matches children/teens with MS with appropriate peers and offers parents the opportunity to network (call the Denver home office: 303-813-6623) family counseling programs in some chapters, referrals to experienced community counselors in others.

INDEPENDENCE

The National Multiple Sclerosis Society is committed to promoting the highest possible level of independence for people with MS. This category of programs and services does not deal with the immediate needs of people recently diagnosed, but does look at some of the long-term issues of which we all should be aware.

Independent Living and Accessibility

Referrals to centers for independent living, equipment vendors, accessible housing, and others.

All chapter offices and program locations are accessible to people with disabilities.

Employment

Referrals and consultations to help people continue employment despite MS-related obstacles.

Long-Term Services

Programs to help people who are moderately to severely limited by MS-related disability receive necessary personal services and other assistance.

The Multiple Sclerosis Society of Canada

Founded in 1948, the Multiple Sclerosis Society of Canada has a membership of 28,000, with seven regional divisions and more than 120 chapters. The Head Office is located in Toronto, Ontario. Division offices are located in Dartmouth, Montreal, Toronto, Winnipeg, Regina, Edmonton, and Vancouver. The mission is "to be a leader in finding a cure for MS and enabling people affected by MS to enhance their quality of life." The Multiple Sclerosis Society of Canada expends over $4 million annually on medical research programs.

INDIVIDUAL AND FAMILY SERVICES

The Multiple Sclerosis Society of Canada provides a wide variety of services for people who have MS and their families. These include:

Information:

- MS Society of Canada publications
- ASK MS information resource center
- Literature and videos
- Conferences and workshops

Funding:

- Equipment purchase or loan programs
- Special assistance programs

Support:

- Individual advocacy
- Support counseling
- Consultation and referral
- Support and self-help groups
- Recreation and social programs

Services vary across the country depending on the kind of provincial government and community programs available, since the MS Society does not wish to duplicate services already in existence. The Society currently spends more than $7 million annually on services and education programs for people who have MS, their family members, and health care professionals.

PUBLIC EDUCATION

The MS Society is firmly committed to informing Canadians about MS and how they can join the fight against MS. The national office coordinates an overall public awareness campaign that is supplemented and complemented by activities at the divisional and chapter levels.

SOCIAL ACTION

The Multiple Sclerosis Society of Canada has long been aware of its responsibility to bring about changes to government policies and private actions and attitudes that will positively benefit people with MS. Since December 1987, when the National Board of Directors approved the formation of the National Social Action Committee, Society volunteers have been pursuing these goals in a more coordinated manner.

FUND RAISING

The Multiple Sclerosis Society of Canada has total revenues of more than $20 million annually. The funds are used to support research, individual and family services, public education, social action, and volunteer resources. Most of this income comes from public donations, bequests, and special fund raising programs conducted by the MS Society. The five major fund raising programs are the MS Carnation Campaign, the MS Bike Tour, the MS Read-A-Thon, the Super Cities Walk for Multiple Sclerosis, and the Direct Mail Campaign.

HISTORY

The first multiple sclerosis society in the world—the National Multiple Sclerosis Society in the United States—began in 1946. After contact with the American organization, a small group of dedicated volunteers in Montreal founded the Multiple Sclerosis Society of Canada in 1948. Support of MS research began in 1949.

Headquarters for the Society remained in Montreal until the mid-1960s, when the offices were moved to Toronto. Other advances came with the establishment of regional divisions; there are now seven divisions across Canada, from coast to coast. The Multiple Sclerosis International Federation, of which the Canadian Society is a charter member, was established in 1967.

Individual and Family Services Summary Chart

Alberta Division
10104-79th Street
Edmonton, AB
T6A 3G3
780-463-1190

Atlantic Division
71 Ilsley Avenue
Unit 12
Dartmouth, NS
B3B 1L5
902-468-8230

British Columbia Division
1600-1130 West Pender
Street
Vancouver, BC
V6E 4A4
604-689-3144

Manitoba Division
141 Bannatyne Avenue
Suite 400
Winnipeg, MB
R3B 0R3
204-943-9595

Ontario Division
250 Bloor Street East
Suite 1000
Toronto, ON
M4W 3P9
416-922-6065

Quebec Division
666 Sherbrooke Street
West, Suite 1500
Montreal, PQ
H3A 1E7
514-849-7592

Saskatchewan Division
150 Albert Street
Regina, SK
S4R 2N2
306-522-5600

Call toll-free in Canada 800-268-7582.

Glossary

Activities of daily living (ADLs)

Activities of daily living include any daily activity a person performs for self-care (feeding, grooming, bathing, dressing), work, home-making, and leisure. The ability to perform ADLs is often used as a measure of ability/disability in MS.

Acute

Having rapid onset, usually with recovery; not chronic or long-lasting.

Antibodies

Proteins of the immune system that are soluble (dissolved) in blood serum or other body fluids and which are produced in response to bacteria, viruses, and other types of foreign antigens. *See* Antigen.

Anticholinergic

Refers to the action of certain medications commonly used in the management of neurogenic bladder dysfunction. These medications inhibit the transmission of parasympathetic nerve impulses and thereby reduce spasms of smooth muscle in the bladder.

Antigen

Any substance that triggers the immune system to produce an antibody; generally refers to infectious or toxic substances. *See* Antibodies.

Assistive devices

Any tools that are designed, fabricated, and/or adapted to assist a person in performing a particular task, e.g., cane, walker, shower chair, adapted kitchen utensils, etc.

Ataxia

The incoordination and unsteadiness that result from the brain's failure to regulate the body's posture and the strength and direction of limb movements. Ataxia is most often caused by disease activity in the cerebellum.

Autoimmune disease

An immune system malfunction in which the body's immune system causes illness by mistakenly attacking healthy cells, organs, or tissues in the body. Multiple sclerosis is believed to be an autoimmune disease, along with systemic lupus erythematosus, rheumatoid arthritis, scleroderma, and many others.

Autonomic nervous system

The part of the nervous system that regulates "involuntary" vital functions, including the activity of the cardiac (heart) muscle, smooth muscles (e.g., of the bladder and bowel), and glands.

B cell

A type of lymphocyte (white blood cell) manufactured in the bone marrow that makes antibodies.

Babinski reflex

A neurologic sign in MS in which stroking the outside sole of the foot with a pointed object causes an upward (extensor) movement of the big toe rather than the normal (flexor) bunching and downward movement of the toes. *See* Sign.

Blood-brain barrier

A semipermeable cell layer around blood vessels in the brain and spinal cord that prevents large molecules, immune cells, and potentially damaging substances and disease-causing organisms (e.g., viruses) from passing out of the blood stream into the central nervous system (brain and spinal cord). A break in the blood-brain barrier may underlie the disease process in MS.

Brain stem

The part of the central nervous system that houses the nerve centers of the head as well as the centers for respiration and heart control. It extends from the base of the brain to the spinal cord.

Catheter, urinary

A hollow, flexible tube, made of plastic or rubber, which can be inserted through the urinary opening into the bladder to drain excess urine that cannot be excreted normally.

Central nervous system

The part of the nervous system that includes the brain, optic nerves, and spinal cord.

Cerebellum

A part of the brain situated above the brain stem that controls balance and coordination of movement.

Cerebrospinal fluid (CSF)

A watery, colorless, clear fluid that bathes and protects the brain and spinal cord. The composition of this fluid can be altered by a variety of diseases. Certain changes in CSF that are characteristic of MS can be detected with a lumbar puncture (spinal tap), a test sometimes used to help make the MS diagnosis.

Cerebrum

The large, upper part of the brain, which acts as a master control system and is responsible for initiating thought and motor activity.

Clinical finding

An observation made during a medical examination indicating change or impairment in a physical or mental function.

Clonus

A sign of spasticity in which involuntary shaking or jerking of the leg occurs when the toe is placed on the floor with the knee slightly bent. The shaking is caused by repeated, rhythmic, reflex muscle contractions.

Cognition

High-level functions carried out by the human brain, including comprehension and formation of speech, visual perception and construction, calculation ability, attention (information processing), memory, and executive functions such as planning, problem-solving, and self-monitoring.

Cognitive impairment

Changes in cognitive function caused by trauma or disease process. Some degree of cognitive impairment occurs in approximately 50 to 60 percent of people with MS, with memory, information processing, and executive functions being the most commonly affected functions.

Cognitive rehabilitation

Techniques designed to improve the functioning of individuals whose cognition is impaired because of physical trauma or disease. Rehabilitation strategies are designed to improve the impaired function via repetitive drills or practice, or to compensate impaired functions that are not likely to improve. Cognitive rehabilitation is provided by psychologists and neuropsychologists, speech/language pathologists, and occupational therapists. While these three types of specialists use different assessment tools and treatment strategies, they share the common goal of improving the individual's ability to function as independently and safely as possible in the home and work environment.

Computerized axial tomography (CAT scan)

A noninvasive diagnostic radiology technique. A computer integrates X-ray scanned "slices" of the organ being examined into a cross-sectional picture.

Contraction

A shortening of muscle fibers and muscle that produce movement around a joint.

Coordination

An organized working together of muscles and groups of muscles aimed at bringing about a purposeful movement such as walking or standing.

Corticosteroids

See ACTH, Glucocorticoid hormones.

Cortisone

A glucocorticoid steroid hormone, produced by the adrenal glands or synthetically, that has anti-inflammatory and immune-system suppressing properties. Prednisone and prednisolone also belong to this group of substances used in MS to decrease the duration of attacks.

Cranial nerves

Nerves that carry sensory or motor fibers to the face and neck. Included among this group of twelve nerves are the optic nerve (vision), trigeminal nerve (sensation along the face), vagus nerve (pharynx and vocal cords). Evaluation of cranial nerve function is part of the standard neurologic exam.

Deep tendon reflexes

The involuntary jerks that are normally produced at certain spots on a limb when the tendons are tapped with a hammer. Reflexes are tested as part of the standard neurologic exam.

Demyelination

A loss of myelin in the white matter of the nervous system.

Diplopia

Double vision, or the simultaneous awareness of two images of the same object that results from a failure of the two eyes to work in a coordinated fashion. Covering one eye will erase one of the images.

Disability

As defined by the World Health Organization, a disability (resulting from an impairment) is a restriction or lack of ability to perform an activity in the manner or within the range considered normal for a human being.

Double-blind clinical study

A study in which none of the participants, including experimental subjects, examining doctors, attending nurses, or any other research staff, know who is taking the test drug and who is taking a control or placebo agent. The purpose of this research design is to avoid inadvertent bias of the test results. In all studies, procedures are designed to "break the blind" if medical circumstances require it.

Dysesthesia

Distorted or unpleasant sensations experienced by a person when the skin is touched.

Electroencephalography (EEG)

A diagnostic procedure that records, via electrodes attached to various areas of the person's head, electrical activity generated by brain cells.

Electromyography (EMG)

A diagnostic procedure that records muscle electrical potentials through electrodes.

Etiology

The study of all factors that may be involved in the development of a disease, including the patient's susceptibility, the nature of the disease-causing agent, and the way in which the person's body is invaded by the agent.

Evoked potentials (EPs)

Recordings of the nervous system's electrical response to the stimulation of specific sensory pathways (e.g., visual, auditory, general sensory). Evoked potentials can demonstrate lesions along specific nerve pathways whether or not the lesions are producing symptoms, thus making this test useful in confirming the diagnosis of MS.

Exacerbation

The appearance of new symptoms or the aggravation of old ones (synonymous with attack, relapse, flare-up, or worsening); usually associated with inflammation and demyelination in the brain or spinal cord.

Experimental allergic encephalomyelitis (EAE)

An autoimmune disease resembling MS that is induced in genetically susceptible research animals. Before testing on humans, a potential treatment for MS may first be tested on laboratory animals with EAE in order to suggest the treatment's efficacy and safety in humans.

Extensor spasm

A symptom of spasticity in which the legs straighten suddenly into a stiff, extended position. These spasms, which typically last for several minutes, occur most commonly in bed at night or on rising from bed.

Flaccid

A decrease in muscle tone resulting in loose, "floppy" limbs.

Flexor spasm

Involuntary, sometimes painful contractions of the flexor muscles, which pull the legs upward into a clenched position. They often occur during sleep, but can also occur when the person is in a seated position.

Food and Drug Administration (FDA)

The U.S. federal agency that is responsible for establishing and enforcing governmental regulations pertaining to the manufacture and sale of food, drugs, and cosmetics. Its role is to certify benefits of medication and prevent the sale of impure or dangerous substances. Any new drug that is proposed for the treatment of MS must be approved by the FDA.

Foot drop

A condition of weakness in the muscles of the foot and ankle, caused by poor nerve conduction, which interferes with a person's ability to flex the ankle and walk with a normal heel-toe pattern. The toes touch the ground before the heel, causing the person to trip or lose balance.

Frontal lobes

The anterior (front) part of each of the cerebral hemispheres that make up the cerebrum. The back part of the frontal lobe is the motor cortex, which controls voluntary movement; the area of the frontal lobe that is further forward is concerned with learning, behavior, judgment, and personality.

Glucocorticoid hormones

Steroid hormones that are produced by the adrenal glands in response to stimulation by adrenocorticotropic hormone (ACTH) from the pituitary. These hormones, which can also be manufactured synthetically (prednisone, prednisolone, methylprednisolone, betamethasone, dexamethasone), serve both an immunosuppressive and an anti-inflammatory role in the treatment of MS exacerbations: they help control overactive immune response and interfere with the release of certain inflammation-producing enzymes.

Handicap

As defined by the World Health Organization, a handicap is a disadvantage, resulting from an impairment and disability, that interferes with a person's efforts to fulfill a role that is normal for that person. Handicap is therefore a social concept, representing the social and environmental consequences of a person's impairments and disabilities.

Helper T-lymphocytes

White blood cells that are a major contributor to the immune system's inflammatory response against myelin.

Immune system

A complex system of cells and dissolvable proteins that protect the body against disease-producing organisms and other foreign invaders.

Immunocompetent cells

White blood cells (B- and T-lymphocytes and others) that defend against invading agents in the body.

Immunosuppression

In MS, a form of treatment that slows or inhibits the body's natural immune responses, including those directed against the body's own tissues. Examples of immunosuppressive treatments in MS include cyclophosphamide, cyclosporine, methotrexate, and azathioprine.

Impairment

As defined by the World Health Organization, an impairment is any loss of function directly resulting from injury or disease.

Incidence

The number of new cases of a disease in a specified population over a defined period of time.

Incontinence

The inability to control passage of urine or feces.

Inflammation

A tissue's immunologic response to injury, characterized by mobilization of white blood cells and antibodies, swelling, and fluid accumulation.

Intention tremor

Rhythmic shaking that occurs in the course of a purposeful movement, such as reaching to pick something up or bringing an outstretched finger in to touch one's nose.

Interferon

A group of immune system proteins, produced and released by cells infected by a virus, which inhibit viral multiplication by modifying the body's immune response. Several interferons have been approved by the Food and Drug Administration for treatment of relapsing-remitting MS.

Lumbar puncture

A diagnostic procedure that uses a hollow needle to penetrate the spinal canal to remove cerebrospinal fluid for analysis. This procedure is used to examine the cerebrospinal fluid for changes in composition that are characteristic of MS (e.g., elevated white cell count, elevated protein content).

Lymphocyte

A type of white blood cell that is part of the immune system. Lymphocytes can be subdivided into two main groups: B-lymphocytes, which originate in the bone marrow and produce antibodies; T-lymphocytes, which are produced in the bone marrow and mature in the thymus. Helper T-lymphocytes heighten immune responses; suppressor T-lymphocytes suppress them and seem to be in short supply during an MS exacerbation.

Macrophage

A white blood cell with scavenger characteristics that ingests and destroys foreign substances, such as bacteria and cell debris.

Magnetic resonance imaging (MRI)

A diagnostic procedure that produces visual images of body parts without the use of X-rays. An important diagnostic tool in MS, MRI makes it possible to visualize and count lesions in the white matter of the brain and spinal cord.

Minimal Record of Disability (MRD)

A standardized method for quantifying the clinical status of a person with MS. The MRD is made up of five parts: demographic information; the Neurological Functional Systems, which assign scores to clinical findings for each of the various neurologic systems in the brain and spinal cord (pyramidal, cerebellar, brain stem, sensory, visual, mental, bowel and bladder); the Disability Status Scale, which gives a single composite score for the person's disease; the Incapacity Status Scale, which is an inventory of functional disabilities relating to activities of daily living; the Environmental Status Scale, which provides an assessment of social handicap resulting from chronic illness. The MRD assist doctors and other professionals in assessing the impact of MS and in planning and coordinating the care of people with MS.

Monoclonal antibodies

Laboratory-produced antibodies, which can be designed to react against a specific antigen in order to alter the immune response.

Motor neurons

Nerve cells of the brain and spinal cord that enable movement of muscles in various parts of the body.

Muscle tone

A characteristic of a muscle brought about by the constant flow of nerve stimuli to that muscle. Abnormal muscle tone can be defined as: hypertonus (increased muscle tone, as in spasticity); hypotonus (reduced muscle tone (flaccid paralysis); atony (loss of muscle tone). Muscle tone is evaluated as part of the standard neurologic exam in MS.

Myelin

A fatty white coating of nerve fibers in the central nervous system, composed of lipids (fats) and protein. Myelin serves as insulation and as an aid to efficient nerve fiber conduction. When myelin is damaged in MS, nerve fiber conduction is faulty or absent.

Myelin basic protein

A protein comprising about 30 percent of all myelin of the central nervous system that may be found in higher than normal concentrations in the cerebrospinal fluid of individuals with MS and other diseases that damage myelin. Some believe myelin basic protein is an antigen against which autoimmune responses are triggered in MS.

Myelitis

An inflammatory disease of the spinal cord. In transverse myelitis, the inflammation spreads across the tissue of the spinal cord, resulting in a loss of its normal function to transmit nerve impulses up and down, as though the spinal cord had been severed.

Nerve

A bundle of nerve fibers (axons). Fibers are either afferent (leading toward the brain and serving in the perception of sensory stimuli of the skin, joints, muscles, and inner organs) or efferent (leading away from the brain and mediating contractions of muscles or organs).

Nervous system

Includes all of the neural structures in the body: the central nervous system consists of the brain, spinal cord, and optic nerves; the peripheral nervous system consists of the nerve roots and nerves throughout the body.

Neurogenic bladder

Bladder dysfunction associated with neurologic malfunction in the nervous system and characterized by a failure to empty, failure to store, or a combination of the two. Symptoms that result from these three types of dysfunction include urinary urgency, frequency, hesitancy, nocturia, and incontinence.

Neurologist

Physician who specializes in the diagnosis and treatment of conditions related to the nervous system.

Neuron

The basic nerve cell of the nervous system. A neuron consists of a nucleus within a cell body and one or more processes (extensions) called dendrites and axons.

Occupational therapist (OT)

Occupational therapists assess functioning in activities of everyday living that are essential for independent living, including dressing, bathing, grooming, meal preparation, writing, and driving.

Oligoclonal bands

A diagnostic sign indicating abnormal levels of certain antibodies in the cerebrospinal fluid; seen in approximately 90 percent of people with multiple sclerosis, but not specific to MS.

Oligodendrocyte

A cell in the central nervous system that is responsible for making and supporting myelin.

Optic neuritis

Inflammation or demyelination of the optic (visual) nerve with transient or permanent impairment of vision and occasionally pain.

Orthosis

A mechanical appliance (such as a leg brace or splint) that is specially designed to control, correct, or compensate for impaired limb function.

Paresthesia

A sensation of burning, prickling, tingling, or creeping on the skin that is often seen in MS.

Paroxysmal symptoms

Symptoms that have sudden onset, apparently in response to some kind of movement or sensory stimulation, last for a few moments, and then subside. Paroxysmal symptoms tend to occur frequently in those individuals who have them, and follow a similar pattern from one episode to the next. Examples of paroxysmal symptoms include acute episodes of trigeminal neuralgia (sharp facial pain), tonic seizures (intense spasm of limb or limbs on one side of the body), dysarthria (slurred speech often accompanied by loss of balance and coordination), and various paresthesias (sensory disturbances ranging from tingling to severe pain).

Physiatrist

Physicians who specialize in the rehabilitation of physical impairments.

Physical therapist (PT)

Physical therapists evaluate and improve movement and function of the body, with particular attention to physical mobility, balance, posture, fatigue, and pain.

Placebo

An inactive compound designed to look just like a test drug in a clinical drug study as a means of assessing the benefits and liabilities of the test drug taken by experimental group subjects.

Placebo effect

An apparently beneficial result of therapy that occurs because of the patient's expectation that the therapy will help, in the absence of any real treatment.

Plaque

An area of inflamed or demyelinated central nervous system tissue.

Postural tremor

Rhythmic shaking that occurs when the muscles are tensed to hold an object or stay in a given position.

Prevalence

The number of all new and old cases of a disease in a defined population at a particular point in time.

Primary progressive MS

A clinical course of MS characterized from the beginning by progressive disease, with no plateaus or remissions, or an occasional plateau and very short-lived, minor improvements.

Prognosis

Prediction of the future course of the disease.

Pseudo-exacerbation

A temporary aggravation of disease symptoms, sometimes resulting from an elevation in body temperature or other stressor (e.g., an infection, severe fatigue, constipation), that disappears once the stressor is removed. A pseudo-exacerbation involves temporary flare-ups of prior or existing symptoms rather than new disease activity or progression.

Pyramidal tracts

Motor nerve pathways in the brain and spinal cord that connect nerve cells in the brain to the motor cells located in the cranial, thoracic, and lumbar parts of the spinal cord. Damage to these tracts causes spastic paralysis or weakness.

Reflex

An involuntary response of the nervous system to a stimulus, such as the stretch reflex, which is elicited by tapping a tendon with a reflex hammer, resulting in a contraction. Increased, diminished, or absent reflexes can be indicative of neurologic damage, including MS, and are therefore tested as part of the standard neurologic exam.

Relapsing-remitting MS

A clinical course of MS that is characterized by clearly defined, acute attacks with full or partial recovery and no disease progression between attacks.

Remission

A lessening in the severity of symptoms or their temporary disappearance during the course of the illness.

Remyelination

The repair of damaged myelin. Myelin repair occurs spontaneously in MS but very slowly.

Sclerosis

Hardening of tissue. In MS, sclerosis is the replacement of lost myelin around CNS nerve cells with scar tissue.

Secondary progressive MS

A clinical course of MS that initially is relapsing-remitting and then becomes progressive at a variable rate, with or without relapses and remissions over a progressive course.

Sensory

Related to bodily sensations such as pain, smell, taste, temperature, vision, hearing, and position in space.

Sign

An objective physical problem or abnormality identified by the physician during the neurologic examination, including altered eye movements and other changes in the appearance or function of the visual system; altered reflexes; weakness; spasticity; sensory changes.

Spasticity

Abnormal increase in muscle tone, manifested as a springlike resistance of an extremity to moving or being moved.

Sphincter

A circular band of muscle fibers that tightens or closes a natural opening of the body, such as the external anal sphincter, which closes the anus, and the internal and external urinary sphincters, which close the urinary canal.

Steroids

See Glucocorticoid hormones.

Symptom

A subjectively perceived problem or complaint reported by the patient. In multiple sclerosis, common symptoms include visual problems, fatigue, sensory changes, weakness or paralysis of limbs, tremor, lack of coordination, poor balance, bladder or bowel changes, and psychological changes. *See* Sign.

Tonic seizure

An intense spasm that lasts for a few minutes and affects one or both limbs on one side of the body. Like other types of paroxysmal symptoms in MS, these spasms occur abruptly and fairly frequently in those individuals who have them, and are similar from one brief episode to the next. The attacks may be triggered by movement or occur spontaneously. *See* Paroxysmal symptom.

Trigeminal neuralgia

Lightning-like, acute pain in the face caused by demyelination of nerve fibers at the site where the sensory (trigeminal) nerve root for that part of the face enters the brain stem.

Urinary frequency

Need or urge to urinate more frequently than normal due to small hyperactive bladder.

Urinary hesitancy

The inability to void urine spontaneously even though the urge to do so is present.

Urinary urgency

The inability to postpone urination once the need to void has been felt.

Vertigo

A dizzying sensation of the environment spinning, often accompanied by nausea and vomiting.

Additional Readings

NOTE: National Multiple Sclerosis Society chapters have lending libraries of books and videos. Call 1-800-FIGHT-MS and select option one to be connected to your local chapter.

Books

Bowling AC (2001). *Alternative Medicine and Multiple Sclerosis*. New York: Demos.

Burnfield A (1997). *Multiple Sclerosis: A Personal Exploration*. London: Souvenir Press.

Cooper L. (2001). *Insurance Solutions—Plan Well, Live Better: A Workbook for People with a Chronic Disease or Disability*. New York: Demos.

Coyle PK., Halper J (2001). *Meeting the Challenge of Progressive Multiple Sclerosis*. New York: Demos.

Garee B (ed.) (1989). *Parenting: Tips from Parents (Who Happen to Have a Disability) on Raising Children*. Bloomington, IL: Accent Press.

Giffels JJ (1996). *Clinical Trials: What You Should Know Before Volunteering to Be a Research Subject*. New York: Demos.

Holland NJ, Reingold SC, Murray TJ (2001). *Multiple Sclerosis: A Guide for the Newly Diagnosed* (2nd edition). New York: Demos.

James JL (1993). *One Particular Harbor: The Outrageous True Adventures of One Woman with Multiple Sclerosis Living in the Alaskan Wilderness.* Chicago: Noble Press.

Kalb RC (2000). *Multiple Sclerosis: The Questions You Have—The Answers You Need.* (2nd edition) New York: Demos.

Kalb RC, (1998). *Multiple Sclerosis: A Guide for Families.* New York: Demos.

Kraft GH, Catanzaro M (2000) *Living with Multiple Sclerosis: A Wellness Approach.* (2nd edition). New York: Demos.

Lechtenberg R (1995). *Multiple Sclerosis Fact Book.* Philadelphia: Davis.

LeMaistre J (1994). *Beyond Rage: Mastering Unavoidable Health Changes.* Dillon, CO: Alpine Guild.

MacFarlane EB, Burstein P (1994). *Legwork: An Inspiring Journey Through a Chronic Illness.* New York: Charles Scribner's Sons.

Perkins L, Perkins S (1999). *Multiple Sclerosis: Your Legal Rights* (2nd edition). New York: Demos.

Peterman Schwarz S (1999). *300 Tips for Making Life with Multiple Sclerosis Easier.* New York: Demos.

Pitzele SK (1986). *We Are Not Alone: Learning to Live with Chronic Illness.* New York: Workman.

Polman CH, Thompson AJ, Murray TJ, McDonald WI (2001). *Multiple Sclerosis: The Guide to Treatment and Management* (5th edition). New York: Demos.

Register C (1987). *Living with Chronic Illness: Days of Patience and Passion.* New York: Free Press.

Rogers J, Matsumura M (1990). *Mother to Be: A Guide to Pregnancy and Birth for Women with Disabilities.* New York: Demos.

Rosner LJ, Ross S (1992) *Multiple Sclerosis: New Hope and Practical Guidelines for People with MS and Their Families.* (2nd edition). New York: Prentice Hall.

Schapiro RT (1998). *Symptom Management in Multiple Sclerosis* (3rd edition). New York: Demos.

Vazquez TC, DeThomas PF (2001). *Esclerosis Múlitiple: Guia para el Recién Diagnosticado.* New York: Demos.

Wolf J, Miles, M, Pickett K (1993). *Vignettes: Stories from Lives with Multiple Sclerosis.* Rutland, VT: Academy Books.

Wolf J (1991). *Fall Down Seven Times, Get Up Eight*. Rutland, VT: Academy Books.

NATIONAL MULTIPLE SCLEROSIS SOCIETY PUBLICATIONS
(212-986-3240; 800-344-4867)

Booklets:

- *Living with MS*—Debra Frankel, M.S., O.T.R., with Hettie Jones
- *What Everyone Should Know About Multiple Sclerosis*
- *Research Directions in Multiple Sclerosis*—Stephen C. Reingold, Ph.D.
- *ADA and People with MS*—Laura Cooper, Esq., Nancy Law, L.S.W., with Jane Sarnoff
- *The Win-Win Approach to Reasonable Accommodations: Enhancing Productivity on Your Job*—Richard T. Roessler, Ph.D., and Phillip Rumrill, Ph.D.
- *Managing MS Through Rehabilitation*—Lisa J. Bain and Randall T. Schapiro, M.D.
- *Food for Thought: MS and Nutrition*—Jane Sarnoff, with Denise M. Nowack, RD.
- *Multiple Sclerosis and Your Emotions*—Mary Eve Sanford, Ph.D., and Jack H. Petajan, M.D.
- *Solving Cognitive Problems*—Nicholas G. LaRocca, Ph.D., with Martha King
- *Controlling Bladder Problems in Multiple Sclerosis*—Nancy J. Holland, Ed.D.
- *Understanding Bowel Problems in MS*—Nancy J. Holland, Ed.D., with Robin Frames.
- *MS and Intimacy*—Tanya Radford
- *PLAINTALK: A Booklet About MS for Families*—Debra Frankel, M.S., O.T.R., and Sarah Minden, M.D.
- *Taming Stress in Multiple Sclerosis*—Frederick Foley and Jane Sarnoff
- *Someone You Know Has MS: A Book for Families*—Cyrisse Jaffee, Debra Frankel, Barbara LaRoche, and Patricia Dick

- *When a Parent Has MS: A Teenager's Guide*—Pamela Cavallo, M.S.W., with Martha Jablow
  - *A Guide for Caregivers*—Tanya Radford

Other MS Society Publications:

- Facts and Issues (reprints of articles that originally appeared in the National MS Society magazine
- *Inside MS*, covering such topics as diagnosis, pregnancy, pain, gait problems, genes and MS susceptibility, fatigue, etc.)
- *Inside MS*—a 24-page magazine published four times yearly

Monograph Series (1995)

- *Families Affected by Multiple Sclerosis: Disease Impacts and Coping Strategies*—Rosalind C. Kalb, Ph.D.
- *Long-Term Care and Multiple Sclerosis*—Debra Frankel, M.S., O.T.R.
- *Employment and Multiple Sclerosis*—Nicholas G. LaRocca, Ph.D.
- *Economic Costs of Multiple Sclerosis: How Much and Who Pays*—Carol Harvey, Ph.D.
- *Utilization and Perceptions of Healthcare Services by People with MS*—Leon Sternfeld, M.D., Ph.D., M.P.H.

EASTERN PARALYZED VETERANS ASSOCIATION PUBLICATIONS
(800-444-0120)

- *Understanding the Americans with Disabilities Act* (English and Spanish)
- *The ADA: Resource Information Guide* (bibliography of books and videotapes)
- *Air Carrier Access* (defines the Air Carrier Access Act and gives information about air travel for wheelchair users)
- *Accessible Building Design* (a description of the essential components of an accessible building, including dimensions)
- *Planning for Access: A Guide for Planning and Modifying Your Home*
- Programs of EPVA (a summary of 15 programs designed to improve the lives of spinal cord injured veterans and people with disabilities)

GENERAL PUBLICATIONS

- *Inside MS*—A quarterly magazine for members of the National Multiple Sclerosis Society (733 Third Avenue, New York, NY 10017; 800-FIGHT-MS.

- *Mainstream*—A monthly magazine available from Exploding Myths, Inc. (2973 Beech Street, San Diego, CA 92101; 619-234-3138)

- *MessageS*—A newsletter sponsored by an unrestricted grant from Berlex Laboratories) available at no cost from Phase Five Communications (114 Fifth Avenue, NY, NY 10011; FAX 212-866-3271)

- *A Positive Approach*—A magazine available from A Positive Approach, Inc., a non-profit organization that services individuals with disabilities (P.O. Box 910, Millville, NJ 08322; 609-451-4777)

- *Real Living with MS*—A monthly newsletter available by subscription from the Cobb Group (9420 Bunsen Parkway, Louisville, KY 40220; 800-223-8720)

- *The Very Special Traveler*—A bimonthly newsletter for people with disabilities who travel, published by Beverly Nelson (The Very Special Traveler, P.O. Box 756, New Windsor, MD 21776-9016; 410-635-2881)

- *'We're Accessible': News for Disabled Travelers*—A newsletter from British Columbia for world travelers with disabilities (Lynne Atkinson, 32-1675 Cypress St., Vancouver, B.C. V6J 3L4; 604-731-2197)

Resources

A vast array of resources is available to help you in your efforts to meet the challenges of multiple sclerosis. This list is by no means a complete one; it is designed as a starting point in your efforts to identify the resources you need. Each resource that you investigate will lead you to others and they, in turn, will lead you to even more.

INFORMATION SOURCES

EASTERN SEALS MARCH OF DIMES NATIONAL COUNCIL (Canadian Rehabilitation Council for the Disabled [CRCD]) (90 Eglinton Avenue East, Suite 511, Toronto, Ontario M4P 2Y3, Canada; tel: 416-932-8382). The Council is a federation of regional and provincial groups serving individuals with disabilities throughout Canada. It operates an information service and publishes a newsletter and a quarterly journal.

NATIONAL HEALTH INFORMATION CENTER (P.O. Box 1133, Washington, D.C. 20013; tel: 800-336-4797). The Center maintains a library and a database of health-related organizations. It also provides referrals related to health issues for consumers and professionals.

ELECTRONIC INFORMATION SOURCES

One of the most flexible ways to obtain information about multiple sclerosis is via the Internet. Simply type in "multiple sclerosis" to the "find" or "search" feature of your favorite browser, and you will immediately have access to a wide range of MS information. Keep in mind, however, that the World Wide Web is a free and open medium; while many of the web sites have excellent and useful information, others may contain highly unusual and inaccurate information. We strongly recommend that, before following any recommendations made on web sites other than those from reputable organizations with which you are familiar, that you carefully check them out in the reference materials provided in this book, with your physician, or with your local chapter of the National Multiple Sclerosis Society.

Some of the best sources of information about MS available on the Internet are:

- National Multiple Sclerosis Society: www.nmss.org
- Multiple Sclerosis Society of Canada: www.mssoc.ca
- Multiple Sclerosis Society of Canada/Société canadienne: www.mssociety.ca
- Multiple Sclerosis International Federation: www.msif.org

RESOURCE MATERIALS

COMPLETE DRUG REFERENCE. (Compiled by United States Pharmacopoeia, published by Consumer Report Books, A division of Consumers Union, Yonkers, NY.). This comprehensive, readable, and easy-to-use drug reference includes almost every prescription and non-prescription medication available in the United States and Canada. A new edition is published yearly.

AGENCIES AND ORGANIZATIONS

CONSORTIUM OF MULTIPLE SCLEROSIS CENTERS (CMSC) (c/o Gimbel MS Center at Holy Name Hospital, 718 Teaneck Road, Teaneck, NJ 07666; World Wide Web at http://www.mscare.org). The CMSC is made up of numerous MS centers throughout the United States and Canada. The Consortium's mission is to disseminate information to clinicians, increase resources and opportunities for research, and advance the standard of care for multiple sclerosis. The CMSC is a multidisciplinary organization, bringing together health care professionals from many fields involved in MS patient care.

DEPARTMENT OF VETERANS AFFAIRS (VA) (810 Vermont Avenue, N.W., Washington, D.C. 20420; World Wide Web at: http://www.va.gov). The VA provides a wide range of benefits and services to those who have served in the armed forces, their dependents, beneficiaries of deceased veterans, and dependent children of veterans with severe disabilities.

EASTERN PARALYZED VETERANS ASSOCIATION (EPVA) (75-20 Astoria Boulevard, Jackson Heights, NY 11370; tel: 718-803-EPVA; World Wide Web at http://www.epva.org). EPVA is a private, non-profit organization dedicated to serving the needs of its members as well as other people with disabilities. While offering a wide range of benefits to member veterans with spinal cord dysfunction (including hospital liaison, sports and recreation, wheelchair repair, adaptive architectural consultations, research and educational services, communications, and library and information services, they will also provide brochures and information on a variety of subjects, free of charge to the general public (see "Additional Readings").

NATIONAL MULTIPLE SCLEROSIS SOCIETY (NMSS) (733 Third Avenue, New York, NY 10017; tel: 800-FIGHT-MS, press #1 to be connected with your local chapter); World Wide Web at http://www.nmss.org. The NMSS funds both basic and health services research. An office of professional education programs maintains a speakers' bureau and supports professional education programs both nationally and in the individual chapters. Over 105 chapters and branches of the Society provide direct services to people with MS and their families to meet their MS-related needs and improve quality of life. Services include information and referral, counseling, equipment loan, and social and recreational support programs.

PARALYZED VETERANS OF AMERICA (PVA) (801 Eighteenth Street, N.W., Washington, D.C., 20006; tel: 202-USA-1300; World Wide Web at http://www.pva.org). PVA provides extensive services to veterans; members increasingly include those diagnosed with multiple sclerosis.

ASSISTIVE TECHNOLOGY

NATIONAL REHABILITATION INFORMATION CENTER (**NARIC**) (1010 Wayne Avenue, Suite 800, Silver Spring, MD 20910; tel: 800-346-2742; tel: 301-562-2400; fax: 301-562-2401; World Wide Web at http://www.naric.com). NARIC is a library and information center on disability and rehabilitation, funded by the National Institute on Disability and Rehabilitation Research (NIDRR). NARIC operates the REHABDATA databases. NARIC collects and disseminates the results of federally funded research projects and has a collection that includes commercially published books, journal articles, and audiovisual materials. NARIC is committed to serving both professionals and consumers who are interested in disability and rehabilitation. Information specialists can answer simple information requests and provide referrals immediately and at no cost. More complex database searches are available at nominal cost.

REHABDATA (1010 Wayne Avenue, Suite 800, Silver Spring, MD 20910; tel: 800-346-2742; tel: 301-562-2400; fax: 301-562-2401) REHABDATA is a database containing bibliographic records with abstracts and summaries of the materials contained in the NARIC (National Rehabilitation Information Information Center) library of disability rehabilitation materials. Information specialists are available to conduct a database search on any rehabilitation related topic.

ABLEDATA (8401 Colesville Road, Suite 200, Silver Spring, MD 20910; tel: 301-608-8998; 800-227-0216; fax: 301-608-8958; World Wide Web: http://www.abledata.com.

ABLEDATA is a national database of information on assistive technology designed to enable persons with disabilities to identify and locate the devices that will assist them in their home, work, and leisure activities. Information specialists are available to answer questions during regular business hours. ABLE INFORM BBS is available twenty-four hours a day to customers with a computer, modem, and telecommunications software.

TRAVEL

DIRECTORY OF TRAVEL AGENCIES FOR THE DISABLED. (Written by Helen Hecker, published by Twin Peaks Press, P.O. Box 129, Vancouver, WA

98666-0129). This directory lists travel agents who specialize in arranging travel plans for people with disabilities.

INFORMATION FOR HANDICAPPED TRAVELERS (available free of charge from the National Library Service for the Blind and Physically Handicapped, 1291 Taylor Street, N.W., Washington, D.C. 20542; tel: 800-424-8567; 202-707-9275). A booklet providing information about travel agents, transportation, and information centers for individuals with disabilities.

WILDERNESS INQUIRY (808 14th Avenue S.E., Minneapolis, MN 55414; tel: 800-728-0719; 612-676-9400). Wilderness Inquiry sponsors trips into the wilderness for people with disabilities or chronic conditions.

PUBLISHING COMPANIES SPECIALIZING IN HEALTH AND DISABILITY ISSUES

DEMOS MEDICAL PUBLISHING (386 Park Avenue South, Suite 201, New York, NY 10016; tel: 800-532-8663; World Wide Web at http://www.demosmedpub.com).

RESOURCES FOR REHABILITATION (33 Bedford Street, Suite 19A, Lexington, MA 02420 tel: 781-862-6455; fax: 781-861-7517; World Wide Web: http://www.rfr.org).

TWIN PEAKS PRESS (P.O. Box 129, Vancouver, WA 98666; tel: 800-637-2256).

WOODBINE HOUSE (Publishers of the Special-Needs Collection) (6510 Bells Mill Road, Bethesda, MD 20817; tel: 301-897-3570; 800-843-7323).

Index